THOMAS MANN

ARTIST AND PARTISAN

IN TROUBLED TIMES

by

Walter E. Berendsohn

Translated and with a Preface

by

George C. Buck

The University of Alabama Press
University, Alabama 35486

Translated into English from
Thomas Mann: Künstler and Kämpfer in bewegter Zeit
Copyright (c) by Verlag Schmidt-Römhild, Lübeck,
Federal Republic of Germany
English translation Copyright (c) 1973 by
The University of Alabama Press
ISBN 0-8173-8062-0
Library of Congress Catalog Card Number 73-57
Manufactured in the United States of America

CONTENTS

TRANSLATOR'S PREFACE

Professor Berendsohn has made liberal use of quotations from Thomas Mann throughout this book, often undocumented. In many cases the passages are quite lengthy. Where they are easily identifiable, I have chosen to use standard, previously published translations for the longer passages and, in some instances, even for brief quotations. Unless otherwise indicated by specific reference, all other quotations are my own renderings, with no further attempt to identify the precise source in Mann beyond what Berendsohn's text offers. The titles of all German works cited with a few obvious exceptions have been rendered in English. If the book has been translated, it can be found under the title given. German readers can easily recreate the original title.

To reproduce in translation the metrical structure of two poems by Eichendorff and Mann, respectively, with any unusual degree of competence is beyond my modest abilities but is surely not necessary for our purposes. I have tried to create a text faithful to the import, while retaining as much as possible of the imagery and basic structure.

The manuscript was typed by Ms. Sigrid Hokanson. The Indexes were alphabetized and typed by Ms. Renate Hanson. To both of them I would like to express my sincerest appreciation.

One of the most memorable moments of my career was to interview Thomas Mann for the school paper when I was an undergraduate at Amherst College. The years have not diminished a whit my feelings of admiration for him as a person nor my fascination with his literary achievements. This little effort is a humble tribute to the memory of a man who has afforded me so many hours of lasting enjoyment.

George C. Buck

Seattle, Washington
May, 1973

iv

ABBREVIATIONS OF TRANSLATIONS CITED

BB   Buddenbrooks (1924)

BR   The Beloved Returns (1940)

BS   The Black Swan (1954)

SL   Stories of a Lifetime (1936)

ES   Essays of Three Decades (1947)

FK   Confessions of Felix Krull, Confidence Man (1955)

JB   Joseph and His Brethren, 4 volumes (1938)

        I.   The Tales of Jacob
        II. The Young Joseph
        III. Joseph in Egypt
        IV. Joseph the Provider

MM   The Magic Mountain (1927)

OD   Order of the Day (1942)

NOTE: All the translations listed above were published by Alfred A. Knopf, New York.

AUTHOR'S PREFACE

Whoever dares to write a book about Thomas Mann today must be conscious that he is doing it before the eyes of the whole literary world, that above all the literary critics and historians are watching him carefully, and that his work will be subjected to an unusually sharp analysis. I do not imagine that I am the one to write the Thomas Mann book. All too many documents are still inaccessible. In order to separate the wheat from the chaff with more assurance, it is necessary to have a broader perspective on him and his time. Many preliminary researches are still required before a total character study can be definitively made. After more than thirty years of dedication, I hope to contribute its fruits to the understanding of Mann's personality and his creative effort.

In the title of my book, **Künstler und Kämpfer in bewegter Zeit,** I indicate actually both subjects which I take as the chief basis for my work—Mann's artistic achievement and the conflict in his public life. Most informed people would agree that his writings are vital expressions of the inner world of Thomas Mann, that art is his proper occupation. His writings must therefore take precedence and occupy the most of our attention. The Conclusion of this book is also dedicated solely to the creative artist. But I do consider it inadmissible to concentrate on the creative fiction at the expense of the rest of Mann's activity and literary achievement. That would not do justice to Thomas Mann's complex personality. In fact, he himself has sharply criticized the questionable aspect of artistry at that point where it disengages itself from life. He apparently felt deeply the need to play a role in the world as an active citizen and as a controversialist, in addition to his role as an artist. Admittedly, strong demands had to be made on him from the outside before he decided to leave his workshop and enter directly into political life. Nevertheless, he fulfilled his citizen's duty with passion and great moral courage.

Both the artist and the partisan derive from the personality of Thomas Mann, but separately they are not to be equated with the whole man, who assumes a quite different corporeal shape in art and in public life. There are countless relationships between both areas; many threads run back and forth between them. Still, one must not try to reduce the whole life's work of this man to an all-too-simple formula; but, on the contrary, one should separate the two spheres; the world which he creates poetically, and the real world around him whose demands he fulfills, oftentimes reluctantly and under duress but always with fidelity to his obligations. His literary legacy testifies to both spheres of influence in various ways, and his assured position in world literature rests on the fact that he was one of the most outstanding masters of the word in his age and at the same time one of its boldest fighters for humanity, freedom, and peace.

I am familiar with a large part of the voluminous literature that is written about Thomas Mann all over the world. Each time I read a book about him, I ask myself whether it makes my own superfluous; but, after mature consideration, I put it aside reassured. Much of what I have worked out in these thirty years and have reflected on again and again is not to be found in the books on Thomas Mann that I know.

Though I did not invent the method of structural and stylistic analysis, for more than fifty years I have practised it on quite different literary forms and have developed it in detail. It rests on the premise that fantasy is a force which is fed by the dark realm of the emotions, represents it in the intellectual world, and creates in it effects other than those of strict reason. The imaginative events in the soul of a poet can only be investigated to a very slight extent, but can indeed be established quite precisely in his writings through the awakening of language. His language blossoms in rich profusion at the point where his soul is heavily involved, where his interest is strongly engaged. In structural and stylistic analysis, the structure corresponds approximately to the steel frame of a concrete building, the style approximately to the details of the decoration and inner arrangement. Such analysis is esthetically-philologically oriented—esthetically because it makes the artistic intention the main concern, philologically because it never lets the linguistic structure out of sight. It aims at the relationship of both, the unity of the work of art.

The independence of my studies encourages me to permit this work to reach publication.

Walter E. Berendsohn

I

THE WORLD OF YESTERDAY

INTRODUCTION
THOMAS MANN AND HIS TIMES

When, on 12 August 1955, Thomas Mann closed his eyes forever and went to his eternal peace, his life was fulfilled in the
deepest sense of the word. After all, he had already exceeded
the biblical age of man by a decade. His life was fulfilled beyond the mere temporal sense because in it all the forces—
human, artistic, and moral—reached their full blossom. His
life was fulfilled to the last breath by a powerful intellectual
striving which included a great deal of self-education, tough
patient artistic work, world-wide successes, and the most
glorious honors that mankind can bestow. How very much
Thomas Mann was permitted to enjoy even in the last year of
his life! The gigantic success of the first volume of his adventure novel, **Confessions of Felix Krull, Confidence Man,**
which was distributed in over sixty thousand copies in Germany
alone; the request to deliver the memorial lectures in Stuttgart,
Weimar, and Amsterdam on the occasion of the   150th
anniversary of Friedrich Schiller, a task which he solved in
masterful fashion, both factually and stylistically, as the "Essay
on Schiller" (Frankfurt am Main, 1955) and the lecture preserved on phonograph records demonstrate; the ceremony in
his birthplace, Lübeck, which finally reached a reconciliation
with its famous son and granted him an honorary citizenship;
the golden wedding anniversary with his life-long companion
Katja Pringsheim, and the eightieth birthday in which the whole
intellectual world took part, among others the French writers
with their volume "Hommage de la France à Thomas Mann"
and the students of the Norwegian capital city Oslo with a
Festschrift which bears the title: "The responsibility of the
intellectual man." In it they paid their respects to the great
artist, one of the most outstanding of our age, and at the same

1

time the bold fighter for freedom, justice, and human dignity, the militant humanist. To be sure, this year 1955 was especially rich in festivals and celebrations, but his whole life was filled with experience, creation, and activity even before the First World War; and these were intensified in the second half of his life.

We can readily discern the world-wide effect of the works of Thomas Mann during his lifetime in the bibliographies of Hans Bürgin and Klaus W. Jonas. According to Bürgin, up to 1956, translations appeared in 31 countries: in Japan 56, USA 49, in Italy 45, Sweden 39, Hungary 35, England and Czechoslovakia each 29, France 28, the Soviet Union 25, Denmark 22, Argentina and Holland each 20, etc. In addition, German school editions numbered in the USA 7, in Holland 4 (one has gone through six printings), in England 2, in Denmark, France, Latvia, Sweden, and Czecholsovakia one each. Up to 1956, there were 51 translations of **Tonio Kröger**, **Buddenbrooks** 48, **Tristan**, 45, **Mario and the Magician** 35, **Disorder and Early Sorrow** 29, **Royal Highness** and **The Magic Mountain** 28, **Confessions of the Confidence Man, Felix Krull** 27, **The Beloved Returns** 17, **The Transposed Heads** 16, **Joseph and his Brothers, The Black Swan**, and **Doctor Faustus** each 15, **The Holy Sinner** 9, etc. According to Jonas, up to 1954, 190 books and dissertations were devoted exclusively to Thomas Mann; and 250 more in substantial part. Of the 2900 listed studies, which include only a selection of the reviews, approximately 1730 are German, about 900 English, 150 French, 70 Italian, 65 Japanese, 50 Hebrew, 13 Norwegian, 11 Polish, 10 each Czechoslovakian and Danish, 2 each Yiddish and Serbo-Croatian. Jonas himself describes the figures from Poland, Russia, and Hungary as insufficient.

Thomas Mann never took the easy way, always worked slowly and carefully, never attached himself to a fashionable movement or school, went his own way in accordance with his own inner laws, never pandered to the cheaper tastes of the reading public, but on the contrary always wrote only for the more elevated discernment of demanding intellectual circles. This makes the eager reception throughout the world of his actionless, ponderous, psychologically exhaustive narratives all the more astonishing. The critics have a good right to raise objections to many details; but, if they measure his life's work even in Germany against irrelevant yard sticks just to devalue it completely, as (for example) Hans Egon Holthusen did in "The World without Transcendence" (1949), it only proves that broad segments of the German population had not been able to find a connection to humane world opinion. The cited numbers indicate graphically how heavily entrenched a postion Thomas Mann had gained in world literature by the end of his life.

But this position does not rest simply on his fiction. Bürgin also affords us an insight as to how much space the essays and articles take up in the legacy of Thomas Mann—67 of 117 titles from the period 1918-1956 compose twelve stately volumes. If we add the letters which are estimated to be from 15,000 to 20,000, then these answers of Thomas Mann to the demands of the day, representing his direct attention to the times and the world about him, exceed his writings in scope. As a morally courageous personality, especially as the champion of humanity in a politically disturbed time, he has had just as strong an effect as through his art.

His life's span, 1875-1955, is separated almost precisely in the middle into two very different periods by the outbreak of the first world war in 1914, which many historians also regard as the beginning of a new epoch in world history. In the earlier period lies the "World of Yesterday," in which the great powers of Europe were not carrying on wars with one another, the world economy was developing quickly, well-to-do segments of the citizenry believed steady progress toward better relationships on earth to be a natural law, and they gained from this a feeling of security but did not seriously relate the situation of the masses to their concept of the times. In this first half of his life, Thomas Mann could be apolitical, could enclose himself on a modest economic basis in his purely intellectual world, occupying himself above all with the problems of the artist and with being a poet through and through. In the second part of his life, however, he entered upon a wildly disturbed epoch in which devastating political events followed quickly upon one another—two world wars; inner upheavals in many countries, above all Communistic and Fascistic; grave economic jolts and collapses; the revolt and liberation of the colored, undernourished colonial peoples; and in addition the revolution in technology, industry, world commerce, and world economics developing out of nuclear physics, all of which justifies speaking of a new age. These events also caused a far reaching change if not confusion in the intellectual life. The whole development was completed so quickly and surprisingly that the majority of people in all strata were unable to grasp the monstrous transformations, the disappearance of all the bases of the former bourgeois world. Although against his will at first, Thomas Mann was drawn into the vortex of the political arguments and in them matured to a political morality, while basically remaining a man who thought apolitically. The graphic instruction in the world history of his time, which extended so deeply into his personal fate that he lost his homeland and fatherland, transformed him into a bold fighter against barbarism and fanaticism, into a citizen of the world for humanity after the manner of Goethe.

The secondary works before 1914 treat almost exclusively artistic subjects. These continue to be numerous even after 1914, but eventually are outweighed in volume and effect by the political manifestos which distinguish many of the volumes of his collected papers. Even the essays on literary and philosophical themes of this period are closely related to the struggle for threatened humanity; as, for example, the title **Nobility of the Spirit, 16 Essays on the Problem of Humanity** [1945] bears witness. To be sure, the concept of humanity, like **Nobility of the Spirit**, in the essay volume, takes on in the political struggle a wider-reaching content, that of the great period of the eighteenth century, in which it embraces the total economic, social, and political life, not only humanity but also society. Naturally, this phase of Mann's effort is reflected in his total literary production, but, in the second half of his life, the political happenings penetrate gradually even his poetic writings.

In 1950, the 75-year-old man entitled a lecture **My Times** whereas his brother Heinrich, 4 years older, published in 1946 at the same age his book **An Age is Reviewed**. Both titles, as I see it, typify the differing relationships of the two to their times: In the one, the ego stands in the foreground; in the other, the objective world, the age. Heinrich Mann utilized, much earlier than his brother, the possibility that intellectualism offered to emerge from the tradition of the social group into which he was born; he then took the political pulse of the time, became a sharp critic of bourgeois society, and finally a friend of the Soviet Union. He is especially critical of German Romantic literature, within whose circle Thomas Mann always remained as an artist despite his regard for Goethe; Heinrich opposes to German Romanticism the Russian and French literature of the nineteenth century that gave their peoples an insight into the reality of their social and political situation. Heinrich's novels are critical of society and also political because politics had become a matter of the heart for him. Thomas Mann on the other hand stresses, above all in his lecture **My Times**, his indissoluble bond with the "bourgeois" world, although he is of the opinion that this world has not existed since 1900. Social criticism and politics have never been main themes in his novels. He is interested primarily in the unusual destinies of individual representative human beings who live in isolation, necessarily removed from society or in contrast to it. Whatever the brothers may have in common, their relationship to their times remains basically different. The answer is not at all to be found in their milieu. It is rather a question of the difference in their natural disposition and intellectual decision.

Whereas Heinrich and Thomas Mann had to leave their homeland because of their disagreement with National Socialism and never again lived there, their younger brother Viktor, as he himself reports in his book **We Were Five**, which appeared shortly before his death in 1949, remained in the Third Reich and adapted to such an extent that he at one time denied his relationship to the older brothers.

In the Mann family, literary talent is inherited. Consequently, we are able to comprehend the relationship to their times of even the next generation, the children of Thomas Mann. Erika and Klaus Mann grow up in the shadow of the First World War and its consequences, but deviate far from the bourgeois mode of life of their parents, surrender passionately and without reservation to life, and take a political position in a disturbed time without hesitation. We can see and read all this especially in the son's description of his life, **The Turning Point** (English version, 1942; thoroughly reworked and expanded in German, 1949), as he develops into an independent writer despite all the intellectual relationships with his uncle and his father. He regards with due criticism the political attitude of his father in **Irony and Radicalism: Reflections of an Unpolitical Man.**

Golo Mann, historian by profession, published in 1958, **A German History of the 19th and 20th Centuries,** in which a much too severe judgment is rendered on the political attitude and effectiveness both of his father and his uncle (p. 702 ff.); it is unjust because he disregards the moral effect of their personalities and writings; he only praises Thomas Mann's energetic rejection of National Socialism and his often repeated exhortations that the bourgeoisie improve Franco-German understanding and reconcile itself to social democracy. How different the relationship to their times are the two generations!

If we go beyond the literary Mann family and turn to the literature of the time in general, it becomes convincingly clear that there are many other possibilities of coming to terms with contemporary society and representing it in literature. Despite a few verses Thomas Mann is not the born lyricist; despite **Florence,** not a born dramatist, though it already reveals his special way of experiencing the world about him. But even in his own territory, the narrative, there is a large group of writers who, like Tolstoi earlier in **War and Peace,** anchor the individual destinies which they depict penetratingly and attractively in a popular or mass destiny. I shall only name a few: Heinrich Mann's **Henry** IV, Arnold Zweig's unique novel series in German literature on the age of the First World War, Alfred Neumann's **There Were Six of Them,** Leonhard Frank's **The Disciples of Jesus,** Leon Feuchtwanger's political novels. Thomas Mann read Tolstoi's book on Napoleon's Russian campaign, **War and Peace,** marvelled at it very much, and regarded its monumental size as a model. But he hardly recognized that its size reflected its political character.

It is worthwhile therefore to describe penetratingly the very personal relationship of Thomas Mann to his experience of the contemporary world; for the special nature of his total literary creation is most closely related to it. He is not **the** representative of the time and its literature, its culture, its intellect, and its humanity; but, on the contrary, one among its great humane voices. We can do justice to his greatness as Artist and Partisan only if we observe these limits.

I

THE WORLD OF YESTERDAY

1. ORIGIN AND EARLY IMPRESSIONS

How the forces of nature mix the various elements of a broadly spreading family tree to make possible an important creative personality will probably always remain an impenetrable secret. Still, in the case of Thomas Mann, the influence of heredity is apparent: when the wholesale merchant and senator from Lübeck, Thomas Johann Heinrich Mann, took as his wife, in 1869, the lovely Julia da Silva-Bruhns, the daughter of a Brazilian Creole mother, a very exotic strain came into the German family—one that brought much discord and unrest, tensions and difficulties into the life of the children, and that definitely did not sublimate into artistic work in all cases.

In 1926 in **Lübeck as an Intellectual Form of Life,** Thomas Mann depicts his father:

How often in my life did I discover with a smile, yes even caught myself in the process, that it was actually the personality of my late father who as an unconscious image determined all my actions and omissions. Perhaps one or another is listening to me today who knew him then, saw him in action here in the city, in his many offices, who still remembers his dignity and astuteness, his ambition and industry, his personal and intellectual elegance, the friendliness with which he knew how to accept—in a patriarchal manner still genuine—the common people who clung to him, and his social gifts and his humor. He was no longer a simple man, not robust but on the contrary nervous and capable of suffering, but a man of self-control and success who early achieved honor and respect in the world—his world, in which he established his lovely house.

We are not talking here about artistic gifts but surely about

8

the sense for beauty which affected the ordering of the house as well as the selection of his exotic wife. In a letter to Agnes E. Meyer, 29 June 1939, Thomas Mann writes about his mother:

> Her sensuous preartistic nature expressed itself in musicality—tasteful, bourgeois-trained piano-playing and a fine singing voice to which I owe my thorough knowledge of the German lied. She was transplanted at a very tender age to Lübeck and conducted herself, as long as she managed the huge household, completely as an adopted child of the city and its upper society. But suppressed longings for the "South," for art, in fact for bohemianism, were present and persevered after the death of her husband and the change of relationships, which explains the prompt resettlement to Munich. In her childhood she had been very pretty in a Spanish style. I believe that I, the second one, was closest to her heart. Our relationship to Mama was very much more intimate and confidential than that to Papa, who was a somewhat withdrawn, even feared, terribly busy dignitary but who, at the same time, made an even stronger impression from an educational point of view than our mother.

Following the well-known verses of Goethe, Thomas Mann derives his "serious conduct of life" from the paternal side, "the desire to tell stories," "the artistic sensuous direction," from the maternal heritage from which his musicality also derives. But in his artistic creation, the bright, critically sifting, and ordering powers play at least an equally great role as the dark forces of the blood, of the passions, of the emotions and the inspirations of fantasy; in fact, it is partly characteristic of his works that the ordering powers predominate, exclude intoxication and recklessness, and try to subdue the demonic by all means, so that even here the inheritance from the father plays its role.

Perhaps it seems paradoxical to place the bourgeois origin at the beginning of the characteristics of Thomas Mann since he has indeed varied the contrast between the artist and citizen in many narratives; but he himself has again and again placed them at the focal point of all his observations about himself all his life long and out of them derived very far-reaching consequences for his life and effectiveness, among other things his sense for elegance and solidity, indeed even his innate claim to dignity and a comfortable surplus on the material side of life. In the **Reflections of a Non-Political Man,** for example, it is said:

> Who am I, where do I come from, that I am as I am and cannot make myself otherwise nor wish it? I am an urbanite, a citizen, a child and a greatgrandchild of German bourgeois culture. Indeed I am a citizen, and that is in Germany a word whose sense is as little strange to the intellect and to art as to dignity, graceful solidity, and comfort.

He then reaches beyond his Lübeck forefathers and points to his ancestors, who were craftsmen in Nuremberg, the city of the plastic artists Albrecht Dürer and Peter Vischer, and the Meistersingers, the craftsmen who wrote lyrics in melody. Mann does this with the intention of relating the nature of his own creation to them. This is therefore much more than a question of class consciousness. It is a question of the ethical attitude toward work, of industry, sense of duty, conscientiousness, perseverance toward completion in work, together with self-criticsm and self-discipline.

Thomas Mann's concept of the bourgeoisie however embraces even more than this occupational ethic. It is not merely related to the concept that the age of German humanity, which for the first time gained world importance for the German spirit in the second half of the eighteenth century, is an outgrowth of the cities and their citizenry. Erich von Kahler, for example, in his book, **The German Character in the History of Europe** [Zurich, 1937], has depicted in masterly fashion how humanity grows, as the spirit of the German bourgeoisie, out of the management "of the German city and the holy Empire," whereby the strong influence of antiquity and Christianity is adequately taken into account. Thomas Mann equates humanity with urbanity (from "urbs—the city"). This shows that his "humanity" does not refer to the whole all-embracing, worldly view of life and the world of Wieland and Lessing, Kant and Herder, Goethe, Schiller, and Wilhelm von Humboldt; but, on the contrary, to certain personal characteristics—engaging kindness and indeed politeness in deportment, a gracious or even benign attitude toward the world around us, toward human beings and animals. He is not a passionate warrior, not a hunter, not a fisherman, he is against all crudity; his appearance is tactful and tasteful; he is the cultured, solid man of the world.

But Thomas Mann's action and being are by no means exhausted with these inherited and precociously formed traits. Where does his unique intellectual energy come from which enables him even in his eightieth year to solve difficult tasks successfully at a high level? Whence the inexhaustible thirst for knowledge and new things which makes him receptive above all to the literatures of the West and drives him to penetrating studies in many areas? Whence the deep melancholy which he tries to overcome and the gay side of his nature which lets him surrender so fully to joyous laughter? Whence the oversensitive irritability of his nerves, which causes him to be upset so often and at the same time makes him so receptive to the thousands upon thousands of impressions of the world about him? Whence his powerful, all-embracing memory from which he constantly draws in conversations and in his literary creativity? If we knew a great deal about all his ancestors on both sides, we could perhaps determine the origin of this or that trait, but there will never be a satisfactory answer to all these and similar questions. Mann was not a "simple man" but a complicated personality, difficult to fathom, with many inner tensions and contradictions.

This special nature, together with his precocious writing, brings it about that even as a boy he withdraws from the world about him, disdains school, produces very little in it, displeases the teacher, and among his comrades finds only a few similarly disposed friends. As a child and young man, he lives with his tender soul in a proud and aching loneliness. The patrician world of Lübeck in itself forms a good soil for an individualism which has little understanding of social restrictions on personal ambitions; but it does not lead to loneliness. The incipient poet, however, becomes a clearly defined, idealistic individualist, estranged from the world about him, who experiences in it a great deal of "misery and comedy." The mass of the people remains beyond his field of vision for a long time.

Therefore, Thomas Mann includes, in his concept of the bourgeoisie, ties reaching back to the romantic movement of the nineteenth century. But the German bourgeoisie in its totality was definitely not romantic, and the nineteenth century was not quite that either; indeed, even the bourgeois literature of this period conceals all sorts of testimony that economic, social, and political problems were not excluded by it in any way; for example, Georg Buchner's **Wozzeck** and **Danton's Death,** Heinrich Heine's satire, **Germany, a Winter Fairy Tale,** as well as his poem "The Weavers," and Gerhard Hauptmann's drama of the same title. No, the romantic movement is only one of the main tendencies of the nineteenth century, and the fact that Thomas Mann felt so completely under its spell depended on his personal disposition and his spiritual individualism, which developed from it. That is not the case with his brothers Heinrich and Viktor, nor with his children Erika, Klaus, and Golo.

The romantic movement attracted him in many ways. The seven-starred constellation of German humanity which I have already mentioned, its most outstanding banner carriers, had together constructed the new intellectual space for the German nation in the shape of an arch high over the wretched economic, social, and political conditions of the eighteenth century, an arch in which philosophy and poetry had intimately joined hands. These had created an empire in which all the intellectually alive brains, all the warm receptive hearts, could meet beyond the three hundred boundaries of the splintered state system. Along with the predominant theology of the day, there was a secular world view which took a position on all questions of personal and public life, including obviously both everyday work as well as politics. In it the idea of the human personality and the idea of the human community were firmly related, tied to each other by the idea of the love of mankind, the heart of so many religions and philosophies; and thus a happy balance was established between the subjective and the objective world. This clear, transparent order of thought which derived from the Enlightenment, the intellectual release from church dogma, they called humanity. In his early period Thomas Mann did not adhere to this world and life view. As late as the **Reflections of an Unpolitical Man,** he speaks quite scornfully of the

Enlightenment of the eighteenth century. He means that humanity has atomized the bourgeoisie and made them into individualists, and he calls Goethe apolitical. The basis for the world view of that time remained foreign to him.

The chief contrast between the creators of German humanity and the Romanticists who stand on the grounds which their predecessors have prepared is that the Romanticists, because they are completely different kinds of human being, displace the accent in their view of the world and life more and more from the idea of the human community to the idea of the human personality. They release the ego from time, the world around, and reality and allow it to unfold in an endless inner universe such as is clearly represented in E. T. A. Hoffmann's fairy tale, **The Golden Pot.** That is the beginning of a gradually intensifying spiritual individualism which casts about itself in philosophy and poetry and, at the middle of the nineteenth century—for example, in Max Stirner's **The Only One and his Possessions** [1849]—finds a characteristic expression and high point. This individualism had a persistent effect in bourgeois circles right down to our time in a further intensified, sick form, very broadly diffused in protest against the simultaneous mass gatherings of the workers, who aim through their organizations to obtain for themselves a life worthy of a human being. Individualistic philosophy, insofar as it is not restricted to epistemology and scientific doctrine, becomes personalism and existentialism and has a difficult time bridging the gap to the idea of the human community. Art, formerly a common word and a common value, is now used among the majority of artists only as an expression of individuality; they no longer have the capability and hardly the willpower to draw together the world around them and their isolated ego into one intellectual unity.

In the eulogistic tones of the **Reflections**, Thomas Mann selects three figures from the romantic movement of the nineteenth century for special praise:

Schopenhauer, Nietzsche, and Wagner: a stellar trio of eternally related spirits—their creative and dominant destinies are deeply and indissolubly joined—the three are one. The reverent pupil for whom their powerful careers have become a culture would like to wish that he could talk about all three at once, since it is so difficult for him to separate what he owes to each one individually.

Very early, around 1890—that is, in his developmental stage—Thomas Mann experienced for the first time the elemental sensual power of the music of Richard Wagner.

Gerhäuser from the City Theatre sang Tannhäuser with his impetuous ardor. Every second evening he sang Lohengrin. He floated fitfully on the crest of the instruments and sang with delicate motions: "Now be thanked." He came forward with softly shuffling steps and sang: "Hail, King Henry," and his voice sounded like a silver trumpet. It was at that time that the art of Richard Wagner came to me.

It excited him deeply and entranced him for his whole life, it became a fruitful motive in his early works, and he presented the results of his penetrating studies in two lectures: **Sufferings and Greatness of Richard Wagner** (1933) and **Richard Wagner and the Ring** (1937).

In bold characterization of the nineteenth century, he compares in 1933 the monumental accomplishments of Zola, Tolstoi, Ibsen, and Wagner. He then refers to myth and psychology as the forces which elevate Wagner's musical dramas high above the level of all the older musical drama; and adds his personal confession:

My passion for the Wagnerian enchantment has accompanied my life ever since I was first conscious of it and began to make it my own and penetrate it with my understanding. All that I owe to him, of enjoyment and instruction, I can never forget: the hours of deep and solitary bliss in the midst of the theatre throngs, hours of nervous and intellectual transport and rapture, perceptions of great and moving import, such as only this art vouchsafes. My curiosity about it has never jaded; I have never become sated with listening, marvelling, and watching—not without misgivings, I admit; but the doubts, objections, and oppositions detracted from it as little as Nietzsche's immortal criticism of Wagner, which I have always felt to be a panegyric with the wrong label, like another kind of glorification (ES, 314).

Is it not characteristic of the poet's musical experience that he speaks of the nerves and the intellect, not of the emotional tensions? Does perhaps the difference between Mann and those musical people who reject Wagner lie here?

The love of Thomas Mann for Wagner is not blind; rather, it is knowing and clairvoyant. Thomas Mann calls Wagner a "theatrical person," indeed a "theatromaniac." "The genius of Richard Wagner is put together out of streams of pure dilettantism." He calls Wagner's language bombastic, baroque, childlike, and uncalled for. He does not conceal the neurosis of the artist who is kept on an even keel solely by application to his life's work. The analysis of the personality is as penetrating as that of the works and lays bare every weakness; indeed, the entire dubiety of the artist and his art is noticed in order then to praise all the more enthusiastically, despite everything, the genius of the accomplishment. Mann lauds Wagner as a psychologist, as a discoverer of myth for the opera, as a synthesizer of the arts. "The general tone of Wagner's music is heavily pessimistic, laden with sluggish yearning, broken in rhythm; it seems to be wrestling up out of confusion toward redemption in the beautiful; it is the music of a burdened soul." (ES, 321). Then, however, he names a whole series of genial musical images in the individual operas.

The phenomenon of the two—Richard Wagner and Thomas Mann, their appearance, their character—are very different; their relationship lies in art. What Thomas Mann says about this in the **Reflections** is astonishing.

Rarely, I imagine, would the influence of Wagner be as strong and determining on a non-musician—and on an even more decidedly non-dramatist—as I must confess to be the case with me. It did not have any effect on me as a musician or as a dramatist or even as a "musical dramatist" but as an artist as general as the modern artist par excellence, as Nietzsche's criticism has accustomed me to seeing him, and in particular as the great musically epic prose writer and symbolist which he is. What I know about the economy of the means, about the effectiveness in general—in contrast to the effect, this "effectiveness without cause"—about the epic spirit, about beginning and ending, about style as a secret adaptation of the personal to the factual, about symbolization, about the organic closeness of the individual work, of the life unity of the total work, what I know about all this and have tried to practise and develop it within my limits, I owe to my devotion to this art.

From this master teacher, the poet appropriated many tricks of the craft that one must command in order to be able to create independently. On the way to his own mastery, he gained a part of his means of expression from Wagner.

Thomas Mann soon moved (in the 1890's) from Richard Wagner to Friedrich Nietzsche. In the **Reflections,** he stresses first of all the concept of **life,** "which Nietzsche imbued with a new feeling, clothed with beauty, power, and sacred innocence; raised to the highest rank and guided to intellectual leadership." Mann's efforts were concentrated above all on **Thus Spake Zarathustra** and the late works of Nietzsche. But Mann often stresses that he never allowed himself to be overwhelmed by the prayers and hymns to the point of an intoxicated affirmation of life as did the great part of the youth of Europe around the turn of the twentieth century. The prophecy of the "Superman" and the fanatic doctrine of the "Blonde Beast" left him cold. Above all he studied the early volumes of aphorisms and revered in Nietzsche the genial psychologist of decadence; the writer of world rank, the stylist who surpassed even his great teacher Schopenhauer; the master of irony from whom he learned a great deal. "I have often felt that Nietzsche's philosophy could have become the lucky discovery of a gold mine for a great poet in quite similar fashion as that of Schopenhauer's for the creator of Tristan; namely, as the source of a supreme **irony,** slily erotic, darting between life and spirit." Thomas Mann has been called the "ironic German." Under the influence of Nietzsche, irony became for him the chief means of rescuing art in a critical age. Thomas Mann's ties to Nietzsche are, by far, not so firm and lasting as those to Wagner. At various times of his life, Mann takes elements from Nietzsche's work that give him confirmation in his creative efforts. Accordingly his judgment also changes and wavers, but he always regards with reverence Nietzsche's intellectuality, which transcends itself and his tragic fate.

Still in the nineties, Mann has moved from Wagner and

Nietzsche to the philosophy of Arthur Schopenhauer, to whom indeed both these artists are deeply indebted. He passed his experience on to Senator Buddenbrook who, for a short time before his death, reads in his garden for four hours in **The World as Will and Imagination** and feels overcome above all by the chapter **about death and its relationship to the indestructibility of our being in itself:** "He felt his whole being expanded in an uncanny fashion and filled with a heavy dark intoxication; his senses clouded over and completely befuddled by something rather unspeakably new, enticing and promising which reminded of a first, hopeful desire for love." Also in a Schopenhauer essay of 1938, the poet gives testimony of this intoxication: "the organic upheaval which is signified can only be compared with that which the first acquaintance with love and sex creates in the young soul." The young man was gripped by Schopenhauer in just as elementary a fashion as by Wagner and indeed as artist just as strongly as man.

> The philosophy of Schopenhauer has always been felt as outstandingly artistic, indeed as the philosophy of the artist par excellence ... its composition is of such a perfect clarity, transparency, tightness, its presentation of a power, elegance, aptness, a passionate wit, a classic purity, and a magnificently gay severity of linguistic style such as has never before been attained in German philosophy: All this is only "phenomenon," the necessary and innate expression of beauty simply for the being, the innermost nature of this thought process, a tension-filled, emotional, in short dynamic artistic nature, playing between violent contrasts, instinct and intellect, passion and release, which cannot reveal itself otherwise than in forms of beauty or otherwise than as personal creation of truth giving testimony through the power of its being experienced and suffered.

Added to this is the great importance Schopenhauer attributes to art and above all to music in his system of philosophy. According to him, music is a form of self-negation of the will since it develops out of the pure observation of life. Furthermore, the concept that the total phenomenological world, filled by the metaphysical will, is condemned to suffer in accordance with its nature, appeals to the poet who after all feels excluded from the very beginning from the world about him and joins up with those who recognize the misery and comedy of life. The philosopher praises sympathy as lofty moral and his negation of the will leaves the way open to religiosity without rigid adherence.

In his essay, Thomas Mann establishes that one can live and die with this philosophy:

> I dare to assert that the Schopenhauer truth and its acceptability is adapted to stand firm in the final hour and in fact to resist **effortlessly** without exertion of the thought processes, without words. Not in vain does Schopenhauer say: "Death is the actual inspiring genius of philosophy. Furthermore without death it would in fact be difficult to philosophize.: He is a great intimate and herald of death.

Schopenhauer is of greater importance than Wagner and Nietzsche for the formation of the persisting world and life view of Thomas Mann. In the feeling and imagination of the poet, the three personalities melt into a unity although there are strong differences (indeed, contrasts) between them, which find violent expression in Nietzsche's hostility to Wagner at the time of the **Parsifal.** No firm rational world and life view, such as is offered by the devolvement of ideas from **humanity,** developed out of Mann's tie to this triumvirate. His intellectuality remained determined by the dark subcurrents of his soul within the liquescent boundaries of concepts. Furthermore, as an attentive observer of life in its various aspects, he did not want to permit himself to be pinned down with rigid concepts to current opinions. This evasion corresponds to his individualistic independence and originality. His subjectivity is the basis of his artistic creation, which gains its special stamp thereby and not through acquired ideas!

All three—Schopenhauer, Wagner, and Nietzsche—stand in close relationship, long since thoroughly investigated, to romanticism itself. Thomas Mann also had arrived at romanticism and had buried himself primarily in the writings of Friedrich Schlegel and Friedrich von Hardenberg (Novalis). The philosophical contribution of the eighteenth century lay primarily in the fact that it created the solid core of ideas (summarized under the simplified concept of humanity) that represented an ideal, eternal task of being human in human society. It is never quite to be solved, but rather it always remains a goal toward which one strives. Romanticism, which gradually turns its interest more and more to the individual, opens up new possibilities of intellectual life and new vistas for the soul; for, because of it, all relationships of man become new problems. Tensions, polarities, contradictions in the inner life of man, the relationships of the human spirit to life and death, to night and sickness are experienced and endured. A new freedom of the superior intellect over time and the world about us is practiced and leads to the serious play of irony. Thus, Thomas Mann garners from the study of romantic writings an abundance of problems that enter into his work as essential components. The romanticists Wilhelm Wackenroder, Ludwig Tieck, and E. T. A. Hoffman are after all the first ones who take up music as a central motive in their stories, a technique which Thomas Mann follows.

All these sources of Thomas Mann's education also expressed something about his own nature, because he selects them for himself. The relationships to romanticism which are occupied so much with sickness and death; to Wagner's work, which he calls "the music of a burdened soul"; to Schopenhauer's pessimistic world view; and to Nietzsche's decadence psychology, point jointly to the deep melancholy that can also be perceived in Mann's script. The graphologists regard a handwriting in which every line inclines downwards as an expression of an inclination to melancholy, to sickness, indeed to suicide. In the case of Thomas Mann, the handwriting lies like a row of roof tiles; it falls somewhat off in every word. This points to melancholy, which his intellectual powers are constantly struggling against.

When the poet visited Vienna in 1936, an inhabitant of that city with its old charming way of life said to him: "Mr. Mann, you always live like this (balled fist) we like to live like this (the hand opens, the fingers relax indifferently)." That aptly characterizes the constant summoning of the intellectual powers to overcome the disposition inclining toward stodgy melancholic lassitude.

Naturally, there are still other sources of the literary culture of the poet during the early period. He himself mentions the German narrative art of the nineteenth century, above all Theodor Fontane, Theodor Storm, and Fritz Reuter; beyond that, the French, the "holy" Russian, the admired Scandinavian and English literatures—all of them, according to his own confession at that time, mostly in translations. The science which attempts to classify him historically will have to work at it for a long time in order to illuminate these relationships in all their details. An example: In a previously unprinted letter to the literary historian Professor Vilhelm Andersen in Copenhagen, 8 July 1903, Mann writes:

> In contrast to my older brother Heinrich, the author of the novels In Fool's Paradise and The Goddesses, in which the addition of Romantic blood makes itself artistically strongly evident, I am of a completely Nordic temperament and perhaps it is J.P. Jakobsen who influenced my style up to now the most.

But Thomas Mann's own artistic achievement must not be minimized because of all these influences.

In accordance with the model of his father and his counterbalance to the son's strong inner inclination to Romanticism and to the challenge and dubiety of his artistry, Thomas Mann strove to lead the life of a serious citizen. This life needed two bases—the clarification and establishment of a profession, and the founding of a family. In both of these endeavors, the poet was favored with unusual good fortune. After he had worked for a short time in an insurance company and then as an editor on Simplicissimus, he became a free lance writer on the basis of a modest allowance from his father's legacy. In May 1897, the short story Little Herr Friedemann was accepted by the Neue Deutsche Rundschau of the firm S. Fischer in Berlin; and in 1898 a volume of short stories appeared in the same press under this short story's title.

The publisher furthermore urged Mann to write a novel. On receiving the manuscript of Buddenbrooks in 1900, the publisher demanded from the author first of all a reduction by about half. When Thomas Mann refused in a letter which he himself describes as the most beautiful which he has ever written but which unfortunately is not extant, Fischer let him wait so long for the answer that the author became impatient and asked whether Fischer wanted to let him drop. At that time he wrote to his brother Heinrich that he was toying with the idea of becoming a bank official. Then finally, on 4 February 1901, came the welcome report that the novel was to appear unabridged in two volumes. Fischer immediately offered the young author the unusually high honorarium of 20 percent. In 1903, the second and third thousand appeared; in 1905, the editions had already grown to 35,000 copies. That was the beginning of his association with the highly respected printing house. Thomas Mann had found a permanent outlet for his literary work.

With these satisfying results of his novel in the background, Thomas Mann could think about founding a family. Among other places in Munich, he frequented the home of the wealthy, art-loving professor of mathematics and Wagner enthusiast Alfred Pringsheim and his wife, the daughter of Hedwig Dohm of Berlin, which resembled a museum and in which the best society of the Bavarian capital city met. He fell in love with the spoiled and much-sought-after daughter Katja, in whose genealogy, as in his own, greatly varied elements were mixed. The letters from the long period of courtship are preserved and published. In 1904 they became engaged, and in 1905 they married. He fell in love with a "fair princess from the East."

Katja delivered six children into the world for him and transformed herself into an unusually clever and capable mother and wife who stood with both feet firmly planted on the ground. She willingly took over the education of the children because Thomas was always involved in his work; in addition, she took a motherly interest in all the young friends of either sex who came into the house. She made sure that there was quiet during Mann's morning work hours; she relieved him so far as possible of all business details; she became his secretary as the correspondence grew, prepared the manuscript for print when the first typewriter came into the house, and was often his adviser when difficulties arose in his work. One cannot at all imagine how his life might have been shaped without this vital, warm-hearted, independent, active woman who accompanied him along his life's path to its end. The long delay in her acceptance of him was probably the result among other things of the fact that she suspected what a huge, difficult task faced her at the side of this artist. His mighty works are also a monument to her lifelong faithful love and self-sacrificing fulfillment of duty.

Usually, Mann the father worked in his study, removed from the daily life of the children. It was exciting and festive on the occasions when they were led into the room where so much cigar smoke hovered below the ceiling. Then he read aloud to them from his library of stories—for example, from the fairy tales of the Grimm brothers, from A Thousand and One Nights, or from the folk tales of Tolstoi, depending on their age. When they sang, he accompanied them with a melodic whistling and clear high tones. If difficulties really arose, he reached in with the hand of a master pedagogue. If, for example, an evil spirit plagued the fantasy of a child during the night, he knew how to contain it. They called him for this reason the "magician," a nickname which he accepted and in his old age even used in his letters to them, shortened to M. Or he cured a half-grown child of his desire to invent lies constantly. He was the highest authority in the house, against whom there was no further appeal. Thus he bore his proper share in the children's education. He obviously suffered whenever his work prevented him from being as much to the children and standing as close to them as the mother. There are countless testimonies to his love for them. He took his fatherhood just as seriously as everything else that was part of the conduct of a good citizen's life.

Buddenbrooks

The major work of the period to the first world war is the Lübeck novel of a merchant family, Buddenbrook, on which Thomas Mann worked for the three years from 1898 to 1900. Originally he wanted to write a narrative of merely moderate scope about the musical Hanno and his father Thomas; but, as with Richard Wagner in the **Ring of the Nibelungs**, he was driven to present the whole background. As a result, a huge epic material fell to his disposal, the history of his own family in the nineteenth century, with countless oral and written traditions—a raw material from which he graphically shaped the external relationships and inner conditions of four generations; many very lively, individual human beings with their words, gestures, personal peculiarities, thoughts and actions, and from which he created an exciting plot in a long chain of eventful happenings. **Buddenbrooks** is the only popular work of the novelist that extends to all social levels. He added an intellectual context, which appeared in the sub-title "Decline of a Family," reminiscent of Nietzsche and Schopenhauer. The intensifying refinement from which art blossoms is a decadent product of the bourgeoisie: that is the theme. The point of view is pessimistic, the fate of the family very sad. Despite the realistically penetrating depiction of the external and inner life, the book is not merely an imitation of reality but one in which the problems of life are of real concern.

It is understandable that Lübeck's society did not receive **Buddenbrooks** enthusiastically. It is truly not an emotionally patriotic representation of the city of Mann's birth. The tone is parodistic. Right at the beginning, a festive family dinner with many heavy courses is depicted in detail in nine short chapters and the house doctor pronounces melancholy observations at the bedside of the sick Christian, a motif that recurs:

> Dr. Grabow smiled to himself—a thoughtful almost a melancholy smile. He would soon meet this young man again. He would do as the rest of the world did—his father and all their relatives and friends: He would lead a sedentary life and eat four good, rich, satisfying meals a day. Well, God bless us all! He, Friedrich Grabow, was not the man to upset the habits of these prosperous, comfortable tradesmen and their families. Young as he was, he had held the head of many an honest burger who had eaten his last joint of smoked meat, his last stuffed turkey, and, whether overtaken unaware in his counting house or after a brief illness in his solid old four-poster had commended his soul to God. Then it was called paralysis, a 'stroke,' a sudden death. Well, God bless us all. (BB, 32)

Midway in the story, there are insights into the condition of the grain firm, into its main ledger book with gains and losses, their refined business procedure which has already been abandoned by the competition, the gradually dwindling respectability and honor of the house. These are indeed unhappy truths, painful to read.

The novel begins in 1835, reaches into the eighties, and depicts in eleven parts the steady decline of the four generations. The great grandparents are presented very briefly as happy people from the enlightened Biedermeier period who stand firmly and surely on solid ground; their death is reported in the second part. The grandfather, Consul Jean Buddenbrook, is already under the spell of a pietistic movement and maintains a pious house rule which his wife intensifies after his death, so that many preachers consort in the patrician home, at times even live there. The third generation—Thomas, Christian, and Tony—take up the greatest space in the work. The daughter (Tony) has to sacrifice her personal inclination for a certain student to the will of the parents and marry a Hamburg merchant whom she despises. The fact that her pious father allows himself to be deceived by this unsympathetic smooth talker, who is only angling for her dowry and soon feigns bankruptcy, does not speak for his knowledge of human beings. In order to restore the honor of the family, Tony enters upon a second marriage with a man from Munich, who retires—once in the possession of the dowry—as a man of independent means and soon, through his coarseness, drives Tony out of the house and back to her birthplace. The twice-divorced woman must then experience, on top of this, that the husband of her daughter winds up in jail through his business dealings as director of an insurance firm.

In Christian's case, the family decadence appears as a sickness. He is a psychopath who can never summon up his energies for regular middle-class work; leads a gay, pleasure-filled life, always entertains his circle of friends with his stories—apparently his is an artistic nature but without creative power; naturally, he constantly incites the older brother to sharp criticism.

Thomas treads bravely in the footsteps of his forefathers. Having been introduced to the business early, he becomes a hard-working, imaginative, well-liked president, who at first leads the firm to new heights and soon is elected a senator of Lübeck. He has a splendid new house built and takes a beautiful, musically gifted wife from Holland. All of that seems easy for him; but appearance does deceive. His public appearance is a kind of theatrical performance for which he prepares himself daily by a tedious, careful toilet, and he has to strengthen himself with a selected wardrobe and frequent changes of linen. Inwardly, he is overworked and dead tired and is unable to believe in a happy conclusion. His lethal collapse comes surprisingly early.

Like his uncle Christian, Hanno is equally unable to fulfil the severe demands of his father, who lives in heroic self-discipline. Hanno belongs completely to the musical mother. Music has become the total content of life in his case, but he lacks the vigor and the will to be an arist. He himself says to his friend:

What about my music, Kai? There is nothing to it. Shall I travel around and give concerts? In the first place, they would not let me; and in the second place, I should never really know enough. I can play very little. I can only improvise a little when I am alone. And then, the

> traveling about must be dreadful, I imagine. It is differ-
> ent with you. You have more courage. You go about
> laughing at it all. You have something to set against it.
> I can't. I get so tired of things. I would like to sleep
> and never wake up. I would like to die, die! No, I am
> no good. I cannot want anything. I don't even want to be
> famous. I am afraid of it, just as if it were a wrong thing
> to do.

He dies during puberty of typhoid fever. One time when he was
reading in the family chronicle, he drew a diagonal line of
conclusion over the last page begun and explained, to his
father's outraged question: "There will be nothing more."

The depiction of deaths is penetrating in this novel. After
each of them, a family council takes place. Finally, only
three mourning women are still sitting together. The family
Buddenbrook is at an end.

It is still clearly discernible that Thomas and Hanno were
originally the figures who lay closest to the novelist's heart.
He accompanies them into loneliness and allows them to reveal
their innermost soul. He gives his own intoxicating and rewarding experience of the consoling philosophy of Schopenhauer
to the father tired of life. The parodistic tone of the narrator
softens; he depicts the philosophy very extensively in a winged,
almost hymnlike language so that one perceives the heartbeat
of the novel.

> A great unknown, and welcome peace flooded his being.
> He felt the incomparable satisfaction of how a truly su-
> perior brain masters this powerful, strong, cruel,
> mocking thing called life in order to conquer and con-
> demn it. The satisfaction of the sufferer who has always
> had a bad conscience about his sufferings and concealed
> them from the gales of a harsh, unsympathetic world,
> until suddenly, from the hand of an authority, he receives,
> as it were, justification and license for his sufferings—
> justification before the world, this best of all possible
> worlds which with playful scorn was proven to be the
> worst of all possible ones! (BB, 256)

After a few hours of deep sleep, deeper than he had ever
slept before, he awoke and thought thoughts such as he had

never known, in an intoxicated language such as he had never spoken.

And behold, it was as though the darkness were rent from before his eyes, as if the whole wall of the night parted wide and disclosed an immeasurable, boundless prospect of light. What was death? The answer came not in poor, big sounding words: he felt it within him, he possessed it, death was a joy, so great, so deep that it could be dreamed of only in moments of revelation like the present. It was the return from an unspeakably painful wandering, the correction of a grave mistake, the loosening of chains, the opening of doors—it put right again a lamentable mischance.

Individuality?—All, all that one is, can, and has, seems poor, grey, inadequate, wearisome; what one is not, cannot, has not, that is what one looks at with the longing desire that becomes love because it fears to become hate.

Have I ever hated life—pure, powerful gruesome life? Folly and misconception! I have but hated myself, because I could not bear it. I love you, I love you all, you blessed, and soon, soon, I shall cease to be cut off from you by close constriction; soon will that in me that loves you, that is my love for you be free and be in you and with you—in and with you all. (BB, 256)

Those are only a few fragments of his monologue after the philosophic reading is interrupted by tears.

The stylistic elevation recurs in the description of Hanno's improvisation at the piano, which is perhaps the gem of the whole novel. It is a marvellous example of Thomas Mann's early artistic mastery. "It was quite a simple motif that he presented, a nothing, the fragment of an absent melody, a figure of one and a half bars ..." which "basically consisted of a single dissolution, a longing and painful sinking down from one tonal quality to the next ... a breathless, wretched invention." The way it is varied comes into conflict with other musical elements, becomes elevated and grows and overwhelms everything; that is the content of three pages. The poet employs countless musical technical expressions, which awaken musical experiences. He also likes to select images and comparisons from the musical sphere, only one from the world of colors, "in a tone color of age-old silver," which tied together with the basic motif is repeated again. Psychological meanings constantly accompany the music; for example, he speaks of the pianissimi: "which were like a gliding away of the ground under the feet and like a sinking down into the desire." It is the confusion of the feelings during Hanno's years of puberty, which find their expression on them. "I know what you are playing about," his friend Kai, the poet, had said to him in school. In order to indicate the varying recurrence of the basic motif, Thomas Mann varies the words "sinking down from one tonal quality to the next" five times. At the height of the variation he lets its content appear twice in images which for the most part are taken from Richard Wagner's **Siegfried** and **Walkure**. The countless words that emphatically expressed temporal course, like "suddenly," "soon," "until finally," conceal at the same time the element of the musical tension that demands solution. Otherwise, images of motion dominate the linguistic field; for example, "a restless coming and going," "a striving upwards," echoing the tonal movements. Here and there the poet looks the performer himself in the eye; "he was sitting a little bent over the keys, with parted lips and distant glance, and his brown hair covered his temples with soft locks." This portrait takes up exactly the middle of the whole episode. Even this linguistic construction in which the otherwise suppressed inner pathos of the poet breaks forth in rhetorical questions, piling up of words, intensifications, repetitions, and moody word combinations, contrasts with the ironic presentation of the world about. The language blossoms with musical motives and is itself borne along on a sweeping melody whose rhythms, extending widely, overreach the bars and sentence structure, a poetic composition which affords us the illusion of a genial musical improvisation by the young Hanno.

These two entrancing descriptions are the strongest testimony that this novel, despite its slightly parodistic tone, is not a sharp social/critical satire. Humorous shafts of light frequently illuminate this family history, tragic in its core. The author regards the life represented with compassionate love. Tony is a touching and charming figure with her naive family pride and her conventional chatter about her fate. The figure of Christian is also sunny when he talks about his half-imagined suffering. When the young Thomas Mann read aloud from the manuscript in the family circle, they laughed until they cried. The powerful dosage of humor gives his work artistic balance; the recurring gathering about the dead has serious dignity; and the end of the senator Thomas and his son Hanno, tragic grandeur.

It was an unusually mature literary performance for a young man who was just twenty-five years old when he finished it. He knew that epic breadth was indispensable for a story that spanned a century of middle-class life, and he therefore rejected the demand to substantially shorten it. But at that time he did not yet know that his family history was representative and that the development presented was typical. This he discovered with surprise in Paris in 1926, where it was told him that the story could have been set in the middle-class circles of Marseille. If one but penetrates deeply enough into the individual phenomena of life, one brings truths to light which have far-reaching validity.

Here and there the attempt was made to interpret the story of the Buddenbrooks as the decline of the middle class, an attempt that Thomas Mann disavowed. A sociological kind of observation was completely foreign to this individualist. Furthermore, such an interpretation is factually untenable. The story depicts biological weakening, with its intellectual and psychological consequences. Furthermore, even today one can probably speak about the danger to the small middle-class but not of the decline of the middle class. The middle class produced the whole powerful twentieth century development of science, technology, and the world economy; and it created for itself even in fascism a dangerously sharp weapon against the rise of the masses. As far as the Mann family is concerned, which after all furnished the raw material for the novel, two generations of people after the dissolution of the Lübeck grain firm have managed to achieve success and reputation in the world for themselves and, indeed, through their literary work. The end of the Buddenbrooks is pure poetry, nourished on the romantic sympathy of the poet for sickness and death.

Rejected Narratives

I will now consider six narratives of Thomas Mann which
he did not incorporate into his works. **Vision** (1893) is a melancholy narrative which the eighteen-year-old brings to life in
an enthusiastic style. It corresponds to the attitude of Tonio
Kröger during the period of the dance lessons or a little later,
and never recurs. The boy in **Vision** remembers a girl's hand,
and the lost love forces tears to his eyes. In **Fallen**, 1894, we
read of a shy young man who, egged on by a friend, gains the
favor of a young actress but one day comes upon an elderly
gentleman with her. She has taken a lover for the sake of better clothing, among other things. **Avenged**, 1899, is a "scene"
between a twenty-year-old, somewhat dissolute young man and
an ugly thirty-year-old woman who have formed an intellectual
friendship. One day he tells her right to her face that she exercises no sexual attraction for him. She takes revenge by
telling him about herself and a love affair, and rejects him
now that he desires her. **The Hungry**, 1903, are two opposite
types, an artist, who longs in vain for the love of a girl; and
the girl, who talks harmlessly with a young painter, dances,
and then leaves the festival hall. Outside, the artist sees a
savage individual who is really hungry and envies him. They
should be brothers! **Blood of the Walsungs**, printed 1906, but
recalled at the wish of Professor Pringsheim, tells of a sibling love under the influence of Wagnerian opera. **Anecdote**,
1908, reports of an attractive woman who is the ideal of society
in a little city, loved by women young and old. When a gentleman at an evening party in her house initiates another cheer
for her, her husband takes the floor and reveals the hell of his
marriage. After that, the couple moves to another city. Mann's
reason for excluding the six stories is that, in general, they
lack the mature artistic balance which, very early, is essential to him. There may have been other reasons; for example,
The Hungry became superfluous as a result of the thorough
treatment of its theme in **Tonio Kröger**.

Tonio Kröger; Tristan; Death in Venice

From the other narratives of this period, I shall select for
discussion first of all the three poet-portraits: **Tonio Kröger**,
Tristan, and **Death in Venice**.

Thomas Mann's narrative art rests on a musical basis. The three narratives are composed to a certain extent in three different tonalities. **Tonio Kröger** is set in spring: the young poet travels from Munich to his birthplace Lübeck and further to the North to the Danish Øresund coast. The story closes on a hopeful note.

The famous aging poet Aschenbach in **Death in Venice**, on the other hand, is traveling from Munich southwards to the Adriatic, where the spirit of the ancient world blows over him from the Mediterranean Sea, and, entranced by a handsome young boy, he remains in stricken Venice to fall victim to cholera. A foreboding of death permeates the writing.

In the short story **Tristan**, the poet Spinell, much like his protagonist, the merchant Klöterjahn, is parodistically described; but he joins with Klöterjahn's wife for a few hours in the realm of music, a spiritual union that she pays for with her death. This short story, with its class contrasts, is a disturbing tragicomedy.

Style is always for Thomas Mann the secret fusion of the impersonal with the factual. This fusion gives each of these three works of art its uniform stamp.

Tonio Kröger stands closest to the poet. As a child and young man, Tonio lives in Lübeck like Hanno Buddenbrook and has, like the latter, a beautiful musical mother; but he bears the sufferings of his artistry with more power or resistance. He could be Hanno's friend Kai. He plays the violin, like Thomas Mann, and composes as he does. His school experiences resemble Hanno's. Later he lives in Munich and knows Italy, like Thomas Mann. One could list even more parallels to Mann's life. Yet basically **Tonio Kröger** is neither an autobiographical report nor actually a short story. There is a complete lack of exciting plot. Thomas Mann wants to throw the brightest spotlight on the central problem of the artist, especially the contrast between literary art and the naive life.

In the first three sections of the story, he depicts the development of Tonio Kröger: First, his unhappy love for a blonde school comrade; then, a much more sensual unexpected attraction for a blonde girl during a dancing lesson. What happens is as good as nothing. There are living vignettes and conversations. The whole emphasis lies on the inner world of the inchoate poet, in whom the intellect is already beginning to stir and who finds the dull, naively existing human being, the activity and the vain gestures of the dance instructor ridiculous and despicable, yet still in his loneliness longs for union with the banal everyday world. In the third section, in Italy and Munich, he matures into a poet already successful in creating distinguished literary images.

The long conversation of Kröger with his Russian friend Lisabeta in her painter's studio takes up the middle of the work. It is a monologue. She paints and, here and there, throws a few words in to encourage him to make further confessions. The conversation, resembling the dialogues of Socrates in Plato, gives the philosopher an opportunity to present his opinions almost in essay form. Tonio Kröger begins with the fact that one cannot compose in the spring. It is an error to believe that the warm-hearted feeling itself is artistic, it is dilettantish—only the cold refined ecstasies of the intellect create the work of art. The literary person stands outside life, is an "unperson." He accomplishes everything in words; kills the experienced, endured world; and he himself is cold and dead. Among intellectual men, he is bored to death. So far as he still feels inwardly like a human being, the literary person feels revulsion in the face of intellect. The painter ends the conversation by calling her friend a "lost citizen." He goes home. She has also "finished" him.

The last three sections of the story present the experiences of Tonio Kröger on his trip to the North, with graphic examples of observations made in Munich. In conclusion, he writes a letter to his friend in which he describes his love for life as a bridge leading to naive people. It is responsible for making the literary person a poet. "Don't make fun of this love, Lisabeta; it is good and fruitful. There is longing in it and melancholy envy and a little bit of scorn and a whole lot of chaste bliss." These last words of the narrative also stand at the end of the first section, which Tonio's boyish love illuminates. His heart is still as lively as at that time.

We must certainly not transfer all the details of this story to the biography of Thomas Mann. The Russian girl friend is invented to permit transforming an essay on the antithesis between art and life into a dialogue. Furthermore, the rhetorically intensified excursions of the oversensitive poet whom the spring disturbs in his work are full of exaggerations. Thomas Mann certainly did not lead a debauched life in Italy that weakened his health. It should also not be taken literally that women compare him and his type with castrated male singers. He also does not feel completely finished as a result of Lisabeta's last remark to him. He finds the way to vital poetry.

The central problem of the romantic, middle-class artist Thomas Mann during this period is really the problem we have discussed and illustrated—the tension between art and intellect on the one hand and the naive life on the other, and the solution. In repeated sentences he characterizes himself as a "sentimental" poet in contrast to the "naive" type, to use concepts from the famous essay by Friedrich Schiller. The separation of the intellectual person from nature is basic. Out of the scorn for the unintellectual human world grows a moral and satiric aptitude. But enviously and longingly he tries to achieve the undisturbed happiness of everyday, middle-class life.

Strong threads run from this early narrative to both of the other poet figures—Spinell and Aschenbach; to the novel **Royal Highness**; to the **Confessions of Felix Krull, Confidence Man**, of which five chapters had already been completed by 1911; and to the musical novel **Doctor Faustus**, whose seed and nucleus, the idea that the German Faustian man must be a musician, was already fixed in 1901 in a diary entry. There is always a concern either with an artist or with a parallel to the artist's questionable state of non-manhood. Tonio Kröger therefore always remained close to the heart of Thomas Mann. It conceals the key to the understanding of a great part of his life's work.

In the short story **Tristan,** in which in accordance with classical example a passionate experience between two people becomes life's fate, the antithesis of art and life is represented satirically in the contrast between the writer Detlev Spinell and the merchant Klöterjahn, whose gravely ill wife Gabriele tarries in a private sanatorium with the writer. A great deal of mockery is expended on the two men. Only the lovely musical wife remains untouched by it. Spinell loves her in shy admiration. One day, when almost all the inhabitants of the house are away on a winter sled excursion, the two of them meet in the salon at the piano, where there is sheet music. Her doctor has strictly forbidden her the excitement of playing a piano. But she cannot resist Spinell's pleading. At first she plays nocturnes by Chopin, then **Tristan.** Richard Wagner's music, as the centerpiece, fills four pages of this narrative just as it influences Hanno's improvisation at the piano. In order to approach closely the melancholy, sensuous, spiritual nature of this tonal art, Thomas Mann abstracted many words, phrases, and whole sentences from the hundreds of florid, clumsy, alliterative verses of the libretto and fitted them into his own rich, melodic, musical description similarly as with the description of Hanno's playing. In his loneliness Hanno expresses in musical tones what fills him, but here two souls are joined for a few hours in the intoxicating experience of the love songs from **Tristan.** Once they are disturbed from their blissful enchantment. The pastor's wife Hüldenrauch, who has brought nineteen children into the world and is mentally unbalanced, walks through the room on the arm of her nurse on one of her rounds. Thus the crude, ghastly reality of everyday life interrupts the noble converse of souls. But they find each other again soon in the mighty elevation of the music. When the pianist has ended, Spinell sinks down on his knees at the door far from her in a shyly reverent gesture of renunciation. A few days later she has to pay for this intemperance with a lethal hemorrhage. To the vigorous screams of Klöterjahn's little son, Detlev Spinell takes flight from the sanatorium.

Death in Venice is a variation on the theme of the mature, famous artist's non-middle class adventuresome unreliability. Originally, Thomas Mann wanted to illustrate this theme with the grotesque and upsetting spectacle of the seventy-eight-year-old Goethe's hopeless courtship of the nineteen-year-old Ulrike von Levetzow, which inspired the moving "Marienbader Elegie." If he had carried out this plan, a poetic creation of completely different character would have arisen, adapted to the other personality, the other time, the other locations, the other incident. The problem of subject is just one element in the composition of the gaily colored, rich tapestry which the artistic work of the poet drapes over it. Sympathy with death gives **Death in Venice** its dark basic tone through which the mysterious charm of the old lagoon city on the Adriatic Sea is contrasted in strong colors to the love of the aging German writer Gustav Aschenbach for a seductively handsome Polish boy. Thomas Mann borrowed the first name and external characteristics of Aschenbach from the composer Gustav Mahler and gave Aschenbach all sorts of characteristics from himself. Among other things he made him into an "author of the clear prose epic of the life of Frederick of Prussia," for which he himself at that time was carrying on penetrating studies. But, as with the over-sensitive Detlev Spinell, he released Aschenbach from his own life and made him into an independent, fictitious figure with a fate of his own. It is rewarding to trace briefly the structure and the style of **Death in Venice**.

The narrative is divided into five sections, two short ones of six and seven pages which reveal the reason for Aschenbach's departure from Munich, and his life and work—the second in retrospect—and three sections of twenty-seven, twelve, and twenty-seven pages which depict the three phases of his passionate love. The surrounding world, a backdrop against which the events take place, is drawn very realistically in compressed factual description without any special decoration—the northern part of Munich, in which Aschenbach takes an afternoon's walk; the island in the Adriatic where he stays for a week and a half; and Venice with its famous docking area and its streets and canals, these latter several times; and finally the hotel on the Lido. There is only one exception: the ocean is described again and again in the most profuse language.

Aside from several secondary figures, four strange shapes appear who stand in a mysterious relationship to Aschenbach's fate and take on symbolic importance. In the portico of the cemetery chapel, a strange man appears who, in a completely surprising manner, awakens in Aschenbach a longing for distant places and a desire to travel. On the steamer which bears him from the island to Venice, there is an old man in the middle of a youthful group who is dressed like a young boy and conducts himself in an especially noisy fashion, drinks too much, and annoys the writer on his arrival in Venice. He foreshadows the transformation which the aging Aschenbach undergoes when his passion is unbound. The gondolier who rows him against his will directly to the Lido is a wild and strange uncouth individual, an intruder in the business without a permit. He disappears without pay while Aschenbach is changing his money in a nearby hotel. In his black, coffin-like boat, he is reminiscent of the ferryman crossing the Styx into the realm of shadows. One evening in the front garden of the hotel, a group of two female and two male street singers appears. The theatrically talented leader who ridicules the elegant society of the hotel resembles the strange man in front of the cemetery chapel. Although all these scenes are painted on a broad canvas with countless realistic details, the impression predominates that the four figures are personifications of death, who lure Aschenbach to his destruction and laugh mockingly all the while.

Gustav Aschenbach, who lives completely alone, is the main figure in whose eyes all the happenings are mirrored and whose inner world is the real showplace of the action. Up to now he has subordinated his life completely to his work and his fame. He has had little success and has granted himself hardly any leisure and enjoyment. The stranger arouses in him the vision of an Indian swamp landscape and the idea for a world trip. This is the area from which, at that time, cholera was spreading over the world. But his clear reason still predominates; and he decides, since his work is at a standstill and he is apparently over-tired, to take a break of a few weeks for his health. The second section of the narrative is an essayistic presentation of his manner of living and working, of his strictly disciplined artistry up to the meeting with the stranger in which, among other things, the mother-like heroism of the artist and the questionability of art are treated as in "**Tonio Kröger.**" Here there is clear evidence that much of the nature of the storyteller Mann is concealed in Aschenbach but since Mann is thirty-six years old, to this fictitious figure— although a greying, aging man of far more than fifty years— he has added many strange elements, and has given him among other things a completely different biography. Where Mann describes Aschenbach's aging, one is reminded of Goethe. Thomas Mann lets us see how the severe self-discipline practiced over decades is transformed in the atmosphere of the lagoon city and gradually becomes, through love for the beautiful Tadzio, a daring sinful passion. Since Aschenbach lives very withdrawn, the narrator leads us into his loneliness and constantly gives us insights into his emotional experience, each time from every possible angle. Initially his reason resists. Although he is already tied down, he wants to leave, since Venice in unfavorable weather has a harmful effect on him. But when a misdirected trunk forces him to return, he is very happy and decides to remain as long as the handsome, young boy is there.

Reason orders him once again to travel on, as cholera is

making the rounds in Venice. At first, only the rotten smell of the canals is mentioned in passing; then rumors crop up. During a visit in the city, he detects the smell of a disinfectant. A subsequent smell makes Aschenbach feel very miserable. Finally, from an Englishman in an official travel-bureau, he gets a long factual report on the origin of cholera from India, its spread, its penetration into the European harbors, its devastating effect, and its worst form, the "dry" form, which brings death quickly. At first the Germans and Austrians, warned by their press, leave. Finally, though most of the guests take flight, Aschenbach no longer thinks about leaving. As life has become savage in the city, so too his passion intensifies. He pursues the boy and his longing for beauty is transformed into wild desire.

Even when he catches sight for the first time of the half-grown, fourteen-year-old boy on the day of his arrival, the boy's perfect beauty enraptures him. One glance from him becomes fate for Aschenbach and binds him. On the following morning on the beach, he tries to occupy himself with his correspondence but puts everything aside in order to observe him. The melodic sound of the name Tadzio delights him. From now on he describes him again and again and loses himself in a hundred details of Tadzio's innate charm.

> He stood at the water's edge, alone, removed from his family, quite close to Aschenbach; standing erect, his hands clasped at the back of his neck, rocking slowly on the balls of his feet, day-dreaming away into blue space, while little waves ran up and bathed his toes. The ringlets of honey-colored hair clung to his temples and neck, the fine down along the upper vertebrae was yellow in the sunlight; the thin envelope of flesh covering the torso betrayed the delicate outline of the ribs and the symmetry of the breast structure. His arm pits were still as smooth as a statue's, smooth the glistening hollows behind his knees, where the blue network of veins suggested that the body was formed of some stuff more transparent than mere flesh. What discipline, what precision of thought were expressed by the tense youthful perfection of this form! His eyes took in the proud bearing of that figure there at the blue water's edge; with an outburst of rapture he told himself that what he saw was

beauty's very essence; form as divine thought, the single and pure perfection which presides in the mind, of which an image and likeness, rare and holy, was here raised up for adoration. This was very frenzy—and without a scruple, nay, eagerly, the aging artist bade it come. His mind was in travail, his whole mental background in a state of flux. Memory flung up in him the primitive thoughts which are youth's inheritance, but which with him had remained latent, never leaping up into a blaze. (SL, II, 43 f.)

Tadzio senses Aschenbach's attentive adoration and oftentimes exchanges a serious glance with him. But one time when he smiles at him, Aschenbach's equanimity is gone. His love for Tadzio fills his soul with joyful intoxication. He no longer leaves it to chance, but follows the boy everywhere, pursues him in the confusion of alleys in the city. This does not escape Tadzio. There arises a kind of agreement between them. When all the people at the hotel are caught up by the wild laughing refrain of the street singers, both of them remain unmoved and exchange a serious glance. On the day of Aschenbach's departure, Tadzio stands alone in the shallow water on a sandy bank. Aschenbach, already deathly sick, believes he sees him beckon to him and he calls him Psychagogue, the leader of souls who accompanies the dead into the underworld. The ambiguous experience of beauty has seduced him, the artist, and enticed him to his death.

With this transformation of the Polish boy into a Greek god of the dead, the most important element of the style of this short story is touched upon. From the very beginning it is aiming at the Grecian world; and, wherever the language of Thomas Mann waxes enthusiastic during factual description in the novel, it revolves around Greek images and traditions, figures of the gods and men. Even at the cemetery chapel, a Greek cross is mentioned. The boy reminds Aschenbach of the "thorn remover." Later he compares him with Eros, then with Hyacinthus, with Narcissus. The love of boys is after all an essential element in ancient Greece in the formation of youth. Thus it is natural that the narrator allows a vivid image to arise in Aschenbach's fantasy—Socrates and Phaedrus in the conversation on love. In a feverish monologue, Aschenbach addresses Tadzio with the name Phaedrus. In a frightening, betraying dream, he experiences the way the dissolute Bacchanalian procession of the strange god Dionysus storms up and the way he is rended in a turbulence of desire.

The Greek stylization also extends to the representation of nature and the ocean which Aschenbach loves as contrast to the strict discipline and form of his profession, and the language is intensified to a hymnlike quality, as at the beginning of the fourth section:

Now daily the naked God with cheeks aflame drove his four fire-breathing steeds through heaven's spaces; and with him streamed the strong east wind that fluttered his yellow locks. A sheen, like white satin, lay over all the idly rolling sea's expanse. The sand was burning hot. Awnings of rust-colored canvas were spanned before the bathing-huts, under the ether's quivering silver-blue; one spent the morning hours within the small, sharp square of shadow they purveyed. But evening too was lovely: balsamic with the breath of flowers and shrubs from the nearby park, while overhead the constellations circled in their spheres, and the murmuring of the night-girted sea swelled softly up and whispered to the soul. Such nights as these contained the joyful promise of a sunlit tomorrow, brim-full of sweetly ordered idleness, studded thick with countless precious possibilities.... (SL, II, 40 f.)

In the description of the sunrise ten pages later:

... he rose and, wrapping himself lightly against the early chill, sat down by the window to await the sunrise. Awe of the miracle filled his soul new-risen from its sleep. Heaven, earth, and its waters yet lay enfolded in the ghostly, glassy pallor of dawn; one paling star still swam in the shadowy vast. But there came a breath, a winged word from far and inaccessible abodes, that Eos was rising from the side of her spouse; and there was that first sweet reddening of the farthest strip of sea and sky that manifests creation to man's sense. She neared, the goddess, ravisher of youth, who stole away Cleitos and Cephalus and, defying all the envious Olympians, tasted beautiful Orion's love. At the world's edge began a strewing of roses, a shining and a blooming ineffably pure; baby cloudlets hung illumined, like attendant amoretti, in the blue and blushful haze; purple effulgence fell upon the sea, that seemed to heave it forward on its welling waves; from horizon to zenith went great quivering thrusts like golden lances, the gleam became a glare; without a sound, with god-like violence, glow and glare and rolling flames streamed upwards, and with flying hoofbeats the steeds of the sun god mounted the sky. The lonely watcher sat, the splendour of the God shone on him; he closed his eyes and let the glory kiss his lids. (SL, II, 47 f.)

These examples must suffice. Style is the fusion of the personal with the factual. Aschenbach's love of the boy requires a style of language to connect it to the Grecian world. The rich fabric of relationships, so characteristic of all Mann's narrative art, is at least made suggestively manifest.

Death in Venice, the longest story from this period, appeared separately in 1911. Mann did not include it in the collection, The Infant Prodigy, 1914; with its macabre impact it would have smothered those five little narratives.

The Infant Prodigy; The Dilettante

The Infant Prodigy (1903) belongs with the artist stories.

To term the four 'artist stories' variations on the same motive says nothing significant; for, as artistic structures, they have nothing in common. This one on the prodigy is just a vivid image of the emergence of a virtuoso. The prodigy is an eight-year-old Grecian pianist who plays his own compositions for one hour. The critic summarizes everything that takes place on the podium in the packed auditorium of the elegant hotel and is described carefully by the narrator with all the details of the inner and external life:

Look at him, this bébé, this little monkey! As an individual human being he still has a little to grow, but as a type he is completely finished, as a type of the artist. He has within himself the artist's loftiness and his lack of dignity, his charlatanism and his holy spark, his scorn and his secret intoxication. But I don't dare write that; it is too good.

It is a parodistic glorification of artistry within the broad framework of a biting satire on the public.

The Dilettante, 1897, also possesses talents which he uses to entertain the people around him in order to make himself popular. But he is lacking essential characteristics—the urge to know, industry, concentration, the power to give shape and form—all necessary for the artist. When his father dies and leaves him a legacy, he first does some extensive traveling and then settles down at the age of twenty-five to a comfortable life of tasteful enjoyment and idleness in a little capital city. But he falls in love with a beautiful girl from a fine family, experiences a bitter disappointment, and is seized with disgust for his own useless existence.

The Remaining Stories

The way Tonio Kröger matures into an arist is depicted in the third section of **Tonio Kröger**. He becomes clairvoyant. "But what he saw was this: Comedy and misery—comedy and misery." With these two words we can characterize almost all the rest of the stories of this period. To be sure, Thomas Mann loves the naive life and longs for it, but he does not represent it in a pleasing manner. On the contrary, under the influence of his melancholy nature and the pessimistic world view which he has adopted for himself, he selects unusual, out of the way, shadowy figures and events. He presents them in a ruthless realism of external phenomena and an inexorably penetrating spiritual analysis. Wherever a plot develops, it leads mostly to a bad end, often to death. The main figures live for the most part in loneliness, whether this is dictated by their special predisposition or by an unusual fate. This problematic living of lonely people with all its consequences is the actual misery. Lacking a viable relationship with the world around them, they suffer, are misunderstood, become unhappy, all subject to strange imaginings and ideas which usually bring them to the point of madness. Their contrast to naive everyday society leads to harsh contrastive effects. Typically they themselves occasion a tragi-comic effect or else the satire is sharply directed against all weaknesses of the unintellectual people around them. There is never a complicated action in which major interests or strong passions collide with one another; the two worlds smash into each other senselessly. The occupation, the social and political life, are only alluded to, so that one cannot speak of social criticism but only of moral illumination and unmasking of the social life.

With this general explication, everything significant about these narratives has been said. The richness of variation is astonishing: not one of the stories in the collection resembles the other. Each one concerns a completely unique human fate or at least an event or scene which is shaped quite individually. For each motif Thomas Mann develops a style appropriate to it and, in every case, finds surprising, fortunate words and turns of phrase. Thus in the three collections **Little Herr Friedemann** (1898), **Tristan** (1903), and **The Infant Prodigy** (1914), exquisite images are brought together which capture always a sharply observed, transitory segment of experienced life—balanced writing on an intellectual level and with a personal stamp. Earlier I compared them with the old art of the goldsmith; but even for this comparison their content is too rare and exciting.

In the last collection, there is an autobiographical report, **The Fight between Jappe and Do Escobar** (1911), a remembrance from the childhood of Thomas Mann when he was about thirteen years old and had Mr. Knaack as a dancing instructor (cf. **Tonio Kröger**). The matter is presented factually, with a great deal of mockery for the grown-up who plays the part of the judge in the "duel." A second autobiographical story is **The Train Accident**, 1909. In the story **At the Prophet's**, 1904, Thomas Mann hides behind the short story writer whose book is "read in middle-class circles."

The Wardrobe, 1899, deviates most from all the others. Mann calls it "a story full of puzzles." A rather young man of indefinite age marked for death interrupts a trip in a strange place on awaking and rents a poorly furnished room in a side street. When he opens the clothes closet late in the evening, he sees a naked girl and at the same time sees that the back wall consists only of a cloth. Evening after evening she tells him sad stories and surrenders herself to him whenever he desires. How long the experience lasts remains uncertain; indeed, it remains questionable whether the events really happened or whether the traveller is just dreaming this in his sleeping compartment on the trip. Although it is told with many realistic details, it is still the wish dream of a lonesome, reticent, shy person. The observed reality is different—"misery and comedy."

Florence

In 1906 the dramatic poem **Florence** appeared. As early as 1902, Mann wrote a story called **Sword of God**. A fanatic monk goes into an elegant Munich art shop and demands the removal from the show window of a much too sensuously painted madonna with the Christ child; in profile, the monk resembles Savonarola. This is a prelude to **Florence**. Furthermore, in Daniel's room in the narrative **At the Prophet's** there hangs among other things a picture of Savonarola. In **Florence**, the plot is laid in the time of the Dominican monks, and the contrast between ascetic Christianity and the sensual Renaissance is broadly and vividly presented. Thomas Mann regards art as questionable and does not allow himself to be carried away by enthusiasm for Nietzsche's self-sufficient Renaissance Man.

Savonarola is very successful with his fanatical preaching, not only among the broad masses but also among the young nobles and well-to-do citizens—indeed, even among individual artists—although he attacks the rich and their culture and stands up for the poor. All the dialogues contain passages which bear witness to his power over people. In contrast to this, the situation of Lorenzo de Medici and his circle as representatives of the Renaissance is depicted much less sympathetically, so that the impression can arise that the poet is taking a position against them. The world-wide businesses of the house of Medici are retrenching. The oldest son, haughty and disliked, profligate and deep in debt, will not be able to maintain the mighty position of his father in the future. The throng of artists about Lorenzo with their vain boastings and frivolous quarrels is unattractively presented.

In the face of death, Lorenzo himself demands the unvarnished truth which the toadies around him do not express. He calls his opponent to himself, recognizes his stature, and begs for his understanding, although, even at the deathbed, the visitor appears full of hate and curtly forbidding. But gradually the two arrive at a fruitful conversation and finally at a common antiphonal song on the nature of rulers.

The **prior:** I am chosen. I am permitted to know and

still desire. For I must be strong. God performs miracles. You are looking at the miracle of innocence retained. (Looking at the bust of Caesar) Did he ask by what means he rose?

Lorenzo: Caesar? You are a monk. And you have ambition?

The prior: How could I not have, I that suffered so? Ambition says: My suffering must not have been in vain. It must bring me fame.

Lorenzo: By God, that is it. Did I not know it? Monk, you have weighed all these matters miraculously well. We rulers of men are egoists and they blame us for it, not knowing that it comes of our suffering. They call us hard and understand not it was pain made us so. We may justly say: Look at yourselves, who have had so much easier a time on this earth. To myself I am both torment and joy enough.

The prior: But they do not rail. They marvel, they reverence. See them come to the strong ego, the many who are only one; we see them serve him, see them tirelessly do his will—

Lorenzo: Although his own self-serving is plain to any eye—

The prior: Although he leaves their services quite unrewarded and takes them for granted —

Lorenzo: Cosimo, my forebear—I was old enough to know him; he was a cold and clever tyrant. They gave him the title Pater Patriae (Father of the Fatherland). He took it with a smile and never a word of thanks. I shall never forget it. How he must despise them, I thought. Since then I have despised the common people.

The prior: Fame is the school of scorn.

Lorenzo: Ah, the worthlessness of the masses! They are so poor, so empty, so selflessly self-forgetful.

The prior: So simple, so easy to dominate.

Lorenzo: They know nothing better than to be dominated.

The prior: They write to me from all the quarters of the earth, they come from afar to kiss the hem of my robe, they spread my fame to the four winds. Do I ask them for it, have I ever thanked them?

Lorenzo: It is amazing.

The prior: It is quite amazing. Are you so worthless, one thinks, so idle yourselves that you know nothing prouder than to serve another?

Lorenzo: Absolutely! Ab–so–lutely! One cannot believe one's eyes to see them bowing low and so willingly—and on top of that they are satisfied.

The prior: One is forced to laugh at the docility of the world.

Lorenzo: And, laughingly, one grasps hold of the world like a willing instrument on which to play.

The prior: To play one's own tune.

Lorenzo (feverishly): Oh, my dreams! My power and art! Florence was my lyre. Did it not resound? Sweetly? It sang of my longing, it sang of beauty, it sang of great desire, it sang, it sang the powerful song of life. (SL, II, 321 f.)

This is the heart of the whole poem. Behind the psychological analysis of the two powerful figures, the contrast between Christianity and Renaissance loses its significance in the view of the poet, especially since both powerful movements are not captured in their significant features and in their most productive representatives (for example, Francis of Assisi; Michelangelo, Leonardo da Vinci). Thomas Mann reveals the weaknesses of both his heroes and in this sense administers justice.

There are contradictory opinions about the poem as a drama and its effectiveness on the stage. It shows clearly that Thomas Mann is not a born dramatist but rather an epic writer because he does not bring a number of highly dramatic events onto the stage. He simply allows them to be narrated in detail. In this category above all belong the sermons of Savonarola in the cathedral of Florence, especially the scene wherein, before all the people, he pillories Fiori—who always appears disturbingly a half an hour too late with a large following—as the great Babylonian Whore, and injures her irreparably. She herself reports to Lorenzo how Savonarola as her neighbor begged passionately for her favor in his youth, and not until she rejected him did he enter a monastery. A burlesque folk scene on the stage would be the beating of Aldo Brandini in front of the cathedral, which he himself and a witness describe. Botticelli who, moved by a sermon of Savonarola, destroys a painting in his studio, would yield an effective scene. A dramatist like August Strindberg who has the stage and the auditorium within himself and writes for them would not have let such things get away from him. But there is no lack of dramatic scenes in **Florence**. Fiori says to Piero de Medici, who is pushing her around brutally, that he bores her and that she will never belong to him. His brother Giovanni, the future cardinal, refuses to lend him a hundred ducats. The last argument between Lorenzo and Savonarola with its mighty pathos—a grand conclusion (it is only weakened by Fiori's following speech)—stands in especially effective contrast with the wild tale of Leone and the laughter following it. After the death of his opponent, Savonarola is the unrestricted master of Florence and of the embodiment of the Renaissance city—Fiori. He has reached his goal.

Royal Highness

Thomas Mann called his novel **Royal Highness** a modern fairy tale and a comedy even in the face of negative criticism aimed at the underlying seriousness of the work.

The fictitious plot is truly like a fairy tale: a German by the name of Spoelman has emigrated to America and come into a chance fortune; his son returns with his only daughter Emma as an heir to a billion dollars into a capital city of his father's German homeland and rescues a backward, heavily indebted country from ruin when his daughter reveals to him that she loves the successor to the throne, Klaus Heinrich with the crippled left arm, and wants to marry him. A number of romantic elements strengthen the fairy tale-like impression. A gipsy woman predicted a hundred years ago that a prince with one hand would free the country in dire necessity. In the old castle there are noisy ghosts in one chamber whenever important events are about to take place in the grand ducal house. There are no flowers there. Only, in one of the courtyards there is a stalk of beautiful dark red roses which smell of mildew; but sometimes they have a pleasing aroma. Quite often there are references to fairy tales by Hans Christian Anderson which are read aloud to the princess' children, who identify themselves with the storied princes and princesses. At the end, the grand duke presents his brother, on his wedding, the rose bush from the castle courtyard; and it is planted in the park of his castle, so that the roses, prospectively, will have a pleasing aroma in the future. The old prophecies are fulfilled.

Since the narrative ends happily with a marriage in the midst of the joyous people, as is so often the case with the orally transmitted fairy tales of love, one can also call it a comedy—all the more so, as many bright spots are scattered throughout the whole work; for example, in many a name such as Dr. Raoul Upperleg, Baron von Rubbleheap, and Countess Lionjowl, as well as among the titles and ranks of the court. The film of this novel is much more effective than those of **Buddenbrooks**, of the **Confessions of the Confidence Man, Felix Krull,** or indeed of the actionless short story **Tonio Kröger;** it is a film like the comedy **The Difficult One** by Hoffmannsthal, even if the undertone of the narrative is a few degrees more serious and sinister.

In **Tonio Kröger** the questionable extra-human existence of the poet is compared with that of the prince, the actor, and the swindler. The novel **Royal Highness** centers on princehood. But it is wrong to regard it as a satire—for instance, on Wilhelm II—simply because he had the same deficiency as Klaus Heinrich. The poet really takes the problems of princehood seriously. The motive of the unusual existence separated from the naive life is varied in all sorts of ways. It is illuminated with searching, one might almost say loving, interest. The somewhat sentimental comedy which pervades the tiny principality is captured in a broad panorama.

To be sure, the talk is of decline just as in **Buddenbrooks,** but decline of a state, not of a family with a sad end. Even the former belief in the grace of God shared by the royal house declines along with the distress of the state. Johann Albrecht still lives in an untouchable arrogance, with the result that the plight of the country cannot be made clear to him. The three siblings—two brothers: Albrecht, who follows his father on the throne, and Klaus Heinrich; and a sister Dietlinde, age three—rebel, just as in **Buddenbrooks,** each in his own manner, against the royal form of life. The deathly sick Albrecht II despises popularity, calls it in fact "a disgusting thing," and leaves the representation of the monarchy so far as at all possible to his brother. Dietlinde disregards royal prejudices: although she marries someone of equal birth, he is a prince who has become an industrious, successful big businessman with substantial revenues. The history of Klaus Heinrich's development and education is the chief content of the novel. At the beginning (like Thomas Buddenbrook), he is a duty-conscious servant of tradition and is strengthened in this by his teacher, Dr. Raoul Upperleg. For a long time he leads a dreamy, irrelevant, spurious existence and regards it himself as a difficult, taxing actor's performance which is far superior to that observable on the stage from the actors. He does not fulfil his duties entirely without relish, however, because—with the help of Upperleg—he understands that the people, by acclaiming him with their homage, raise themselves above their everyday existence and celebrate their own lives. He is serving mankind; but, at the moment when he falls passionately in love with Emma Spoelman at first sight, he breaks out of this empty form of life. He abandons the pose he had practised for two long decades, strives for a long time for her confidence, impetuously and importunately, since she (like her father) takes a critical attitude toward the representational pomp and circumstance of royalty; and he does not win her until he occupies himself seriously with the difficult problems of his country, which are treated in detail in several passages in the book. In addition to this three-fold view of the main theme, the fates of a number of secondary people are penetratingly depicted.

The mother of the three, the Grand Duchess Dorothea, a beautiful woman who has been on public display her whole life long without any kind of inner commitment; even love for her children was only acted out for the people. As she ages and declines, her life has no more meaning and she becomes mad.

The meeting of Klaus Heinrich with the poet Martini is a sharp satire. The poet is victor in a contest with a poem on the joys of life, but he confesses to the prince that he is not able to enjoy any of life's pleasures because of his poor health. Klaus Heinrich calls him "frightening" and "repulsive."

The highly gifted Dr. Raoul Upperleg, an illegitimate child, grew up in starvation and by ambitious striving worked himself into a high position. He renounced all human happiness after a frustrating life with a married woman. He is an outstanding teacher but inwardly without any balance so that, as the result of an unhappy event in his school duties, he takes his life. His

friend, the Jewish Dr. Summit, emerging from modest circumstances like himself but hardened by suffering, persists by
virtue of his calm objectivity. The Countess Lionjowl, who
has suffered terribly in her marriage, is at times confused
and "chatters" at such times about her fantastic experiences.
None of the three experience a life similar to that of the royal
existence, though they live by virtue of their fate in a self-
created isolation.

On the other hand, even Emma Spoelman is excluded from
the naive life of the masses by the wealth of her father and an
admixture of Indian blood. She is beautiful, "like the daughter
of the mountain king," by destiny precocious and serious, very
intelligent and in many areas eager and well read, full of goodness and compassion for the misfortunes of others; but for a
long time she keeps the prince at a distance with sharp, scorn-
ful words because his actor-like pose, seemingly devoid of
love, chills her and embarrasses her. Only gradually does
she allow herself to be convinced of his love's genuineness.
The zeal for life, of which Tonio Kröger writes at the end to
Lisabeta, reaches fruition here. Klaus Heinrich finally says
to Emma that it is now up to both of them to unite "nobility and
love." In its happy mixture of seriousness and gaiety, **Royal
Highness** is a charming, warmhearted, vital book.

There are good reasons for that. In her personality, Emma
has taken over many of the traits of Katja Pringsheim, as has
Samuel Spoelman from her father Alfred Pringsheim, who was
also a rich heir, art collector, and devotee of music. It is
superfluous to cite many details. A letter of Thomas Mann's
from this period of the wooing of his "fairy tale princess" reports that the father once presented him with a piece of used
gutta percha for throat wrappings, which he interpreted as a
good sign. This episode is included in the novel. Likewise
the passionate, persistent wooing of Klaus Heinrich and the
joyous festive conclusion are also nurtured and enlivened from
the personal life of the writer, no matter how much had to be
omitted and added in this royal book. It is a disguised confession of poetic transformation which reports how Thomas Mann,
after ten years of lonely suffering in his lofty and difficult
profession, pursued his life's happiness and won it.

The understanding between the prince and Emma is not
reached so quickly as in the popular fairy tale of love but pro-

ceeds quite slowly. In the fairy tale, the obstacles are external; in **Royal Highness**, internal. Once in Emma's library in the castle "Delfinenort," Klaus Heinrich goes on his knees before her in his Major's uniform, and she kisses his withered left hand. But when about three weeks later they go riding together as they often did and he asks her whether she can perhaps not have a little bit of confidence in him, she answers:

> No, prince Klaus Heinrich, that I cannot do ... because you prevent me from doing so ... by everything, by your attitude, by your nature and manner, by your whole royal personality ... you prevent me from letting myself go, you kill my enthusiasm by everything, by your words, by your plans, by your way of sitting and standing, and it is quite impossible to have any confidence in you. I had the opportunity to observe you in your relations with other people ... you hold yourself upright and ask questions but not out of interest. You are not concerned with the content of the question; no, you are not concerned with anything, and nothing is close to your heart. I have seen it often—you speak, you express an opinion, but you could just as well express another one, for in reality you have no opinion and no belief and nothing is a matter of concern for you except your princely posture. You say at times your profession is not an easy one, but since you have asked me I will tell you that it would be a lot easier for you if you were to have an opinion and a belief—that is my opinion and my belief. How could anyone have confidence in you? No, it is not confidence which you inspire but coldness and embarrassment, and if I were to make an effort to approach you more closely, this kind of embarrassment and helplessness would prevent me from it —now I have answered.

But Klaus Heinrich remains stubborn and persistent in his courtship of her, and this conversation is followed by many a similar one. Not until Prime Minister von Knobelsdorff has informed him as to the distressful situation of the principality and he has buried himself in political and economic studies is there the slightest beginning of an approach. She insists on reading his books together with him. She gains confidence in him as she notices that he is seriously concerned about the welfare of his people. Only this leads to the happy end. It is certainly possible that similar conversations also took place between Thomas Mann and Katja Pringsheim.

The charm of the work is substantially increased by the creative use of language adapted to the motif. As in **Buddenbrooks,** each person has his particular characteristics which recur in variations through the whole book; each is penetratingly characterized. The interiors of the castles: those of the court disintegrate; those of Dietlinde and Spoelman in their cultured splendor are carefully described. A number of detailed conversations are reproduced partly in direct speech and part in indirect summary; and to all these external phenomena the inner meanings of the events are contantly related —most detailedly in the case of prince Klaus Heinrich, who, as a result of this, is elevated to the central figure. All this is similar to the narrative art in **Buddenbrooks** and the short stories. But if one compares the total vocabulary of the two novels, one easily sees that Thomas Mann has created a special world of language for this princely story with its own words and phrases, images, comparisons, and symbols.

3. REFLECTIONS OF A NON-POLITICAL MAN

Reflections of a Non-Political Man is a mine for the scholar, a rich, intelligent book worth reading today, although it has the external form of a fiery polemic, intended to pillory and destroy the opponent. Its author is really apolitical. He has never occupied himself with the unfortunate political history of the German people, touches only casually on the democratic movement of the first half of the nineteenth century, passes over the party politics of the second half, the privileges of the conservatives in Prussia, the political Catholicism, and arrives at the social democracy which Bismarck fought against with socialistic law in the Kulturkampf. He has no insight into the fateful role of Wilhelm II, who discharged his annoying mentor Bismarck and dabbled himself in world politics, and he passes lightly over the influence of the Prussian land owners and the Rhenish industrialists on the wartime goals of the German army leadership. How was it even possible that the astute, careful artist who proved his mastery of structuring life and language so early in **Buddenbrooks**, became entangled in the wild adventure of this quarrel and lost three years in it? During this time, he often felt like a chained slave on a galley and longed for freedom and his artistic work.

Thomas Mann lived through the outbreak of World War I at the beginning of August, 1914 in exuberant emotion. His people who broke out in enthusiasm to defend the fatherland seem beautiful to him. He saw the war as an elevating, clarifying sacrificial pilgrimage, as the beginning of a great period, as a turning point in world history, as the beginning of a new historical epoch. Two works he had begun had to lie untouched for the time being. As early as 1911, he had carried the picaresque novel **Confessions of Felix Krull, Confidence Man** up to the fifth chapter but had then broken off in order to write the short story **Death in Venice.** In 1912, his wife's stay in the tuberculosis sanitorium at Davos gave him the initial thrust for a narrative which eventually developed into **The Magic Mountain.** But the excitement of the war made all artistic work impossible, and it was four years before Thomas Mann could return to it again. The invasion of Belgium by a Germany surrounded by enemies was in his eyes ordered by necessity, and he found the forthright speech of Bethmann-Holweg magnificent. Although he himself was incapable of serving in the field, he wanted to do his part for the state which he had just come to understand, and he served with his weapon, the word. He wrote **Thoughts during the War** (November 1914), **Frederick and the Great Coalition** (January/February 1915), and an answer (May 1915) to an open letter from **Svenska Dagbladet,** Stockholm. The three writings are closely related. In all three, there is reference to King Frederick of Prussia, who invaded Saxony in 1756 in order to anticipate the mighty European coalition which threatened to overwhelm him. He thus defended the surprise attack on Belgium, the matter of his threatened fatherland. It was truly no transfigured image which he drew of the Prussian king but quite on the contrary an accurate one with evil features in firm hard strokes, but he still celebrated him as the hero who sacrificed himself for the future of his people and fulfilled a mission which fate had placed upon him. He was well equipped for this literary performance because for a long time he had planned an "epic" about the king.

Initially, **Reflections of an Unpolitical Man** is a continuation of this battle, which was directed against the war propaganda of the enemy and in which many other admired writers also took part. Up to the end of 1915, Thomas Mann had already written about 200 pages. At the beginning of 1916, however, he read the essay **Zola** by his brother Heinrich in **Die Weissen Blätter,** which René Schickele published, a passionate hymn to the French novelist who, in his novel cycle Les Rougon-Macquart, defended the working people and who, in the press, fought for the Jewish captain in the French General Staff, Alfred Dreyfus—a man innocently condemned for treason and sent to Devil's Island. The name Thomas Mann did not occur in the essay **Zola,** but Heinrich had followed his lead and had selected Zola as an historical example in order to oppose his judgment of German war politics to that of his brother. The French writer had predicted the collapse of the Third Republic under Napoleon III because it was erected on swampy ground. Heinrich Mann wanted to predict the defeat of Germany against whose leading lights he had already written novels of social criticism.

Heinrich Mann's **The Subject** appeared in 1918. Its author had already stood for a long time outside the middle-class aristocratic circle from which he originated. Heinrich was genuinely dismayed at the literary military service of his brother. He was of the opinion that every thinking person, even writers, should stand at the side of the working people and fight against the war which the masses had to pay for with their blood and goods. Therefore, he did not take long to select the words for the attack on his brother Thomas, who rightfully felt deeply wounded.

The "literary mouthpiece for civilisation" (Zivilisationsliterat) became Thomas Mann's chief opponent in his answering polemic. For 100 pages Heinrich is scorned and abused, crushed by countless hammerblows. The immoderate violence of Thomas Mann's language is not at all directed against the political reality but against the literary propaganda of Germany's enemies and against the literary attack by his brother Heinrich and against Heinrich's espousal of Western democracy.

At the beginning, Thomas Mann goes very far in his conservative defense of German political conditions. In the preface [**Reflections of a Non-Political Man**, xxxii], he says among other things: "I confess to the deep conviction that the German people will never be able to love political democracy for the simple reason that it cannot love politics itself and that the much maligned 'dictatorial state' is and will remain the fitting form of government appropriate to the German people and basically desired by it." In the year 1917, however, he explains that he is not at all against democracy if by that a German peoples' state is meant, and he makes suggestions for its configuration: monarchy; an independent government not elected by the parliament; multiple votes according to age, education, and performance; suspension of the educational privilege of property owners and more of the same, because he considers the victory of democracy as unavoidable. But he fears the worst consequences for a German culture of the inner man; he fights against the progress "From Music to Democracy": "The difference between intellect and politics contains the difference between culture and civilization, between soul and society, between freedom and voting franchise, between art and literature; and between Germanicism—that is, culture, soul freedom, art—and civilization—that is, society, voting franchise, literature."

That is the actual contents of this book. Thomas Mann is not writing it as a politician but as an artist. He writes against the literary people without and within because they are attacking his Germanicism. He is a moralistic individualist and not only as an artist who needs isolation for his work. He experiences time and the world about him in individualities, in history and the present, in the great creative personalities who, according to his concept, contribute everything that is essential and represent the intellect of the people. The people, too, appear to him as a uniform individuality. The intimacy of the music-loving German people expresses itself in their lack of relationship to politics. Apparently he projects his own apolitical attitude onto the German people; indeed, he identifies his inner world with that of his people. As far as the meaty and spirited Reflections are concerned, it is of little significance against whom and what he is fighting, but very much what he is defending, the rich, intellectual, and spiritual world which he believed to be close to destruction as a result of the political democratization of the German people. Above all else he fears the loss of the German musicality: This book permits itself to dream—confused and difficult and indistinct, but this and nothing else is the content of its fears: "Finis musicae." The word **progress** occurs somewhere in it, and is only a dream symbol for democracy. The progression from music to democracy—that is what it means everywhere when it speaks of **progress**. But when the book maintains and tries to show that Germany is truly and irresistibly moving in the direction of this progress, this attempt is indeed in the first place a rhetorical means of defense. For Thomas Mann's book is after all obviously combatting this progress, is offering a conservative resistance. In fact, all its conservatism is only opposition in this regard; all its melancholy and half-feigned resignation, all its fawning adoration of romanticism and its "sympathy with death" is also no different. It denies progress in general in order to deny this progress in any case; it argues quite at random and enters into doubtful pacts; it charges against "virtue," covers over "belief" with quotations, issues a challenge to "humanity"—all this in order to oppose this progress, this progress of Germany from music to politics.

Since Mann is convinced of the victory of democracy after the great war, he carries on a rearguard action for the defense of the precious, threatened values of the nation. He defends the conservative, middle-class, romantic, protestant, spiritual, moral world to which he belongs. He defends his idea of Germanicism against the propaganda of the enemies without and within—above all, however, against the spokesmen for civilization, such as his brother. As a result there arises this strange exciting mixture of violently zealous polemics and searching self-confession.

As conspirators in this battle, he calls chiefly upon the three great revered masters—Schopenhauer, Nietzsche, and Wagner—the triumvirate of eternally united spirits to whom he owes so much of his education. Artists, he says, add nothing to the ideological stockpile of mankind. It is their business to shape transitory life as it is experienced and suffered into language and by this means preserve it forever. He gathers his thoughts from history and the world around him. For him they are ingredients of his seriously played game. Furthermore, in his defense he does not hesitate to cite an unbelievable number of quotations from all imaginable writings in order to bring his all-encompassing intellectual world into sharpest focus and to prove the untenability of the opposition's theses. He opens up insights into his most personal nature, he interprets his poetic works, reveals his great learnedness. In the process he often winds up far away from the battlefield. Among other things, we read his enchanting description of Joseph von Eichendorff's **From the Life of a Ne'er-do-well.** At one point he writes about Eichendorff's novel:

> I certainly do not imagine there would be any point in my retelling the story, would there? To call it unpretentious would be saying too much. It is the purest irony and the author himself makes fun of it when he has someone say in the end: "therefore in conclusion, as it is natural and fitting for a proper novel: discovery, regret, reconcil-

iation, they are all happy together again and tomorrow we will have the wedding!" But the novel is anything but proper. It lacks solid weightiness, psychological ambition, social-critical direction, and intellectual discipline; it is nothing but dream, music, self-abandon, the wailing sound of a posthorn, loneliness, nostalgia, the falling of the fire-ball on a park in the night, foolish blissfulness, so that one's ears ring and one's head buzzes with poetic enchantment and confusion. But it is also folk dancing and Sunday finery and a wandering hurdygurdy; an artist in Italy seen with German romantic eyes, a joyful boat-trip down a beautiful river while the evening sun covers the forests and valleys with gold and the banks echo with the sounds of a hunting horn. The song of vacationing students who "swing their hats in the morning rays, health, freshness, simplicity, service to women, humor, drollery, intimate pleasure in life, and a constant readiness for song, for the purest, most refreshing wonderful song ... yes, the melodies which resound there, which are scattered everywhere throughout the text as if they weren't anything special—they are the kind which one just accepts, they are gems of the German lyric, very famous, old, and dearly wedded to our ear and heart; here, however, they stand in their proper place, still completely without the patina of fame, not yet incorporated in the treasury of songs of youth and the people, fresh, and brand new: things like "whither I go and look," or that, "whoever wants to wander afar" with the final cry "Greetings, Germany, from the heart," or "The faithful mountains stand guard," and then the magic strophe which a woman disguised as a wandering painter sings to a zither on the balcony in the warm summer night; like each one of the songs, it is prepared musically in quite a prosaic manner—"far from the vineyards across the way one hears still at times a vintner sing, in between times there is often a flash out of the distance and the whole region trembles and rustles in the moonlight"—and, one which to be sure is no longer popular but is a non plus ultra, a maddening essence of romanticism:

Loud and lusty man is silent:

Earth rustles as in dreams

Marvelous with all its trees

Scarcely dawning on the heart

Old times, tender sorrows,

And mild shivers quiver like

Summer lightning through the breast.

Then there follow four more pages of this description.

Another example:

I have heard Hans Pfitzner's musical legend **Palestrina** three times, and with unusual speed and ease, the delicate and bold product has become an intimately possessed property of mine. This work, something final, and consciously final, from the Schopenhauer-Wagnerian, the romantic sphere, with its Dürer-like, Faustian traits; its metaphysical mood; its ethos of "cross, death, and crypt"; its mixture of music, pessimism, and humor—it definitely belongs "to the matter," to the matter of this book. Its appearance at this time vouchsafed me consolation and a good deal of complete sympathy. It corresponds to my most intimate concept of humanity. It makes me positive, releases me from the polemic, and a great subject is offered to me there, feelings to which it can gratefully hold until it can recover its own configuration again and is quieted and from which vantage point all that is **reprehensible** lies in an incorporeal glow.

Appended to this, Thomas Mann dedicates another twenty pages to the work and personality of Hans Pfitzner!

This music and Eichendorff's poetry, that is the heart of the German world which he defends against German democratization! He occupies himself a great deal and oftentimes very extensively with the "holy" Russian literature, among others with Gogol, Tolstoi, Dostoevski, and Turgenev. In no other of his works does his intellectual personality approach us so directly and vitally as in these **Reflections** in which he is not merely an observer. He is passionate in love and in hate and finds for both of them very impressive literary expression. His nature is full of contradictions. His essential characteristics are a melancholy spirit and a sceptical mind. He is to be sure very musical, but his active mind drives him to language as a means of expression. He falls victim to the poetic art through inner necessity, although he knows of its questionability and expresses it. And yet he considers it indispensible when it is pursued in freedom, conscientiousness, and love of truth. He is convinced he is serving mankind whenever he surrenders himself to his work with all the powers of his mind and soul.

On such an intellectual basis, even the most tortuous thought processes of this aggressive author gain charm and value because they illuminate the questions of the day from a high vantage point and introduce views that lead one to reflect. The untenability of his political stand became clear to the author himself immediately after the appearance of the **Reflections**. When the defeat came, the leadership of the army demanded immediate negotiations for peace, the Kaiser fled to Holland, social democracy took the leadership of Germany upon itself in a reconstruction, and the national assembly met in Weimar, the secret capital of the other Germany. On 3 January 1918 (not 1919 as the copy of the handwritten letter of Kantorowicz proves) he answered another attempted approach from his brother Heinrich sharply and bitterly in the negative. But in 1922, after four years, he became reconciled with Heinrich and espoused the Weimar Republic and its first social-democratic president, Friedrich Ebert. The first meeting with politics at the beginning of 1914 wakened Thomas Mann from his native apolitical attitude, and the course of world history then took care that he never again relapsed into it.

II

THE EMULATOR OF GOETHE

4. TURNING TO GOETHE

Goethe does not stand in the intellectual landscape of the German nation like a mountain but rather like a mighty chain of mountains from which life-giving waters flow down from all sides into the German lands. No German who concerns himself at all with the intellectual tradition of his people can escape Goethe's influence completely. In the early notebooks from the first half of the 1890's, Mann had entered many Goethe quotations, and the name remains constantly before him. Even romanticism, to which Mann is more closely linked, is not at all imaginable without Goethe's poetry—above all, that of his Storm and Stress period. Even in romanticism, therefore, threads connect Thomas Mann with Goethe. As early as 1911, he wanted to write a Goethe short story on the Marienbad episode involving Ulrike von Levetzow. Despite this episode, Mann's attitude toward Goethe was indeed full of respect yet still alien and distant, without the strong emotional ties which bound him so intimately to the romantic movement that Goethe had rejected in part and at times as "sickly." It is therefore a decisive turn in the intellectual life of Thomas Mann that around 1920 at the age of forty-five he turned to Goethe and dedicated to him a quarter of a century of intensive studies. Out of this grew a series of lectures and essays:

Goethe and Tolstoi: Fragments on the Problem of Humanity, lecture at Lübeck (4 September 1921)
On Goethe's 'Elective Affinities': Epilogue to an Edition (Leipzig, 1925), **Die Neue Rundschau,** issue 4, 1925
To the Japanese Youth, a Goethe Study (Tokyo, 1932)
Goethe as Representative of the Age of the Bourgeoisie: Address on the 100th Anniversary of Goethe's death (18 March 1932 at the Prussian Academy of Arts, Berlin)

Goethe's Career as a Man of Letters: Speech given in the
city auditorium at Weimar (21 March 1932)
On Goethe's Faust (from the Princeton Faust course)
Mass und Wert, Zurich, issue 4, 1940
Goethe's Werther (from the Princeton Werther course)
Corona: Studies in Celebration of the 80th Birthday of Sam-
uel Singer (Durham, North Carolina, 1941)
Fantasy on Goethe: Preface to The Permanent Goethe (Dial
Press: New York, 1948)
Goethe and Democracy: Lecture for the Goethe celebration
at Oxford (1949)
The Transformation, Heidelberg, summer issue, 1949
Address in the Goethe Year: at the Goethe celebration in the
church of St. Paul in Frankfurt on Main (25 July 1949)
and in the National Theatre in Weimar (1 August 1949)

Mann interrupted work on his novel Joseph and His Brothers
after the appearance of the third volume, Joseph in Egypt, to
write the Goethe novel, The Beloved Returns, which appeared
in 1939. Thomas Mann did not occupy himself so long and so
thoroughly with any other intellectual personality.

Just as with all the later lectures, no external impulse or
occasion drove him to the first Goethe lecture. His starting
point is Schiller's essay "On Naive and Sentimental Poetry,"
and he opposes Goethe and Tolstoi as "naive" against Dostoevski and Schiller as "sentimental." But he expands and deepens
Schiller's basic differentiation by working out the "sentimental"
trait of the "naive" person and the "naive" trait of the "sentimental" writer. This whole observation has significant importance for Thomas Mann himself. There can be no doubt that he
belongs to the "sentimental" type which appears in Tonio Kröger, especially in the conclusion of the letter to Lisabeta. The
intensive study of Goethe means, therefore, that he is turning
to his opposite type. He does this under the "guidance of reason," as he himself confesses. Whereas he inclines to an intensified individualism and to sympathy with sickness and death
under the spell of romanticism, from Goethe he learns "friendliness toward man in the future," and, at the same time, the
problem of education in an expanded meaning of the concept of
humanity enters his circle of ideas. After the powerful youthful impressions of Wagner, Nietzsche, and Schopenhauer, there
is no other intellectual force which gains so much influence on
Thomas Mann's life and work as Goethe!

Besides this, Thomas Mann not only shows in these essays his familiarity with Goethe's works (including the posthumously printed ones), letters, and conversations, but also with a good part of the literature on his life and activity. As a creative person himself, he penetrates more deeply than most literary historians, who are all too eager to place Goethe historically, into Goethe's position as a middle class writer, his relationship to the public, his manner of permitting his works to ripen and mature in accordance with their own will, the clarity and charm of his literary style, and his ethical endeavors to control the Storm and Stress of his nature and to elevate it to a humane culture. Since Mann himself endeavors to unite his literary activity with his middle class nature, he feels related to Goethe and takes over from him willingly what Mann urgently needs to help curb the dangers of his own romantic inclinations. This leads to the heavy stress on precisely these elements in Goethe's conduct of his life and his life's work, and to penetrating observations on the worldwide influence of his humanity. Goethe after all experienced how, on the basis of his humanity, he became part of the common literary property of mankind and created the new concept of world literature. Thomas Mann's conscious devotion to Goethe soon became fruitful, and vigorously furthered his own rise into the world literature of the twentieth century.

It should not be overlooked, however, that Thomas Mann's observations are here and there very subjective; he reads into Goethe what corresponds to his own concept and attitude. It is, for example, astonishing that he often refers to Goethe—who for decades participated in the government of the Grand Duchy of Saxony Weimar Eisenach in a leading position, at times as president of the cabinet—as "unpolitical" or "apolitical"; and, in fact, Mann expresses the opinion that the unpolitical attitude of the German people might be traced back to his model. This error is based on the narrowness of the concept "politics" which Thomas Mann had formed for himself in his earlier quarrel. Furthermore he is not fully aware of the significance of the idea of humanity in the eighteenth century as it applies to the formation of a community, since he speaks of its atomizing effect on the middle class populace—an effect fully ascribable to the romantic movement.

What Thomas Mann only fleetingly touches upon in the life and works of Goethe must also be noted. Above all, Goethe is certainly one of the great admirers of women, portrayers of women, and love poets, and his love lyric accompanies him throughout his whole life. In his works, the passionate love for women occupies such a central position that again and again he equates his rapture before such a part of God's world with piety and, in words from the religious sphere, celebrates love for fifty years from the **Proto-Faust** through the **Marienbad Elegy.** This is not made clear in Mann's studies.

But this oversight does not preclude the fact that precisely the amatory aspect of Goethe's poetry exercised an influence on Mann. In the "sentimental" type of poet, a powerful tension constantly predominates between intellect and sensuality; and also in the case of Thomas Mann. For this reason a puritanical tone pervades his artistic work of the early period prior to 1914. To be sure he does not ban completely love between the sexes from his early narratives but circles hesitantly and shyly around the physical things. The "naive" young Goethe permits Gretchen in her song of longing in the **Proto-Faust** to confess quite without embarrassment, "My womb, alas, strives toward him" and later changes it under the Weimar influence to: "My breast strives toward him." During intensive study of Goethe, Mann's tension relaxes and loosens up gradually, and the prudish Hanseatic from the North learns the "naive" observation of natural things from the sensual Rhinelander. As early as the **Magic Mountain,** these natural things play a large role without an overt depiction of the physical aspect. In **Joseph and his Brothers** this aspect grows; and in the later works, even more strongly. At the same time, Mann's observation of the oncoming generation during the period after the First World War may have had an accompanying influence along with the increasing transformation of the sexual phase of human life during this period, which weakened many taboos.

In general, Mann's relationship to Goethe remains determined more by understanding than by natural disposition; although, in his lecture on Sigmund Freud's eightieth birthday in 1936, he admits to an "imitatio Goethe." Consequently it is also understandable that, when he takes up an idea of his youth and creates his **Doctor Faustus,** he is not at all following Goethe's tracks, but on the contrary writing a work very far removed from Goethe. According to Mann's own confession, Goethe's influence remains significant for the conduct of his life and his public activities right up to his very last days.

5. WRITINGS TO 1943

A Man and His Dog

The defeat of Germany with its difficult political consequences must have shaken Thomas Mann severely. As early as 1917 in the **Reflections of an Unpolitical Man,** on the occasion of the negotiations for an armistice in the East, he had hoped for a "victory without denunciation." He had declared himself for a strong monarchy and opposed to a parliamentary party rule. Now Germany had to accept the difficult, humbling conditions of the Versailles Treaty. The German royal houses disappeared individually and altogether. The Danube Monarchy dissolved into national states and in Russia the Soviet Union was established.

The four years from 1918 to 1922 were for him apparently a time of reticence, withdrawal, and contemplation after the intellectual caprice of the preceding war years, and his defection from all artistic work. During this period of rest in 1919, two autobiographical works of an idyllic character took form which are completely nourished from his own most personal experience, **A Man and His Dog,** and **Song of the Little Child,** writings without any tortuous problems of everyday life.

The compressed, alliterative title **A Man and His Dog,** establishes firm boundaries for the theme. The family even participated in the acquisition of the dog; the children, through their urgent requests, in fact decisively. Their relationship to the new house-companion is not depicted. There is equally little said about his feeding, because it is left up to the lady of the house and her helpers. The chief object of the idyll is the walks of the two: Bauschhan (Bashan)—his low German name, altered from Bastian, is taken from Frith Reuter—and the narrator. Much space is devoted to description of the landscape.

Thomas Mann had his house built on the edge of Munich in the Isar Valley on the left bank, where a construction firm was planning a mile-long housing project upstream with streets parallel to the river and cross-streets which are now gradually being overgrown again by nature because no inhabitants had applied for lots here. The three zones are accurately sketched in with hundreds of sharply observed details: the valley slope along which a brook flows, the forest at the center, and the bank itself; the walks with their richly varied impressions and experiences were taken in these zones. In the story, the master of human portrayal devotes little attention to persons: the cretin-like shepherdess and her mother in the town, the ferry boatman and his family on the river, the professor in the veterinary institute, the kennel keeper there when Bashan has to be turned over for a lengthy observation of his inner bleeding, and the man on the other bank who carries a gun and shoots it (in contrast to Bashan's master). They all remain types. The poet is completely attuned to his dog and furnishes us with an unusually rich piece of animal psychology; he depicts the dog's relationship to his master, his form, his movements, his eyes and facial expressions, his emotional reactions with respect to all events—all this with vivid empathy. But because he is a hunting dog, the flushing and hunting of animals becomes the high point of the portrait, which includes the hunted animals and their psychology.

The tone changes: Mann can be very factual, observant, descriptive; he can add thoughtful observations and fantastic associations, cast everything in an ironic light, and then climb to hymnic heights. The poet carries on his beloved game in his German mother tongue with countless choice whimsies.

Aside from the nature and animal portrayal, the idyllic report reveals a bit of self-characterization. We get quite close to Thomas Mann, the man. He is the one who loves these walks, this landscape, and his dog Bashan, after working at his desk, or talking with tiring companions. He finds refreshment and relaxation alone with the hairy companion, who actively takes part in his activites as an observer and thoughtful student of life. The master is even carried away at times. Once he confesses his dreamy surrender to the motion of water as a significant trait of his nature. This little prose piece is therefore testimony to the fact that a creative person fills every moment of his daytime activity with intense experience. Again and again it is this experienced fullness that endows his works of art with their lasting charm. In the face of this, the talk of Mann's cold feeling and empty play with forms must grow silent.

A conversation with the dog forms the humorous conclusion to the report. The narrator thinks he sees Bashan sulking, reproaching him, indeed scorning him because he does not kill an animal like the hunter—he never does. He has respect for life and does not want to spill any blood.

> He kept beside me on our whole painful homeward way, and did not hunt. Nor did he run diagonally a little ahead, as he does as a rule when not in a hunting mood; he kept behind me, at a jog-trot, and put on a sour face, as I could see when I happened to turn around. I could have borne with that and should not have dreamed of being drawn; I was rather inclined to laugh and shrug my shoulders. But every thirty or forty paces he yawned—and that I could not stand. It was that impudent gape of his, expressing the extreme of boredom, accompanied by a throaty little whine which seems to say: Fine master I've got! No master at all! Rotten master, if you ask me!— I am always sensitive to the insulting sound, and this time it was almost enough to shake our friendship to its foundations.
>
> "Go away!" said I. "Get out with you! Go to your new friend with the blunderbuss and attach yourself to him! He does not seem to have a dog, perhaps he could use you in his business ..."
>
> With such biting words did I address Bashan as he slunk behind me on our way home. And though I did not utter my words but only thought them—for I did not care to look as though I were mad—yet I am convinced that he got my meaning perfectly, at least in its main lines. (SL, II, 137 f.)

Song of the Little Child

Thomas Mann really knows how to surprise repeatedly his faithful readers who follow his creativity from one work to the next: the **Song of the Little Child** is written in hexameters! Ernst Robert Curtius recommends reading them aloud without scanning them strictly. Then they have an effect like elevated prose. In a slightly parodistic "foreword," the author of this

idyll answers the question positively as to whether he is a poet,
since he otherwise just writes prose, by reasoning that he constructs it conscientiously with the "conscience of the heart and
of the ear," as "moral and music." He confesses that he has
failed in many a lyric attempt as a result of the prosaic damp-
ening of his emotional exuberance. But he says he was familiar with the hexameter from his reading of Homer, and now
his love for the fatherland is making him into a metrical poet.

In the eight parts of the song, however, the cadence is definitely no longer parodistic, but borne by a rising and falling
pathos.

At that time then, when everything inside was in order,
You germinated and were born to me, most precious life,
Dear Child! And how differently my mood was now
Prepared for such a reception in many ways!

                         -- Stormy times
Burst in, the ground trembled, a worldly edifice collapsed.
Great was the distress of the sober-sided man, it had
Made me at once softer and firmer and forced me
Consciously to take the place accorded me,
Honorably or not, but where I was definitely at home ...
Open burst the gate to the fifth decade, we were already through
                    it,
Led by the Horae, —what use, if we would delay! ...
Silvery glisten the temples: Now the world takes on
Another appearance to the traveller, and living too has changed.
The shy youth is only aware of ethereal elements, his gaze has
Strayed groping into the confusion of inward matters,
And he distrusts his senses. But if only the time will come,
Nature will speak more kindly then to a less troubled heart,
Once the burgeoning spring did not disturb us
So, nor its soothing breath; nor did we know the rewarding
                    ardor
As children, with which today we sniff at the magic
Fragrance of the summer rose, nor did the eye cast
Its tender glance, as today, at the image of the white-trunked
                    birch,
Which in virginal decor the locks of its foliage
Leaves hanging in the golden afternoons. —Strange emotion,
What dost thou   mean and what this tender regard?
Will nature warn our hearts with gentle allure,

That we belong to her and are soon to return?
Is she already drawing us gently thither, maturing our sense
to sweetness? —
See, little girl, thus was I attuned and prepared in my heart
To receive you from the womb of the organic darkness
Which guarded you faithfully and formed you precisely
According to the laws of our type.   I knew not yet that I loved
you.
But when the grave, gay, divine miracle happened;
When you had appeared and belonged to the light, toward which
you
Long had been striving, lively, in kicks which I felt;
When I first noticed the minute burden on anxious arms
And saw in quiet rapture how your eye
Reflected the light of heaven; then—ever so cautiously—
Lowered you down to your mother's breast: then at once
Did my heart fill up with feeling, with blessed love.

The loving father addresses his little daughter and tells her
everything at great length so that in the future she can read
what has happened up to her baptism in the autumn of her first
year. The marriage had already lasted for fourteen years, it
says in the "Things of Life" chapter. In the first seven years,
four older children had come into the world; but now seven
years afterward, the late-comer.

In the following five parts—"Early," "Monument," "Little
Sister," "The Conversation," "The Sickness,"—Thomas Mann
describes with charming incisiveness how he occupied himself
daily during this early period with his fifth child, observed her
development and expressions of life, tried to make her happy
and entertain her, gave her consolation and solace when she
was restless, afraid, or even sick. The mother had borne her
during the war. The little red mark between her temple and
forehead and a certain frightened irritability gave testimony to
this fact. It is apparently a completely new experience for the
father, this active love for his child still in such need of help.

In the seventh part ("From the East"), however, the thoughts
of the poet wander from the observation of the facial characteristics of the girl, in which a mixture of North German and
Eastern elements is reflected, to her origin. At this point the
picture of the mother, the "fairy tale princess from the East,"

is fitted in, which so unmistakably resembles that of Emma
Spoelman in **Royal Highness.**

The last part presents as highpoint the solemn baptism in
their own house, for which the father has prepared everything
carefully. He himself has purchased the white and colored
chrysanthemums in order to decorate the rooms and altar in a
festive manner. The church has furnished a crucifix and lavabo
and candle. But the baptismal font, the plate under it, and the
old bible are inherited family treasures which are precisely
described. A young theologian who dedicated his doctoral thesis to the revered writer was requested to perform the church
consecration. The name Elizabeth is traditional among the
women of Mann's genealogy. It becomes apparent in this poem
that he is indeed describing the courtly traditions of **Royal
Highness** with a puckish delight but is not satirizing them. Even
in his personal life, he enjoys cherishing traditions faithfully
and wants to fit his own child into the Christian community and
the rows of generations through baptism. As a cultured human
being, he is conservative.

He certainly does not hold at all to a careful description of
blissful reality but constantly strives to go beyond it into far-
reaching intellectual relationships. Even when he speaks of
his marriage as a union between the North of Germany and the
East, he adds several lines on the philosophy of Schopenhauer,
which after all blended the world views of the West and of the
East. As first godfather, he asked his friend, Ernst Bertram,
the author of the Nietzsche book that he loved above all else in
modern literature. Thus the two revered spirits of his youth
find their way into this idyll. The second godfather is a young,
badly wounded, front-line fighter, Gunter Herzfeld, who had
volunteered out of ardent patriotism. That gives the poet welcome opportunity to present to us an insight into his violent
disturbance over the outcome of the war. From the beginning,
he conceived of it as a judgment of the Lord on the history of
the world. Now the judgment has turned out differently from
what he had hoped. Germany lies there shattered and blames
itself, defenseless in the face of superior victorious force
(whose "virtue" he calls "rascally") that dictates the punishment. He is inclined to confess the German arrogance. But
the young man and the poet had great faith when they volunteered their efforts for the true spiritual Germany. An age

comes to an end, a new one begins. Now it is the question of alleviating human misery. Before God we are all just tools, even the poet whose art is called upon to unite and uplift mankind. From the four years 1918-21, this is the only poetic testimony as to how the defeat of Germany shattered Thomas Mann and how he planned to conquer this torturing experience. That is certainly also one of the driving causes why he buried himself for so long in the world of Goethe. Perhaps Goethe's **Hermann and Dorothea**, written in the time of the French revolution—a description of the simple moral bases of human life has had an effect—even on Mann's hexameter idyll.

The Magic Mountain

It is not strange that many readers, especially physicians, have regarded the novel **The Magic Mountain** as an accusatory satire on the tuberculosis sanatorium in the high mountains of Switzerland. For when Thomas Mann returned home in June 1912 from a visit with his wife in Davos, he planned a short story as a humorous counterpart to the macabre **Death in Venice.** Large segments of this original plan have become incorporated into the work. The depiction of the efficient organization in the "Berghof" is acidly sharp. Ironic lights flicker around the two doctors, Hofrat Behrends with his very witty jovial flow of words and Dr. Krakowsky with his foreign accent and his sloppy clothing. A large number of the patients are satirically categorized, often simply by their names. The whole sanatorium society and its socializing is ironically opened to question. Thomas Mann can be very sharp. But satire is not his chief concern.

No, just as he did with the life-style of the court in **Royal Highness,** he seizes upon the existence of people in the high altitude sanatorium as a serious problem of life to which he devotes the passionate interest of an artist, who, despite the misery and comedy detectible by the sharp observer, reveals love for life and joins satire with humor. It is no longer a question of a parallel to his own artistry but of a release from the "flatland," from the practical life in the everyday world, a release which affects all the sick people up there on the mountain to the same degree and changes them so that they gradually but inexorably stand outside, wrapped in the cocoon of their own world, and become "non-people." The narrator makes this evident among other things by the transformation of the experience of time. Constant and often long observations on time accompany the unraveling of events throughout the entire work. Up there, time-killing predominates—time is wasted, indeed even destroyed. It is the world of timelessness. Hans Castorp who has come for three weeks in order to visit his cousin, the young lieutenant Joachim Ziemssen, stays in the Berghof for seven years, enchanted, and finally maintains no more relations at all with the "flatland."

It is Thomas Mann's first novel in which a long series of variegated and probing descriptions of the same landscape recur regularly, comparably to the touching description in A Man and His Dog and the reverence for nature in Song of a Little Child. Of course the contrast in the seasons is at times blurred in the high mountains, but still this contrast is not extinguished and at least reminds one of the natural course of the cosmic year. As a comparison to this mountain world, the poet likes to use the sea, since these two territories make up his primary experience of nature.

The thorough-going separation of the sensory world from the usual, more stringent formalities of life is related to the negligent waste of time, the idleness of the sick. Two things dominate their thinking—their sickness, obvious in the temperatures which they have to read off their thermometers daily; and flirtation. A general profligacy predominates between the sexes which is more furthered than hindered by Dr. Krakowsky's fascinating scientific lectures about love in all imaginable aspects and about his psychoanalytical practice. Because he knows that it delays, and oftentimes in fact, prevents the cure, Hofrat Behrends raves against the sexual but completely in vain. If he does not want to chase the patients away, he has to close both eyes. Besides, he is also vulnerable with respect to especially attractive women among the patients. Countless examples illustrate the games of love which take place up there with or without passion. One could also call the sanatorium the Venusberg!

Into this world completely strange to him comes Hans Castorp from Hamburg—like Thomas Mann, a scion of a Hanseatic conservative patrician family, early orphaned and raised by his grandfather, anemic and sickly, with an expectant sympathy for the experience of death. Hans Castorp inclines toward the good life with rich food and plenty to drink and a good mild cigar. He does not have much regard for hard work. It strains him and tires him quickly. But he completes his accidentally selected study of naval architecture to the point of being an engineer and is about to begin as an unsalaried apprentice in a Hamburg shipyard when he returns from a three weeks' vacation in the mountains. Since he can live on the income of his inherited fortune, nothing and nobody is stopping him from extending his stay in the mountains as long as he wants to. He is called one of "life's problem children."

Thomas Mann has apparently given this young man very much of his own self, especially the slowness, thoughtfulness, thirst for knowledge, and melancholy of his own disposition. One could fill several pages with the references to this, but there is little sense to it. For Hans Castorp is lacking what makes up the heart of his creator's personality after all—the artistic work, the drive to produce, the creative talent. The poet has stripped Castorp off himself, formed him into an independent personality, and given him his own inner development, his own fate, a way of life which we follow with growing interest because it leads us through so many fascinating intellectual adventures.

Hans Castorp is neither a genius nor a person significant for his achievements, nor is he a naive simpleton. Curiosity and a thirst for knowledge are peculiar to him and he loves to reflect on everything that crosses his path. Very early he questions the meaning of life, but not actively, not passionately searching. He is not a grail seeker; rather, a passive yet very attentive observer and listener in life's theatre with its changing repertoire. He is clairvoyant and keen of hearing.

The main plot of the novel is its very unusual love story. As a boy, Hans had been in love from a distance for two years with a student by the name of Hippe in the class ahead of him. Once, half way through this time, he borrowed a pencil from him. That was the brief climax. In the Berghof he meets a Russian lady, Claudia Chauchat, with the same Kirghizian facial characteristics and eyes as the boy, whose husband is on the other side of the Caucasian mountains. Hans falls completely under her spell, but he approaches her just as little as he did the boy. Finally on a Fasching evening, he asks her for a pencil to play a party game, and a conversation develops between them in which he feverishly declares his passionate love for her in a dream and in French. He returns the pencil to her in her room and receives as a souvenir of this evening the X-ray picture of her insides. On the next noon she leaves on a long-planned trip. That is the end of the first volume. Since that time he has been waiting for her return. It is not the slight sickness, it is this passion which drives his morning temperature above normal again and again. He knows this, but he cannot and does not change it!

During this first period of his stay, he is given a teacher in the person of the Italian Freemason Settembrini, whose grandfather was a revolutionary at the time of Metternich and whose father was an important representative of the philological-humanistic sciences. As heir to his father, he is a literary man of culture, a vanguard fighter for the idea of humanity, of progress, of democracy, of world peace, co-worker on an encyclopedia, **The Sociology of Suffering**," for which he is editing the creative literature on human suffering. All that Thomas Mann was blindly fighting against in the **Reflections** is here presented very factually and lovingly.

The clever pedagogue fights against Castorp's sympathy with sickness and death in vivid rhetoric, ingeniously, and in polished form. Hans Castorp again and again seeks his company and listens to him, eager to learn. But in vain Settembrini advises him twice to leave, and completely in vain is his repeated warning against Asia, against the Russian lady with the Kirghizian eyes. In all the teachings of Settembrini which are directed toward the improvement of social relationships, political in the final analysis, something essential is missing—the depth dimension of personal life in which there is sickness, death, and passionate love.

In the beginning of the second volume, an opponent joins Settembrini, Naphta, born an Eastern Jew, with inherited incisiveness of mind, trained early in Talmudic studies but then taken into a Jesuit school and turned into a fighter for the Catholic Church, with which he paradoxically combines the enthusiasm for terror through the dictatorship of the proletariat. Long, involved quarrels develop between them as soon as the small audience furnishes the occasion; namely, Hans Castorp and his cousin, Joachim Ziemssen. Settembrini is more appealing to Hans; but what he lacks, Naphta offers in abundant measure, and Hans finds it very worthwhile listening to them. Oftentimes, from the point of view of Hans' own disposition, Settembrini is quite correct, although the Jesuit tears down and mocks everything which the Freemason builds up and praises. The two of them show how the European intellectual currents they represent are reflected (a little tenuously) in the minds of two intellectuals frustrated by sickness. After a year and a half, Joachim Ziemssen is no longer able to endure being away from the flatlands. In spite of the serious warning of the doctor, he leaves. After a half year he returns, now hopelessly ill. Loved by all and admired by everyone because of his brave attitude, he fails badly. His death is described in detail. He has followed his cousin Hans in every direction but without altering his own soldierly character in the slightest and without influencing his relative. After his death, Hans Castorp has to make do on his adventures with two other patients who also accompany him to the conversations of Settembrini with Naphta.

Again and again, Castorp, a man of the middle, of balance, who is searching for a reconciliation of the opposites, stands between the two of them who are zealously fighting one another on a high plane on the basis of broad knowledge. But they are unable to furnish him with a fruitful idea for this reconciliation—he has to find it himself.

It becomes his in a very strange manner. Without knowledge of the doctors, Hans Castorp acquires skis for himself. On a bold jaunt into the high Alps, he gets caught in a snowstorm, falls asleep from exhaustion in the protection of a hut, and dreams of a non-existent Grecian landscape in which people move about in friendly communion and of a temple room in which two witch-like old women slaughter and devour a tender child. On awakening he understands that he has escaped death once again. He draws a lesson from this dream vision which has shown him where mankind comes from and whither it strives. One must know about the abysses of the human soul and understand them—those abysses of cruelty, sickness, death, passion, and sin—otherwise one knows nothing of life. But the new humanism is synonymous with friendliness among men in the future. "For the sake of goodness and love, man shall not allow death to dominate his thoughts." That is the formula of life which the adventure in the snowstorm inspires in him.

Life itself adds another exciting adventure to this. Mrs. Claudia Chauchat returns to the Berghof but accompanied by a man, Mijnher Peeperkorn, a rich Dutch colonial from Java, a coffee magnate (for whom Thomas Mann borrowed several traits from Gerhard Hauptmann). No one can escape the influence of his strong dominant personality. From early morning on, he drinks a lot of strong coffee, gin, and wine and lives in a constant intoxication, both in mind and in mood. In the evening he arranges great eating and drinking sessions to the point of complete exhaustion and drunkenness for all concerned. Often he speaks in incompleted sentences and allusions, accompanied by grand gestures and facial expressions. But he can also speak clearly and coherently. Then he displays a rich knowledge of all kinds of things and a keen gift of observation. On a walk we experience with him one of the heated verbal duels between Settembrini and Naphta. In his presence they lose brilliance, color, and significance. He washes them away with a few words and motions of his hand. "One should enjoy the pure gift of God of this mountain air with ardor," he counters to their speeches. High above in the blue he discovers a circling golden eagle:

He did indeed stand still, bent backward, shading his brows with his hat. They followed his gaze. "May," said he, "may I draw your attention upwards—high in the sky to that black, circling point against the blue, intensely blue, shading into black—that is a bird of prey. It is, if I am not mistaken—look, ladies and gentlemen, look, my child, it is an eagle. Most emphatically I call your attention—look, it is no buzzard, no vulture, it is an eagle. If you were as farsighted at my advancing age —yes, my child, advancing age—my hair is white, you would see as plainly as I do, the blunt pinion, it is a golden eagle. He circles directly overhead, he hovers, not a single beat of his wing—at a tremendous height in the blue, and with his keen, farsighted eyes under the prominent bony structure of his brows, he is peering earthwards. The eagle, ladies and gentlemen, the bird of Jove, king of his kind, the lion of the upper air. He has feathered gaiters, and a beak of iron, with a sudden hook at the end; claws of enormous strength, their talons curving inwards, the front ones overlapped by the *death befits a great pas.* *died of isolation of suffering as impotence* *Ariadne* *The failure to l*

long hinder one in an iron clutch. Look!"—and he tried
to put his long fingers in the posture of an eagle's claw.
"Gaffer, why are you circling and spying up there?" He
turned his head upwards again. "Strike! Strike downward, with your iron beak into head and eyes, tear out
the belly of the creature God gives you—splendid! Splendid! Absolutely! Bury your talons in his entrails—make
your beak drip with its blood." He had brought himself
to a pitch; all interest in Settembrini and Naphta's an-
tinomies had fled away. (MM, 746, f.)

Peeperkorn is intoxicated and thrilled by the wonders of
reality, by the things which are comprehensible and enjoyable
to the senses. He calls them holy and divine. He speaks of
the sacrament of rapture. (The failure of the emotions to
respond to woman is the end of the world for him.) He too belongs, like Hauptmann, to the naive type.
  The appearance of the couple in the Berghof is a hard blow
for Hans Castorp. But his passive, somewhat phlegmatic nature permits him even in this case to preserve his equanimity
and take in the Bacchanalian phenomenon of Peeperkorn with
downright admiration. In his quiet, steady manner he has
matured into a charming personality. That is shown in two
conversations with each of the two alone. At the beginning,
Claudia mocks his phlegmatic nature and regrets his intimate
address and his loyal admiration. But in response to his questions, she finally confesses that she has come to him because
it is often oppressive and frightening with the violent man, and
she enters upon a friendship with him. Peeperkorn himself
questions Hans Castorp, who visits him at his sickbed—he
suffers every fourth day from a severely debilitating intermit-
tent fever which visibly robs him of his strength—and tells
Hans directly that he is Claudia Chauchat's lover. Thereupon
the young man relates his own love story in a tender, cautious
way. Peeperkorn, too, establishes an intimate friendship with
him.
  On the last trip to a waterfall, which deafens all ears and
swallows up all the words, Peeperkorn gesticulates a speech
after a picnic, holding a glass of wine in one hand. That is his
departure. During the night he takes his own life by means of
an expensive artificial snakebite which conceals lethal poison.
At his deathbed, Hans Castorp gives Claudia a kiss on the

ıd which he had refused to give her before on Peeper-
order. It is his departure from her. She senses it and
leaves the Berghof. Hans Castorp's love story is at an end.
One might think that what follows is only a kind of postlude.
But as far as he is concerned, there is no lack of intellectually
and spiritually moving adventures for the person who never
becomes tired of them. His apprentice years keep passing. He
takes part in all the fashionable movements in his timeless
world.

There comes a period of great dullness. Hans Castorp plays
solitaire with persistent passion. He procures a phonograph
with a substantial supply of records from the sanatorium. He
develops a technical competence in handling this machine and
arranges concerts of his favorite pieces all alone in the quiet
of the night. At this point Thomas Mann interposes enchanting
musical descriptions. Hans Castorp's inborn sympathy with
death reveals itself anew in Schubert's "The Linden Tree."
Among other things he loves a Carmen recording: Carmen mocks
José because he wants to go back into the barracks when taps
sounds, just when she is ready to dance and sing for him. He
then sings his love aria.

> ... dull notes of fatality arise from the orchestra, a
> gloomy, ominous motif, which, as Hans Castorp knew,
> recurred throughout the opera, up to its fatal climax,
> and formed also the first phrase of the soldier's aria, on
> the next plate, which had now to be inserted. "See here
> thy flow'ret treasured well"—how exquisitely José sang
> that! Hans Castorp played this single record over and
> over, and listened with the deepest participation. As far
> as its contents went, it did not fetch the action much fur-
> ther; but its imploring emotion was moving in the high-
> est degree. The young soldier sang of the flower Carmen
> had tossed him at the beginning of their acquaintance,
> which had been everything to him, in the arrest he had
> suffered for love of her. He confesses: "Sometimes I
> curse the hour I met thee, and tried all vainly to forget
> thee"—only next moment to rue his blasphemy, and pray
> on his knees to see her once more. And as he prayed—
> striking the same high note as just before on the "To see
> thee, Carmen," but now the orchestration lends all the
> resources of its enchantment to paint the anguish, the

longing, the desperate tenderness, sweet despair, in the little soldier's heart—ah, there she stood before his eyes, in all her fatal charm; and clearly, unmistakably, he felt that he was undone, forever lost—on the word undone came a sobbing shole-tone grace-note to the first syllable—lost and forever undone. "Then would an ecstasy steal o'er me," he despairingly asseverated in a recurrent melody repeated wailingly by the orchestra, rising two tones from the tonic and thence returning ardently to the fifth: "Carmen, my own," he repeats, with infinite tenderness but rather tasteless redundancy, going all the way up the scale to the sixth, in order to add: "My life, my soul belongs to thee"—after which he let his voice fall ten whole tones and in deepest emotion gave out the "Carmen, I love thee!" shuddering forth the words in anguish from a note sustained above changing harmonies, until the "thee" with the syllable before it was resolved in the full accord. (MM, 648)

"Yes, yes!" said Hans Castorp, melancholy and grateful. His own love experience had made this record so dear to him.

The most exciting experience of all is a spirit séance. A young Danish girl first revealed surprising talents in social games. She is sent out. They give her a very complicated task, which she solves exactly in rapid fashion, since "Holger" whispers everything into her ear. Dr. Krakowsky, whose lectures have long bordered on the occult, takes her under his wing and discovers in her an outstanding medium. At first Hans Castorp keeps his distance and only allows regular reports to come to him from the events. "Holger" is a poet. A sea poem by him is repeated literally, other things are only indicated, but when "Holger" promises to have every desired dead person appear, Hans takes part in order to see his cousin Joachim Ziemssen. They make him the controller of the medium. He has to squeeze the knees of the young girl between his own and hold her hands firmly. What happens is drastically described. For two full hours with a pause of fifteen minutes, the virginal girl contorts herself as if in birth throes. Then suddenly the cousin with his full beard of the last days is sitting on the psychiatrist's visitors' chair and looks at Hans Castorp seriously and sadly. Castorp sobs deeply several times, murmurs "Pardon" and walks to the switch at the door so that the harsh light chases away the phenomenon. Thomas Mann's **An Experience in the Occult** (Munich, 1924) forms the basis for this scene, but transformed into a visual, realistic, exciting narrative.

There arises also a period of general irritability and quarrelsomeness like an infectious sickness. Terrible examples are described. Even the two controversialists, who always move about in the highest intellectual spheres, are unnerved by them. After all, both are hopelessly sick. Naphta's tone becomes continually shriller and more mocking. At the end of a joint sled trip, in a dining hall of the spa with its peasant-like atmosphere, things become too irritating for Settembrini. He flares up and accuses Naphta of disgracing youth, which the latter answers with a challenge. Hans Castorp is the natural neutral person. Settembrini shoots in the air intentionally, but Naphta shoots himself in the head and thus makes an end to his misery.

Thomas Mann himself thinks that his description of the sanatorium as a whole represents symbolically the wretched conditions of European society before the outbreak of the First World War. In this is concealed a residue of his own intoxicating experience in 1914 that, with the war, a period of moral clarification is beginning, a concept which he had already abandoned in the **Reflections** of 1917. There is nothing more to report about the last years of Hans Castorp on the mountain. The outbreak of the first world war in 1914 shatters the enchantment. He goes into the army as a volunteer. We see him once again in the attack on a chain of hills which had been taken by the enemy two days before. The narrator (who steps forward often and takes a position on the events) leaves it up in the air as to whether he falls or remains alive. More significant is the life which is described, the existence outside the active everyday life that conceals so much misery and comedy but also offers the opportunity for education, culture, and intensification beyond life in the "flatland."

Goethe's influence on this work does not lie merely on the surface but reaches deep. Since **The Magic Mountain** deals with education and culture, we think first of **Wilhelm Meister's Apprenticeship.** The society which observes and guides Wilhelm's career and accepts him into it is replaced in **The Magic Mountain** by the international society in the Swiss sanatorium into which Thomas Mann, forsaking his German homeland which had been the scene of his narratives (except for the short story **Death in Venice**), introduces Hans Castorp. The result of his apprentice years is doubtlessly Goethean—the humane young man in whom the opposites are reconciled. But in accordance with his disposition, Hans Castorp is indeed like his creator, marked by romanticism. Goethe would never have selected a sanatorium as the scene of an educational novel in which sickness and death determine the atmosphere. This timeless existence outside practical life would have seemed to him too shadowy.

Originally, Wilhelm Meister waxes enthusiastic for the theater. But the group demands of its members that they select a profession through which they serve the human community; so Wilhelm becomes a surgeon. In the **Travels**, the circle carries on economic endeavors in Europe and America and establishes a "pedagogical province" in which the demanding arts of handcraft are given preference over the liberal arts, and the art of the theatre is excluded. The leader of the circle writes to Wilhelm: "We have to engage all mankind." He calls the circle's world view and attitude toward life "world piety." In this novel as in the conclusion of **Faust II**, the old Goethe is obviously aiming at a new configuration of the economic, social, and political life.

In **The Magic Mountain**, broad, richly populated depiction of life in the sanatorium conceals a social tendency. Thomas Mann also wants to suggest the sick condition of Europe, prior to the First World War. But all that remains in the background. The chief interest is directed toward Hans Castorp's development. The poet is satisfied to allow him to mature inwardly toward humanity: he stands the test among the people on the mountain. But his maturity is never tested in the practical everyday world. **The Magic Mountain** remains in its core a romantically individualistic novel.

Hermann Hesse's **Magister Ludi**, influenced by **The Magic Mountain**, manifests several related structural characteristics. The utopian novel planted in an indefinite future depicts a circle of men which excludes the practical world with its passions, does not occupy itself with history, and constructs the glass-bead game on mathematics and music. One of the members is an intellectualized embodiment of music. Knecht develops such a great talent for the game that he rises to become grand master of the circle. But he leaves the circle because he grows conscious of the fruitlessness of this irrelevant action and becomes the educator of a young man in whom the harmony he (Knecht) sought for has developed independently of the circle. Before the wisdom of his circle can prove itself in practical life, he meets death while bathing in a cold mountain lake. This fate of his is similar to that of Hans Castorp.

The influence of Goethe's novel, **Elective Affinities**, which Mann loved very much and about which he wrote an essay in 1925, is detectible above all in Hans Castorp's love for Claudia Chauchat. She is foreordained by natural law through his disposition; she is guided by his subconscious; a dream reveals to him her connection with his childhood love. For a long time, this distant connection with her is completely sufficient for him. The exhilarating experience of the Fasching night is a kind of feverish dream. The tenderness of this love story, its slow course, its fateful necessity, corresponds to the happenings in Goethe's novel without imitating it in the slightest. The Russian lady herself is not involved in this respect at all; according to her own confession, she experiences love only as a reaction whenever she is loved.

Of the seven chapters of the novel, the first two, which contain the reception and introduction of Hans Castorp by his cousin and a flashback of his prior history, are kept short. But then the chapters swell up quickly to epic breadth and in the last two attain a scope of about 300 pages, so that the whole work embraces 1100 pages. As a result of the countless interposed secondary episodes, the narrative is indeed profuse in figures, plots, and the fates of many. But the detailed conversations and observations, which often have an essayistic character and give the work living breadth and an intellectual depth, take up much greater space.

The novel is rich in individual motives, described with fascinating artistry. But their charm is substantially increased by Thomas Mann's language mastery, which reaches full bloom and variety in the milieu and landscape descriptions, the careful depiction of people, the speech of Hofrat Behrends, the conversations of Settembrini and Naphta, the lectures of Dr. Krakowsky, the conversations of Hans Castorp with Claudia Chauchat and Peeperkorn, and the observations and inner monologues of the young Hamburger—this whole tissue of motives which makes countless relationships tangible by means of word repetitions. It is an exhaustably rich art that enchants and spellbinds the reader.

Professor Fredrik Böök, member of the Swedish Academy, maintained in his criticism in **Svenska Dagbladet** on 25 August 1925 that the novel would be unreadable and incomprehensible if translated into a foreign language. That quickly proved to be a false prediction. In 1929 when Böök spoke during the award of the Nobel Prize, he praised only **Buddenbrooks** and did not mention **The Magic Mountain** at all. Bürgin lists twenty-eight translations, and the literature about it grows constantly. There are therefore intellectual circles in many countries which find enjoyment in such a demanding piece of literature and feel fascinated and enriched by it.

Disorder and Early Sorrow

As a consequence of the long interruption, **The Magic Mountain** was not finished until twelve years after it was begun. Its author recovered from this laborious work with the delicately written narrative **Disorder and Early Sorrow**, 1925, which leads back into his own family circle, even though in transparent disguise and with changed names. **The Disorder** is the period after the first world war with its inflation, poor nourishment, and rather far-reaching brutalization of the oncoming youth, which Klaus Mann has depicted many times. The youngest daughter, whom Thomas had already addressed so charmingly in the **Song of a Little Child,** now five years old, experiences "early sorrow" when the "big" brothers and sisters organize a dance with refreshments in the house, and a young man, making himself very small, dances with her. She cries unconsolably in her little bed and demands that he should be her brother. When the man, apparently so ardently loved, appears at her bed and wishes her good night, she is happy and soon falls asleep satisfied. Thomas Mann calls himself Cornelius, Professor of History, and wanders through the activities of the youth and children as an attentive but slightly estranged observer, possessed by his work like the writer himself. The mother remains a little bit in the background; she loves the youngest son as the father does the little daughter. The fifty-year-old man broods about his preference for this child and feels that it is connected in an inadmissible manner with his premonition of death.

Mario and the Magician

Even the narrative **Mario and the Magician** is autobiographic. Together with his wife and the two youngest children, the 8-year-old Elizabeth and the 7-year-old Michael, Thomas Mann visited a beach on the coast of Italy south of Rome in the late summer of 1926 during the time of the Fascist rule of Mussolini. Politics plays a part in the events of the story. The atmosphere is laden with an intensified nationalism which is viciously expressed on slight provocation before the German guests at the beach. This is not the main event. It is, rather, the appearance of a man by the name of Cipolla who advertises himself as a clever magician but is a highly gifted hypnotist and mind-reader—a fact which he has to camouflage because of the police. Thomas Mann does not like to see the story interpreted politically although this is obvious, and he himself furnishes the occasion for it. He calls the evening the incarnation and high point of the prevailing mood and situation. The "magician" fits many patriotic expressions into his extremely clever flood of words, certain that they will have their effect on his listeners. Twice he raises his right hand in the Roman greeting and speaks of the leader and the people, interpreting his uncanny performances as command and obedience, in that he forces his will on others and willingly follows the secret instructions of the public. He is bent over and ugly and practices his unusual power with arrogance and mockery so that he is not beloved, and the public wavers between revulsion and admiration. Even with respect to Il Duce Mussolini, there are apparently in the public both followers and opponents. If the political interpretation is carried out, the conclusion resembles a revolution. It is the outbreak of the rage of the people whom Cipolla humbles, scorns, makes despicable, and subjects to his will in a dishonoring way.

Thomas Mann does not desire this interpretation because the psychology of events interests him far more. In his presentation, the political element is only a casually indicated, concomitant phenomenon, whereas all the events of the evening receive a penetrating psychological analysis and are made clear through many brilliant details. At the incessant requests of the children, the Mann family takes part in this evening, although it starts late and ends far past midnight and certainly is not designed for them; at times they fall asleep but are overjoyed that they are permitted to take part in a display of magic about whose evil character they fortunately understand nothing. The parents stay. But probably because, in spite of their uneasiness and revulsion from this trainer of human beings, they are fascinated by his uncanny ability. After all, even in Munich, Thomas Mann had taken part in the séances at the house of Schrenck-Notzing, reported his experiences, and introduced them as a motive in The Magic Mountain.

After taming several obstinate visitors, the "magician" begins with simple arithmetical and playing card experiments and then, after an intermission, proceeds to more difficult proofs of his power. He causes a young man to become as rigid as a board, places his head and his feet on two chairs, and sits down on him as if on a bench. He entices a pretty wife away from her husband after he has warned him to call her by her first name and hold her back. Finally, he makes a number of people dance on the stage against their will. He constantly spurs on his own daemonic will with a lot of alcohol and cigarettes. A symbol of his power is the riding whip which he lets whistle through the air. He breaks the strongest resistance, oftentimes in a tough struggle. His accompanying speeches have the same effects as his hypnotic powers. He denies the freedom of the will if it is directed negatively into the void, so to speak. If they give in, the people really feel relieved and happy. If the public sympathizes with people who are robbed of their own willpower, he contradicts them sharply. He himself is the one, after all, who goes through all these sufferings. The others do not suffer, and they know nothing about it when he releases them. But sympathy with the person who exercises such power, that is asking too much. That does not fall to the lot of the "magician."

The tragic conclusion is brought on by the showstopper of the evening. Cipolla masterfully summons the sympathetic and somewhat dreamy waiter Mario to the podium and speaks to him for a long time. He speaks of his lover's grief, at which another lad in the public laughs scornfully, of the girl Sylvestra whom he loves, paints her charms in full, convinces him that she loves him again, suggests that he, "the magician," the old, ugly cripple, is the loved one and causes the blissful Mario to kiss him on the cheek. When the whistling of the riding whip awakens him, the scorned, humiliated man stumbles away, but then turns around and shoots his tormentor down with two pistol shots. The poet has invented this conclusion to vent his own heart, which is tortured by the mistreatment of human souls every hour of the performance.

Drawn from actual experience, this narrative, which builds up intensively, is at the same time a masterly psychological study that includes the "magician," his victims, the entranced public which fills the hall, and the puzzling forces which are so outrageously immoral whenever they are misused, as here. This is also true without doubt for the political mass suggestion and seduction of Fascism, which incites to violent deeds. But it is understandable that the narrator does not wish to have the personal human fate of this evening covered over by the political parallel. He knows that even the "magician" is an unhappy figure who, out of the necessity of his crippled existence, has selected an occupation on the basis of his gift, which compensates for his lacks and raises his self-esteem unusually high. This insight justifies his calling the story "a tragic experience." Here the word of Franz Werfel is valid: "Not the murderer, the murdered is guilty!" But the narrator is not interested in the legal postlude.

Joseph and His Brothers

> Very deep is the well of the past. Should we not call it bottomless ?
>
> Bottomless indeed, if—and perhaps only if—the past we mean is the past simply of the life of mankind, that riddling essence of which our own normally unsatisfied and quite abnormally wretched existences form a part; whose mystery, of course, includes our own and is the alpha and omega of all our questions, lending burning immediacy to all we say, and significance to all our striving. (JB, I, 3)

Thus begins the novel.

The "prelude" to the mighty poem of mankind, **Joseph and His Brothers**, is in no way an essay, as many critics feel, although in it much that is worth knowing from age-old traditions is presented didactically. As early as the second page, Mann writes of Joseph, his times, and the cults in Babel, Thebes, and the middle land of Canaan; and his name is mentioned six times. Subsequently, the prelude tells of Joseph's ancestor who emigrated from Ur because of his concern for God, and of his father who settles in a tent camp in the middle land near Sichem with everything that belongs to him and is his. It is the imaginative world of these people which is to be presented. The narrator strikes a solemn tone with massive sentence structures, many varying repetitions of words and phrases, and visual comparisons from his own time. For he is entering upon his journey into hell, into the deep well of the past, in order to discover the origin and nature of mankind.

Joseph is educated to think in terms of myth, and he is inclined to equate his father with the first emigrant, although they are separated from one another by 20 generations and 600 years. By many subsequent examples the narrator shows that, behind every beginning, new and larger spans of time open up further and further back, so that the well of the past proves to be bottomless and unfathomable. Among other things, he does it with the Babylonian Gilgamesh epic which Joseph knows partly by heart [I myself have seen a clay fragment in the archeological museum in Jerusalem from the sixteenth century before Christ with a fragment of the Gilgamesh poem, which was found in Israel], with the Egyptian sphinx, with the breeding of domestic animals from wild types and of the various grain types from wild grasses, with astronomy, writing, and language, with the sagas of the great flood and of the great tower. In passing, the narrator reports that the natural scientists estimate the age of this species of man at 500,000 years, which causes the 14,000 years of known human history to appear as a tiny span of time. Mythical thinking bridges the time spans between past and future to our own present, out of which the double meaning of the little word "once" grows where memory and prophecy meet. At the conclusion of the long series of time observations, which are constantly permeated with religious elements, stands the question of paradise. Here the narrator penetrates beyond all earthly history to the doctrine of the primeval Adam, the young man who was always present along with God and matter, the pure soul of mankind. This soul descends from brilliant heights down to matter in order to experience passion and desire in it. Thereupon God created the world for it with the disapproval of the angels.

Shemmael was expelled and banned because he opposed it rebelliously. The proto-Adam coalesced with matter. Thereupon the Lord sent the Spirit to free him and bring him back to the eternal home. But even the Spirit fell into a dilemma. Perhaps it is the Lord's secret conclusion that the soul and spirit should unite so that man is blessed "with the blessing above down from the heaven and with the blessing from the depths which lie below." Thus reads Jacob's blessing on Joseph in the Bible and in the novel!

The people of that mythical time, above all Joseph and his father Jacob, are people such as we, just as their domestic animals and the grains are the same; but they are still deeply committed to meditation about time and eternity, about life and death, about past and future; Jacob is full of worry about the Lord, which makes him restless and melancholy and lends him dignity. Joseph lives in a union with the Lord that permits him to be happy and at ease because he, the son of the lovely Rachel, knows he is loved by his father and by God. At the conclusion, the narrator confesses that he undertook this descent into the unfathomable well of the past with desire and trepidation, but desire had the upper hand; for the narrative is the solemn garment for the festival in which past and future coalesce into the present.

Even from this short abstract, it is apparent that the prelude is the right introduction to the four-part novel—in which, as with the overture to an opera, many significant intellectual motives are hinted at that in the work itself are executed at a more comfortable and visual breadth. Thomas Mann urgently advised the publisher Albert Bonnier in Stockholm, quite correctly, **not** to omit this essayistic, highly charged prelude in the Swedish edition; it is preserved!

With this biblical novel Thomas Mann struck out on a new path in his narrative art. Up to that time, he had typically taken a chunk of reality out of his own time into his workshop as the raw material and transformed it into a writing with his personal stamp. Only in Buddenbrooks had he taken over prehistory in its broad outlines from the chronicle of his family. Now he turned to the past (as he had already done in the drama **Florence**), selected material already enshrined in literature, and followed the basic lines of an existing plot, a procedure which he later repeated in **The Transposed Heads, The Holy Sinner, The Tables of the Law,** and in part also **Dr. Faustus.** The external impulse came in 1926 in Munich from a young artist who had created sketches for the story of Joseph and asked him for an introduction to it. Mann reached first for the family Bible and then for Goethe's **Poetry and Truth** and read how reverently the sixty-year-old had immersed himself in the beginning of the Books of Moses, "the origin and the growth of the human race," and in the stories of the patriarchs; and Mann said in conclusion that even as a boy he had sketched the story of Joseph broadly in a literary piece. Mann had been convinced for a long time that it was part of the nature of art to produce something completely new in every work. Here he saw a totally new type of task.

The whole Old Testament is indeed full of myths which bring to life the belief in God's interventions into the fate of the Jewish people. It intrigued the poet to humanize them with the help of psychology. He praised Richard Wagner among other reasons for making myths fruitful for his music drama. Now Mann wanted to do likewise in this novel. The beginning, "deep is the well of the past," is reminiscent of the music at the beginning of **Rheingold.** All myths are stories that illuminate statement of belief or explain the origin of a religious cult. Above all they have a social function in the period of mythical thinking. They bind men together through belief and combine them into a community of belief. Mann found a psychological interpretation of myths in Sigmund Freud. Even when he was writing **Death in Venice** in 1911, he had occupied himself with Freud's work. In 1916 he got to know him personally in Vienna. In 1929 in Munich he gave a lecture, **Freud's Position in the History of Modern Thought;** and, for Freud's eightieth birthday, the festive speech at Vienna, in 1936, **Freud and the Future.**

The psychiatrist had always been very much interested in mythology. In his psychological treatment of sick people, he had discovered remains of mythical thinking in the subconscious of souls (since, after all, the basic biogenetic law that the history of a tribe is repeated in abbreviated form in the development of the individual being is also true for the soul), and now he was also able to illuminate mythical motives psychoanalytically and interpret them without destroying their social function, as in **Totem and Tabu**. With Freud, Mann did just as before with Nietzsche: he took from his doctrine what he could use fruitfully in the construction of his own work. The socially binding and unitary function of myths interested him less. He was much more interested in how they acted in the soul of individual, highly talented people. Joseph for example is identified with the myth of the torn, buried, and resurrected Lord and plays his role. Mann is of the opinion that all of us in the conduct of our lives pattern ourselves after images—he himself after that of his father and of Goethe. Through such imitation arises the continuity of the intellectual tradition. Past and future are united into a palpable present. It makes it easy to span broad periods of time, indeed to negate them. It is Thomas Mann's romantic individualism which suppresses the social function of myths in favor of their function in individual souls. His psychological humanization of the myth is at the same time an individualization.

To be sure, he regards selected, highly gifted individuals as representative, and hence his mythical work as a poem of humanity. **Joseph and his Brothers** abides under the influence of Goethe. In its structure, with all sorts of completely independent episodes and with its positive attitude toward life, it resembles **Wilhelm Meister's** Travels far more than **The Magic Mountain.** During composition on **Joseph,** Mann read again and again Goethe's poem of humanity, **Faust,** which also depicts the career of a representative human being right up to death; the blessing from above rests on Faust, but he pays no attention to the influence from below which man must experience and endure in order to understand life fully. It is Goethean wisdom when Mann says, "God is not the good but the whole." This biblical novel is Thomas Mann's closest approach to Goethe, the novelist, but does not take over or imitate concrete details.

Mann frequently consulted, during his work on **Joseph,** Laurence Sterne's **The Life and Opinions of Tristram Shandy,** in order to strengthen his humorous treatment of serious material. The solemnly intense tone of the prelude betrays that Mann was genuinely interested in the religious content of the Old Testament, and Jacob is depicted with a great deal of reverence; but a generous dose of humor is mixed with the figure of Joseph. Mann calls his theatrical performance an outright "swindle" and, in contradiction to the charges of his friends, feels that the lighter elements make the diffuse work attractive and give it unity. But in my opinion it is completely off the track to look upon the comic elements as the central theme and to conceive of the whole work as a parody.

As a consequence of many kinds of interruptions, the work was not finished for sixteen years. The narrative of Jacob and his sons, from which Thomas Mann takes his starting point, extends from chapter 25, verse 19, in the first book of Moses to the end of chapter 50 and embraces about seventy-seven pages of the novel, which has a length of 2,046 pages. The story thus has been expanded twenty-six and one-half times; **Tales of Jacob,** twelve and one-half times; **The Young Joseph,** over a hundred times; **Joseph in Egypt,** over four hundred; **Joseph the Provider,** thirteen and one-half times. The question therefore is: Why does a poet of the twentieth century undertake to cause a short Bible passage to swell to such epic proportions?

Like the "Prelude" the four-volume novel also begins with Joseph. The seventeen-year-old is sitting at the well and making eyes at the moon. Then his troubled father Jacob appears, issues a severe warning to him, and enters into a long dialogue with him, which shows his passionate love for him, the first-born son of Rachel, whom he loved about all else. A "beautiful" conversation, a musical dialogue full of age-old common knowledge, concludes the meeting. They are the two chief figures of the work, which could well be called "Jacob and Joseph." All the rest are actually secondary figures.

Disquiet, questioning, harkening and seeking, wrestling for God, a bitter skeptical labouring over the true and the just, the whence and the whither, his own name, his own nature, the true meaning of the Highest—how all that bequeathed down the generations from the man from Ur, found expression in Jacob's look, in his lofty brow and the peering, careworn gaze of his brown eyes; and how confidingly Joseph loved this nature, of which his own was aware as a nobility and
cisely as a
ties, lent t
and solemni
dignity—tha

unabashed fondness Joseph recognized the seal of tradition upon his father's brow, so different from that upon his own, which was so much blither and freer, coming as it chiefly did from his lovely mother's side, and making him the conversable, social, communicable being he pre-eminently was. But why should he have felt abashed before that brooding and careworn father, knowing himself so greatly beloved? The habitual knowledge that he was loved and preferred conditioned and coloured his being: it was decisive likewise for his attitude towards the Highest, to Whom, in his fancy, he ascribed a form, as far as was permissible, precisely like Jacob's. A higher replica of his father, by whom, Joseph was naively convinced, he was beloved even as he was beloved of his father. (JB, I, 50)

The first volume is filled with the **Stories of Jacob,** a long flashback on his life up to the introductory scene at the well. It is not only the need to illuminate prehistory in general. Above all the task is to explain the love of Joseph, the eleventh son of twelve: of the 300 pages of the flashback, three-quarters are dedicated to the events around his mother Rachel.

Not until then does the narrator turn again to Joseph, whose name is repeated in the titles of the three following volumes. The first of these depicts the quarrel with the ten older brothers which grew out of the preference of the father for the highly gifted son of Rachel. The second book tells of his rise and fall in Egypt. The last concerns his renewed elevation and his reunion with the family.

The first two volumes take place for the most part in the simple shepherd and farm circles of Canaan and Babylon; the other two, in the highly cultivated court circles of Egypt. The second and third have the narrowest basis in the Bible and, therefore, harbor the most luxuriant revelation of the poet's inventiveness and interpretative ability, which, however, also plays a part in the other books.

In his broadly conceived novel, the narrator speaks of the lands in which the stories unfold—Babylonia in the Northeast, Canaan in the middle land, and Egypt in the South—and of the countless peoples who inhabit them. He describes the landscapes at various times of the year and day and the alternating weather relationships whereby the maintenance of life is de-

pendent on agriculture and the raising of stock. In the first
two volumes, for example, the wells play a large role; in the
latter two, the rising and falling Nile and the whole irrigation
system. He describes in detail the dwelling places, the tents
of the nomadic shepherds, Laban's farm, the villages with their
craftsmen and bankers, the palaces in Egypt with their gardens
in the big cities. The whole surrounding world of man in his
everyday life is carefully presented in clear detail.

But the narrator deals in even greater detail with people.
He describes their shapes, their clothing, their decoration,
the total furnishings of their dwellings, all their tools, their
meal times, and in addition the expressions on their faces in
the most various situations, their gestures and grimaces. For
it is important to him to make their characters come alive for
us, not only through their actions, as in the Bible, but through
constantly renewed insights into their inner world, into their
emotions, dreams, and thoughts, and above all through the
very thorough treatment of their conversations, which contribute a great deal to the epic breadth of the work. In the third
volume, **Joseph in Egypt**, for example, conversations occupy
two-fifths of the pages. We are supposed to understand the
driving forces behind the active characters and the inner relationship of the events. In this manner the story of the Bible,
which is attractive and gripping in itself, is transformed into
a realistic psychological novel of huge scope. That is a very
significant part of the artistic work of Thomas Mann, although
he goes well beyond the presentation of historical reality. He
is passionately interested in all phenomena of existence and
spares no effort to know them precisely and to present them
charmingly. Especially in this case there was a need not only
for thoroughgoing studies but also for a great deal of creative
fantasy and inventiveness in order to paint such a vivid picture
of a distant age, approximately 1400 years before the birth of
Christ. I am convinced that only those works gain a lasting
place in world literature which, among other things, attain a
realistic image of man's external and internal existence.
Whoever overlooks this artistic accomplishment in the creation of Thomas Mann cannot do justice to him.

As is proper in a novel in the traditional sense, love between
the sexes is a main concern in **Joseph and his Brothers**. In
Tales of Jacob, it is told in the second chapter how Jacob, not

Esau, receives the blessing from Isaac, has to flee from his powerful brother, and is able to rescue himself only after humiliation and the surrender of his possessions to Laban, the brother of his mother. The third book reports of Dina, Jacob's daughter who is kidnapped by Shechem, the prince's son in a nearby city, a welcome occasion for the wild brothers, Simeon and Levi, to instigate a horrible blood bath and enrich themselves immeasurably.

In the other four sections, the twenty-five years which Jacob spends in the Northeast country with Laban are described at length. He marries two women, Leah and Rachel, together with their slaves Zilpah and Bilhah, produces his numerous children, and obtains great riches—above all, cattle. His passionate love for Rachel is the core of the long report. The two of them fall in love at first sight when they meet at the well. The poet has endowed the Jewish girl with the traits of his own life's companion.

Laban's daughter was slender—as one could see despite the shapelessness of her garment, a yellow smock or pinafore with a red border patterned with black moons. It hung free and comfortably from throat to hem, showing the little bare feet, but fitted around the shoulders, displaying their appealing fineness and tenderness, and it had sleeves reaching half way down the upper arm. Her black hair was tumbled rather than curled, and almost short, at least shorter than Jacob had ever seen it on women at home; only two braids, curling at the ends, hung across her cheeks and down upon her shoulders. She played with one of them as she stood and looked. What a sweet face! Who shall describe its magic? ... Rachel was beautiful and well-favored, and both at once in such an arch and gentle way that one saw—Jacob saw, as she looked at him—how spirit and will power, wisdom and courage in their feminine counterparts, were the effective source of all this loveliness, so expressive her whole person was of open-eyed readiness for life. She looked towards him, one hand fingering her braid, the other grasping the staff that rose above her head, and measured the young man, gaunt from his journeys, in dusty, faded, and tattered garments, with the brown and

bearded sweat-marked face that was not the face of a
hireling. As she looked, the nostrils—perhaps too thick
—of her little nose seemed to dilate drolly and her upper
lip, which stuck out somewhat beyond the lower, to shape
with it in the corners of her mouth, all by itself and with
no tension of her muscles, that lovely thing—a tranquil
smile. But loveliest and best of all was the look, pecu-
liarly sweetened and transfigured by her nearsighted-
ness, in her black, perhaps just faintly slanting eyes,
that look which, with no exaggeration, nature had endowed with the uttermost of charm that she can give a
human face—a deep, liquid, speaking, melting, friendly
light, at once serious and playful, and such as Jacob
never before in all his life had seen or thought to see.
(JB, I, 247 f.)

Despite all delays and difficulties, their indestructible union
marks a radiant line through the years. Properly and effi-
ciently, Jacob begets children with three other women, but his
heart belongs completely to Rachel. His rapture makes him
blind to the custom demanding that the oldest daughter marry
first. He should have reacted to Laban's suggestion and wooed
both of them at the same time. His love is without bounds or
measure. It is "idolatrous." Laban considers himself justified in deceiving him and substituting Leah on the bridal night.
God does not approve of Jacob's love, and thus for many years
Rachel remains barren. Her first birth is unusually difficult—
it is described for us in great detail—and her delicate body
fails to outlive the second one on the way home shortly before
their arrival. Thus the Lord punishes Jacob's inordinate passion. Jacob however holds to it firmly and transfers it to
Joseph, who preserves his mother's features; whereas Jacob
always regards Benjamin, whose birth causes his mother's
death, with averted eyes. He loves Joseph much more than all
the other sons put together, even "idolatrously," and is again
punished. In the final analysis he is responsible for the tense
relationship between Joseph and the ten older brothers which
breaks out into open quarrel when the father presents him with
his mother's bridal garment. Mann takes a great deal of care
with the description of this garment, a Babylonian work.

It was splendid to see, a magnificent specimen of the

arts of weaving and embroidering: it seemed an unmer-
ited piece of good fortune that such a thing should have
found its way into Laban's house and his chest. It was
large and broad, a garment and over-garment, with wide
sleeves to put one's arms in at will; so cut that a piece
of it could either be drawn over the head to cover it or
else wound about the head and shoulders, or else left to
hang down the back. And the maiden garment weighed
uncertainly in the hand, for it was heavy and light at
once, and of unequal weight in different places. The
background was of the palest blue, woven thin and fine as
a breath of air, a misty nothing, to be squeezed together
in one hand, and yet weighted heavily everywhere by the
embroidered pictures which covered it with brilliant,
glittering colours, carried out in close, fine work, in
gold and silver and bronze, and every imaginable shade:
white, purple, rose and olive, likewise black and white,
all blended together like paintings in bright enamel. And
such clever pictures in the design! Here was Ishtar-
Mami, in various shapes, a tiny nude figure, pressing
milk out of her breast with both hands, the sun and moon
on either side. Everywhere the five-pointed star was repeated in varying colors, signifying god; the dove, the
bird of the mother-goddess of love, was woven most often in silver thread. Gilgamesh, the hero, two-thirds
god and one-third man, was displayed strangling a lion
in the bend of his arm. One recognized the human scor-
pion pair who at the ends of the earth guarded the gate
through which the sun goes down to the lower world. One
distinguished various animals, sometime paramours of
Ishtar and transformed by her—a wolf, a bat, the same
who had once been Isullanu, the gardener. But Tammuz,
the shepherd, was represented by a brilliant bird, the
first partner of her lust, to whom she had decreed weep-
ing year after year; and there was not lacking the fire
breathing bull of heaven, whom Anubis sent against Gilgamesh because of Ishtar's baffled longing and perfervid
plaints. The garment slipped through Rachel's hands:
she saw a man and woman sitting at both sides of a tree,
stretching up their hands to the fruit, while a snake rose
up behind the woman's back. And again there was em-

broidered a sacred tree, with two bearded angels on either side, touching it with scaly masculine cones to make it bear; while above the tree of life the female emblem hovered surrounded by sun, moon, and stars. And likewise there were sayings woven into the veil, in broad-pointed signs, lying down or standing straight or slanting. Rachel made out: "I have put off my coat, how shall I put it on?" (JB, I, 321-3)

This is what Mann's writing makes of the biblical "coat of many colors," which Joseph begs from his father and which the brothers tear into shreds on his body when they fall upon him.

Such were the circumstances wherein Joseph is driven from his father, who mourns him for a long time as dead while his son is gradually climbing to a position of highest honor in Egypt.

The love affair between Joseph and the wife of Potiphar is placed at the midpoint of the Egyptian events. In the Bible, the story is told very tersely. The mistress is seized by a desire for her slave; and, when he resists her, she lodges a complaint against him so that he has to go to prison. Since that time, she has been regarded as the classic example of the lustful seductress and he as the "chaste" Joseph, throughout world literature and in the idiom of the people.

It is necessary to interpose here that the narrator is not satisfied at all to reproduce the biblical report in detail. He constantly accompanies it with his commentaries, investigations, and additions. He performs biblical criticism, and corrects many statements. He gives nameless people names, and adds new figures and new scenes. This is the case even in the first volumes. For example, along with Jacob he places his oldest servant Eliezer, who is also Joseph's teacher. He describes in detail the charming relationship between Joseph and his younger brother Benjamin. These are only two examples of factual expansion of the biblical text. In the third volume, **Joseph in Egypt,** these additions are most profuse. Potiphar is called Peteprê, his wife Mut-en-emet. His parents are the siblings Huia and Tuia. His majordomo is called Mont-kaw and made into a figure of character. Two dwarfs live at the court who, we might say, buzz around Joseph like a good and an evil angel. Their nature is absolutely opposite:

Shepses-Bes, sexless, receptive to the divine, and thoroughly good hearted; Dudu, who married a well-developed woman and produced two strapping sons with her, a conceited and vicious sex-maniac. Potiphar's wife has many ladies-in-waiting and among her slaves a Negress, Tabuba, who engages in black magic with her in order to tame Joseph. With this cast of characters, Thomas Mann constructs many dramatic scenes. As the silent servant of the parents, Joseph discovers that they have dedicated the manhood of their son to the God Amun as a sacrifice for their no-longer-permissible sibling marriage, and Joseph is overcome with strong compassion for the supreme lord of this great house who is flooded by Pharaoh with honors and riches as recompense for his eunuch-like existence. Like the other members of the harem, Mut-en-emet is his wife for the sake of honor. But in her own right, she is an accomplished dancer and singer in the order of Hathor of the Amun Temple, her womanhood being suppressed by the strict concept of her service.

From this pre-history, Thomas Mann is able to transform the terse, rough-hewn, biblical report into a psychologically searching love story. The cultivated lady awakens from her erotic sleep to a blissful passionate love. Through a dream she becomes conscious of herself:

> She dreamed she was sitting on her stool at table on the platform in the hall of the blue columns at the side of the old Huia and was eating her meal in the protective silence which always predominated during this procedure, but this time the quiet was especially protective and deep because the four diners not only kept from saying a word but were also attempting to keep their actions soundless while eating. She was just about to cut up a pomegranate with a finely honed little bronze knife and through care-lessness the blade slipped away from her and went into her hand, rather deep into the soft part between the thumb and forefingers so that it bled. There was sub-stantial bleeding of ruby red like the juice of the pome-granate and with shame and sorrow she watched it welling up. All of them took great pains to look as if they had not noticed anything of Mut's clumsiness and no one bothered about her distress, which upset the wounded girl further.

Then it occurred to her that because of this suffering she was neglecting her duty to look reprovingly for the sake of Amun at the scandal of the house, the Canaanite slave who was growing up there against all that was proper; and she darkened her brows and looked over severely toward the intended one behind Petetrê's chair, the youth Osarsiph. But when he felt himself called by her severe glance, he left the place of his duty and came and approached her. And he was close to her, and she very much felt his nearness. But he had approached her in order to still the flow of blood, for he took her wounded hand and led it to his mouth so that the four fingers were lying on his one cheek and the thumb on his other, but the wound on his lips. As a result her blood stood still with rapture and the flow was dammed.

This treacherous dream with its transparent symbols opens Mut's eyes to her passionate love.

Joseph, too, was deeply overjoyed by the attentiveness of the mistress and very much receptive to her charms. But there are seven cogent reasons which bind him, above all his relationship to the father on earth and the One in heaven and his love to the highest master in the house to whom he had pledged incorruptible loyalty even in the face of Mont-kaw. His chastity does not last forever, but he resists the seductive woman who develops gradually from "feminine beauty" to "beautiful womanhood" and finally assumes witch-like characteristics.

The narrator permits us to experience the intensifying passion of the woman who now finally wants to gain respect as a female, and likewise the long courageous struggling of the handsome, charming man. Dudu fans the flames on both sides. When the two dwarfs meet after they have listened from behind the curtain to a tête-à-tête between the couple, they begin a quarrel which degenerates into a violent fusilade of name-calling. When the mistress' love begins to glow intensely, Dudu goes to the master and lies to him about it. For he has hated the god-like Joseph from the very beginning and sets everything in motion to destroy him—among other things, even the high priest Amun's Beknachos. While Eny—which is the nickname for the mistress—is still in control of herself, she implores her husband to dismiss Joseph from the house. But the clever young man who shows so much understanding for his precarious existence has already become indispensible to him. He cannot fulfil her request. Potiphar is a high-strung, sensitive, thoughtful man. He listens patiently to the report of Dudu, whose nature is repulsive to him, and then, by means of several clever questions, forces him to unmask his evil character. As a punishment for Joseph, the dwarf suggests emasculation, which he himself will gladly carry out if the prisoner is properly bound. As a reward for his watchfulness, he wants to be his successor as majordomo and to advise the lovely sinner to turn to him so that her guilt will not be exposed to the people. Otherwise, Potiphar would be forced to kill her. Potiphar himself thrashes the upstart.

When Eny is lying before him pressing charges, Potiphar has the whole staff called together and proves to be a mild and wise judge. During all the years of his marriage, he has expected and feared such an event because he has put himself in the unfortunate position of his wife. Therefore, he does not ask a single question. After all, everybody knows of the unhappy passion of Eny and of Joseph's resistance. It must in no way be further exposed. He pronounces his judgment immediately. Dudu is relieved of his office and half of his mischievous tongue is cut off. Shepses-Bes becomes his successor in office. Potiphar sends Joseph into the royal prison on an island in the Nile delta and writes a letter to the Captain Mai-sachme that he has committed no breach of honor but has only become involved in a sexual matter. After a short time the prisoner is even elevated there to become the friend and right hand of the prison director. In this and similar manner, the narrator brings everything else that he finds in the chapters of the first book of Moses very close to us like a vivid slice of reality, a real and gripping human destiny. But as the prelude shows, Thomas Mann aims higher. He regards the depicted people as representative figures of the early history of mankind, through whom he wants to fathom the nature of man and present it. His artistic performance does not exhaust itself in this fascinating realism.

The book of books, the Bible, still one of the most powerful books of all world literature in its broad influence, was written by Jewish priests in order to glorify the Lord, the creator of the world and the almighty leader of the destinies of man and people. Everything human is related to Him and dependent on His word and will. It is a holy book, the revealed word of the Lord, which, according to the concepts of orthodox priests and laymen, must not be questioned. The writer of the novel **Joseph and his Brothers** does not agree with these concepts. We know that he practices biblical criticism and establishes a detailed foundation for every change. Without hesitation, he adds a great deal from every accessible tradition and from his own invention. He accompanies his whole story with discursive clarifications of an essayistic nature. He studies religion and mythology and introduces into his biblical stories all kinds of results from research on divine doctrine and cults about 1400 B.C. in the countries of the Near East.

Mann is dealing with an epoch of mythic associative thinking that is sharply separated in space and time from our logically causal view. A phantasmagoria of myths in which space and time are nullified lives in the heads of the wise men. The recurrence of the same names makes it easy for these people to equate themselves with their forefathers. They live in their imitation. They play their roles, and thus the past becomes festive present and has an effect on the future. Between the heavenly above, the human element in the middle, and the nether world of death below, the sphere rolls in its orbit. Human beings become gods and again people. The cycle of the constellations and of the year are very closely related to the birth, life, death, and resurrection of man. In this early period, the world of reality is flooded over and saturated by myths which teach a multiplicity of gods whose cults are intertwined with natural phenomena and for the most part entail fertility rites that often intensify into sexual orgies. In the middle of this chaos, the Jewish patriarchs created monotheism, the belief in a single, supernatural, spiritual god whose incarnation is the word alone, the solid ground prepared for a spiritualization of religion, a strict ethic, and a development of the moral human personality. This history of origins fascinates Thomas Mann. The mythical and religious motives, however, do not remain for him a separate superstructure above the real human event, but go constantly as effective ingredients into the stories, into the plots, conceptions, emotions, thoughts, and deeds of men.

A section in the second chapter of the novel **Young Joseph** is titled outright: "How Abraham discovered the Lord." Eliezer teaches his attentively listening student Joseph: Abraham only wanted to serve the highest. In his persistent reflection he wandered from one natural phenomenon to the next, from the maternal earth to the rain and to the sun in heaven, then to the moon and stars in the night. But since they all appear and disappear, there must be a Lord over them who guides them and leads them. Thus Abraham discovered God from whom everything came, the good and the evil, a reassuring point in the confusion of the world to which one could cling in all life situations and to whom alone reverence was due. Thus out of the secret of the monstrous world about him, he created the Thou for himself. Between Abraham and the Lord a bond is established for their mutual elevation and sanctification. That is the beginning. Since that time the patriarchs are the bearers of God's cares. They sense that their thinking about the Lord must never cease. God is becoming, and they grow and mature with him.

Thomas Mann is apparently no dogmatist, but he cherishes respect for all life's phenomena and their mysterious origins. He wants to humanize the mythical world through psychological interpretation. He does it by representing a strong effect in all participating human beings and by penetratingly depicting its spiritual conquest in the belief in a single invisible God among individual highly gifted human beings. He certainly knows about the community-forming strength of belief which, for example, is manifested in the preservation of the small Jewish race through the centuries right down to our own days. But he also disregards the centuries-long, quiet, steady work of the rabbis. He clings firmly to his conception that everything important in the history of mankind is performed by individual, creative personalities. In his biblical novel, Abraham, Jacob, Joseph, and the Pharaoh Ikhnaton are the bearers of God's cares. They represent the developmental history of mankind.

Strict logic does not predominate in Thomas Mann's religious history. At many points it seems that he thought man created God according to his own image. At others, the existence of God is presupposed, but it depends on whether man recognizes Him and realizes Him within himself. The bearers of God's troubles are blessed, chosen, highly gifted men who are more strongly united with God than the others. This union with the original basis of the world makes them religiously creative. They know about good and evil, guilt and punishment. They execute the will of God. They teach and spread their divine wisdom.

The stories of Jacob are not purely uplifting, and Thomas Mann does not conceal their humor in any way. When Joseph narrates them in abbreviated form in the house of the young Pharaoh, the latter and his mother laugh heartily over them. Jacob too is filled with the mythic associative thinking of his time. When he flees to Laban and when he moves to his son in Egypt, these are trips to the netherworld for him. In his farewell address to his sons, he associates them with the circle of constellations in the skies. These are only two examples from among many more. But his constant worry for the Lord makes him a strong enemy of all adoration of natural phenomena, all orgiastic cults, customs, and any sort of crude deviation. He does not want to spill any human blood either in sacrifice or in war. He is horrified that Laban has killed his little son and laid him to rest in the cellar of his house in order to assure the continuance of happiness. But it also proves to be in vain, for the blessing does not come.

Jacob proves himself to be a genuine bearer of the blessing, even if a little deception was used to exclude the uncouth Esau. Jacob brings the Lord's blessing on the house of Laban. His body has the capability of acting as a divining rod, and he discovers a rich source of water on Laban's property. The herds increase rapidly under his knowledgeable hands, and he is skilled and beloved in business for his master, who does everything to bind him and his blessing to his house as long as possible. But Jacob becomes rich himself in Laban's service. Among other things, he discovers that when ewes "stare" at mottled, peeled sticks, they bring into the world mottled lambs, which, according to contract with Laban, are awarded to Jacob. All of this Jacob conceives of as the fortunate result of his paternal blessing from the Lord.

Even Jacob's dreams are weighty. On his journey to Laban, he dreams of a God who first appears to him in the form of a jackal. Then he dreams of a handsome youth with the head of a dog, who reveals to him in advance, through a revelation of his own history, the deception which Laban is playing on him with his daughters. Laban is a wretched "clod," thinking only of his own advantage, completely without sense for the Lord's cares and hence also without the blessing. Far more important, however, is Jacob's splendid dream, in which he looks up the stairs into heaven and receives the Lord's promise of a glorious future for his race.

At an advanced age, during the period when he is crying over Joseph, still another joy and satisfaction is bestowed upon him:

> [Tamar] ... sat at Jacob's feet, had sat there a long time now, profoundly moved by the expression on his face, listening to the words of Israel. Never did she lean back, she sat up very straight, on a footstool, on a well-step, on a knot of root beneath the tree of wisdom, with throat outstretched and concave back, two folds of strain between her velvet brows ...
>
> She was beautiful in her way; not pretty—beautiful, but beautiful after an austere and forbidding fashion, so that she looked angry at her own beauty, and with some justice too, for it had a compelling power which left the men no rest; and it was precisely their unrest which had graved the furrows in her brows. She was tall and almost thin, but of a thinness more disturbing than any fleshliness however ripe; accordingly the unrest was not of the flesh and so must be called daemonic. She had wonderfully beautiful and piercingly eloquent brown eyes, nearly round nostrils, and a haughty mouth.
>
> What wonder that Jacob was taken with her, and as a reward for her admiration drew her to himself? He was an old man, loving feeling, only waiting to be able to feel again.
>
> Tamar was a seeker. The furrows between her brows signified not alone anger at her beauty but also strain and searching for truth in salvation. Where in the world does one not meet concern with God? One might have supposed that this country girl would have been satisfied by the wood and meadow nature-worship of her tradition. But not so: it had not answered her urgent need even before she met Jacob. (JB, IV, 303–4).

Jacob speaks among other things of the prince of peace who will come, the son of man before whom all kings will bow down. Tamar decides then to join his family as a wife in this blessed lineage. She first marries one son after the other of Judah, who however are incompetent, rejected by the Lord, and die without producing a child by her. Unpertrubed, she sticks to her plan. She lies in wait like a whore along Judah's way home from a festival, seduces him, and has him give her pledges instead of payment. When she becomes pregnant, the whole world finds out what has happened. She has abased herself deeply. Now she becomes the proud mother of two sons. Perez belongs in the genealogy of King David, from whom Jesus of Nazareth takes his origin. From then on she was intimately united with the tribe of Jacob. Thus, the narrator knows how to lend even this chapter of the book of Moses intellectual depth and make it apparent to us how much solemn dignity radiates from Jacob to all who meet him. The sons honor and fear him. Even Pharaoh Ikhnaton is very impressed when Jacob does not adapt to the courtly forms at all but only raises his hand in blessing toward the courtly assemblage.

There is also genuine concern for the Lord even in Egypt, the land of the intensified death cult and of the many gods who are revered in the form of animals—a cult which Jacob despises deeply. The priests of Amun, of the steer god, who personifies the fruitful Nile, have taken the supreme command unto themselves; and their city of Thebes has become the capital city of the empire. They represent the strong warlike royal power which has subjugated many lands, and they fight against all deviations from orthodox belief and everything foreign which could penetrate and dissipate it. But the young Pharaoh does not love this god and turns ever more decisively to the doctrine of the sun god Atum which has been cherished and taught at the head of the Nile delta since ancient times. Amenhotep IV is a sickly youth, subject to epileptic attacks, in which he is transported to his father the god, and returns from these ecstasies with a deepened knowledge of the god. When he ascends to the throne at the end of the second year of Joseph's stay in the prison with Mai-Sachme, he rejects indignantly Amun's command to lead a military campaign. " ... Amun wants to unite the world in the service of rigid terror that is a false and forbidding unity, not wanted by my father, for he wants to unite his children in joy and tenderness!"

His moral father is the "light" and the sweet sun-disc whose rays embrace the lands and bind them with love—he lets his hands grow weak with love, and "only the evil people whose belief regresses have strong hands." He changes his name Amenhotep to Ikhnaton in order to express his love for Atum-Aton. He builds a new city for the ethereal god of peace and makes it into his permanent residence, the capital city of the country. Like the old Ismaelite merchants before, like Montkaw, the majordomo, like Potiphar the courtier, and like Mai-Sachme the prison warden, the young Pharaoh too is immediately receptive to the radiance of Joseph when he stands before him and his mother Teje to interpret his dreams.

There develops between them a long conversation which forms the intellectual climax of the whole book. Thomas Mann states expressly that be began this descent into hell through the well of the past up to the present of Joseph for the sake of this conversation about God. The young prince listens with growing tension and excitement to the speeches of the young Hebrew who comes out of prison to him. Joseph replies to the prince's enthusiastic description of his kindly father who wants peace: "What do you want to do with robber kings who burn and pillage? You cannot bring the peace of the Lord to them. They are too stupid and evil. You can only bring it to them by hitting them so that they feel that the peace of the Lord has strong hands. You are after all responsible to the Lord that things grow on earth at least half way according to his will and not completely according to the will of the incendiaries." That pleases the politically minded mother very much.

Jacob's son Joseph, whom he dearly loves, is the chief figure of the novel, with whom it begins and ends. Thomas Mann makes him into his mouthpiece. He identifies himself with him to a certain limit, and lets him be the standard bearer of the mankind that looms before him as the ideal. He is the heir of the tender beauty and charm of Rachel, above all, of her black, often slightly veiled eyes and her enchanting smile. He also inherits a great deal from his father, especially the close relationship with God. Just as in the love of his father, so too in the love of God, he always feels safe and entrusts himself completely to his planning. He feels elected and blessed from the beginning. His cleverness must be added to his handsomeness. He is highly gifted and even more greatly talented than his father. Jacob allows only him to be instructed in all higher learning, and Joseph soaks it up eagerly and cherishes it in his reliable memory. Even as a boy, he is familiar with the conditions of transport in which all sorts of future events are revealed to him. His prophetic dreams are known everywhere. Viewed from the figure of Joseph, the whole work is a novel of development and education.

In his youth, Joseph is lost in revery and wasted. His lively imagination makes him conceited. He chatters with abandon and seems arrogant with his older brothers. He undertakes all sorts of things which he has to conceal from his strict father. When he tarries in the grove of Adonis with Benjamin before the burial vault, he tells him of the great festival in which he has taken part twice. It deals with the god who was torn asunder, buried, and resurrected again in the spring.

Joseph's fate is twice shaped after his image when the brothers throw him into the empty well and when Potiphar sends him to prison. Actually Joseph himself interprets the events according to this pattern, or, even better, he himself helps his life to develop according to this fate of the gods through his gifts and through his belief in the wise plans which God has mapped out for him. Joseph's attitude toward the heathen world around him is not so strict as that of his father. As soon as fate lays its hard hand on him, he not only accepts it in suffering but reflects, recognizes his own guilt, grows in his self-knowledge, learns respect for his fellow man, and matures with his experiences. In this sense, he proves himself with the leader of the Ishmaelite caravan, with Mont-kaw the majordomo, with the highest master of the house (Potiphar) in opposition to the seductive Eny, with Mai-Sachme, and with Pharaoh Ikhnaton. He matures to the point of friendliness with man beyond his connections to the family. At the same time, he develops a marvelous fluency with words for which I only cite as an example the calming good-night wishes with which he cheers up the old Ishmaelite Mont-kaw and, as intensification, the reassuring speech with which he accompanies Mont-kaw softly to his eternal rest.

"Peace be with you!" he said. "Rest, rest, my father, beatified through the night! Lo, I keep watch over your limbs, that you may carefree tread the path of consolation. You need not to be careful for aught, and thinking

that may be blithe. Not about your limbs, nor the cares
of the house, nor yourself and what will become of you
and how it may be in the life after this life. For just so
is it, that all this is not your affair nor care and you
need not to have unrest about it. Is that not gloriously
soothing and happy? All toil and moil, all heat and heaviness are past, nor anguish more, no wrestling struggle,
no terror of cramp. No bad medicines, no burning poul-
tices, nor sucking leeches on your neck. The dungeon of
your sore trouble opens its door, you can come out and
stroll strong and hale down the path of consolation, which
leads you deeper with each step into the ways of peace.
At first you will go through vales you know, those which
each eve received you when I said good night; you have
still some heaviness and scantiness of breath, of which
you are scarce aware; they come from your body, which
I hold here in my hands. But soon—you will not know the
crossing—you will gain the meadows with light tread,
where no distress from afar can hang on or plague you
even unaware, for all at once you are free of all doubt or
care as to how it will be with you or what will become of
you, so that you are amazed how they could once have so
concerned you; for all is as it is and in the most natural
way, the most right and best, in happy harmony with itself and with you, since you are Mont-kaw to all eternity.
For what is, is; and what was, shall be. For since you
are Mont-kaw, you cannot fall out of your role nor look
before the people as though you believe I was nothing else
but Osarsiph, the bought slave from afar, for secretly
you will know, with silent intuition, from the other time,
who I am and whose bow I draw, that I prepare the way
of the gods, my brothers. Farewell, then, my father
and chief! In light and in lightness shall we see each
other again." (JB, III, 367-9)

Beyond this he proves to be unusually gifted from the practical standpoint. After all, he can read, writes a beautiful
hand, learns foreign languages easily, and with these gifts can
make himself useful everywhere. He sizes up a situation
quickly, has a fortunate touch in all dealings and businesses,
and understands how to guide and plan the work of others. It is
that which helps his climb in the house of Potiphar, in the

prison, and with the Pharaoh. After he instructs the young king in interpreting for himself his dreams that first seven fat years and then seven lean years face him, he develops a plan to prevent the famine of the second period and, at the same time, gains great advantages for Pharaoh's fortune and position by having grain presented to the poor but by making the rich dependent on the Pharaoh through weighted prices, and by only protecting the temples. This proves economic, social, and political astuteness on a grand scale, which is recognized without exception by the queen mother.

During his rise in Egypt, he has to adapt quickly to his surroundings. In living with Peteprê, he becomes more and more an Egyptian. Ikhnaton marries him to the daughter of the high priest at the Aton Temple in On. Jacob would be horrified if he were to see the cult ceremonies which are practiced during the marriage. Many times he also takes part in the burnt offering to the sun god. In these ways he separates himself from his family and becomes estranged. Once when Jacob presented him with his mother's bridal garment, he thought about giving the handsome, highly gifted son the parental blessing too. But the blessing of the Jewish god no longer suits the man of the world, Pharaoh's minister of agriculture, the people's provider in the time of the great famine, who settles him and his tribe with all their belongings in the land of Goshen. When he sees his son whom he believed dead for so many years, he reveals to him immediately, in a confidential dialogue at this emotional meeting, that he is not going to give him the parental blessing. On his dying bed however, he does bless him, the ardently loved son, with great lovely words:

"Joseph, my scion and seed, son of the virgin, son of my dearest one, son of the fruit tree by the spring, fruitful bough whose branches overhang the wall, I greet you. You who are the heart of the spring, first-born bull in his adornment, greeting!"

Jacob had spoken loud and clear, a solemn address, to be heard by all, but then he dropped his voice almost to a whisper, obviously desirous, if not to shut out the public, at least to limit its numbers during this blessing.

"Most dearly beloved," came from the painfully smiling lips, "chosen and preferred by the daring heart for the sake of the only beloved, who lived in you and with whose eyes she looks, just as once she first looked at me at the well ... In you I kept my darling here, when the Almighty tore her from me, in your loveliness she lived, and what is sweeter than the double and the doubtful? Well I know that the double is not of the spirit, for which we stand, but is the folly of the peoples. And still I yielded to that ancient mighty spell. You too, my joy and my care, have already made half the journey towards that land, and yet you were once little and then young and were all that my heart understood of loveliness and charm. Serious was my heart but soft, therefore was it soft before beauty. Called to the heights and to the sides of diamond-sharp steeps, secretly I loved the gentle hills ... Be not proud, my child—have I need to warn you? No, your shrewdness saves you from presumption. It is a charming blessing, but not the highest and sternest, to find favor before God and man. Lo, thy dear life lies open in its truth before the dying days. It was play and playing, familiar, friendly appealingness, approaching salvation yet not quite seriously a calling or a gift. Love pierces my heart at sight of that mingled gladness and sadness; not so can anyone else love you, my child, who sees, not as the father-heart can the sadness, but only the brilliance of your life. And so I bless you, blessed one, with all the strength of my heart in the name of the eternal who gave you and took you and gave you again and now takes me from you. Higher shall my blessing mount than the blessings of my fathers upon my own head. Be blessed, as you are blessed, with the blessing of heaven above, blessings of the deep that lieth under, with blessings gushing from the breast of heaven and the womb of earth! Blessings, blessings on Joseph's head, and in your name shall they sun themselves who come from you. Songs shall stream far and wide singing the story of your life, ever new, for after all it was a sacred play and you suffered and you could forgive. So I too forgive you that made me suffer. And forgive us all!" (JB, IV, 586-7)

The old gnostic myth that the soul and the spirit will coalesce into a fruitful worldly unity is fulfilled in Joseph. The other bearers of God's concern place the blessing from above over all else. Joseph does not barricade himself against the netherworld. This leads to a world view which is effective in practical life. As is maintained in the prelude, it is probably the secret goal in the plan of the Lord, and it leads to worldly success.

Abraham and Jacob, the bearers of God's concern, are dull, dignified, strict, and solemn in their appearance. Ikhnaton, the Egyptian theologian, is zealous and remote. In the propagation of his enlightened doctrine, he collapses before the resistance of the dull masses. Compared with these three, Joseph is dedicated to the Lord but is still a child of the world who regards the Egyptian descent into hell as an adventure and knows how to further his ascent everywhere with smooth talk. Pharaoh compares him with Hermes, the messenger of the Gods, in whose myths many picaresque tricks are reported. He is the mediator between the gods and man, the god of the merchants and writers, labile, resourceful, ready to help. Thus Joseph transmits the worldly blessing which he bears to man and peoples.

As a conclusion to his adventurous journeys into the unknown where he is to be elevated, Joseph always imagines the reunion with his family. He will have them sent for when his dream has been fulfilled and he has become a great man. When the famine takes place, he knows that even his brothers will come to buy grain, and he awaits them excitedly. But he does not want them to know right away; he wants to put on a dramatic festival play that people will talk about for centuries and that will even garner a smile from God. And so he discusses it with Mai-Sachme, whom he has made his majordomo, and carries it out as it is reported in the Bible. Thomas Mann contributes all sorts of things to the festive creation, but especially priceless is the return of the brothers with the joyous knowledge that Joseph lives. The brothers rack their brains as to how they should tell it to their old father so that he will believe it and so that the joyous shock will not kill him. They receive surprising help. Serah, Asher's daughter, awaits them in the flower-burdened spring landscape of Canaan with her lovely resonant voice, which she enjoys displaying to the accompaniment of a lute. On hearing the great news, she improvises a song in doggerel rhyme and wanders ahead to the grandfather. The people hear her and join with her. At first the old man reproves her for such frivolous singing, but she persists in it. Thus Jacob finally has to believe the truth that Joseph is living in high honors, is sending him rich presents, and is happy that his father tarries among the living.

The report extends over a dozen pages and begins as follows:

Sing, Serah, Asher's child, what thou hast learned
From the eleven now out of Egypt returned.
Sing how that God in His mercy has blessed them
That to the man down below they addressed them.
Who then the man, who but Joseph is he,
My uncle as tall and as fine as can be.
Old one, look up, it is thy dear son,
Greater is Pharaoh only by his throne.
Lord of the lands his name they call,
The state's first servant they name him all,
Kings of the earth his praises sing,
Stranger folk kneeling to him tribute bring.
Over uncounted lands is he set,
To all the people he giveth their meat,
From thousands of barns he spendeth them bread
To carry them over their hunger and need.
For he it was in foresight wisely hoarded
And therefore is his name o'er all belauded.

For a word of beauteous rareness
In my music interweaves,
Matching all it hath of fairness,
And it says: Thy darling lives!
Match, O soul, in exultation
Golden music of the strings;
For the grave no longer hath him—
Heart, he is arisen—sing!
Ah, he was no longer present,
Desolate the barren earth—
Till we heard: He is arisen.
Dear old Father, pray have faith! (JB, IV, 481-3)

The writer of the Joseph novel feels related and attracted to his hero whenever he imparts the myths and religion of the early times to his reader. But he is unable to accept them continually in complete earnest and solemnly. Without delay he weaves the tradition of the criticism of the higher ranks of the angels into his report on the Lord. This criticism was discussed in the prelude. The introduction to the third volume is completely dedicated to it, and the man of the Moses book who leads Joseph to Dothan becomes an angel who expresses freely his contempt for the human race in facial expressions and words. All the way through the work, the narrator does not overlook any opportunity to use his sense of "the misery and comedy" of human life and activity in order to bathe the presentation in an ironic light. For example, the narrator oftentimes draws comparisons from his own time, such as the similarity of the figure of Pharaoh Ikhnaton to a young Englishman or when he has the aristocratic circles of Egypt spicing their affected speech with French phrases (instead of Babylonian). It is romantic irony that Joseph refers the mistress Eny to the "history" in which they are playing a part in order to decoy her from her desire. Those are only two of the countless forms of the ironic game. The people in the novel laugh copiously and frequently. Perhaps the readers do not laugh aloud, but they smile gaily just as often as they are moved to tears. That which contributes especially to the enjoyment of the attentive, intelligent reader is the constantly rich and varied play with words and phrases which Thomas Mann carries on so artfully and well in this extensive work, in the descriptions of the surrounding world, the representations of people, and their often discursive conversations.

In the fourth volume, we sense in the beginning to a certain extent that the narrator is having difficulty finding his way back into the long interrupted work. He forgets that he had already given Eny's father the name Mai-Sachme. It is also strange that the prison director of this name immediately relates the love story which he has experienced and on which he is writing, to a visiting priest while receiving the new captive. How much more sensible it would have been, had he confided it later to Joseph of an evening. After that, however, the story again gets back on the right path.

If we wanted to summarize the meaning of **Joseph and his Brothers** very briefly, we might say that it is not primarily a divine doctrine but rather a paean on the creative spirit of man in its variety of forms and accomplishments and, to this extent, a poem of mankind which can exist alongside Goethe's **Faust**, which is also a game conducted seriously, though thoroughly interlarded with humor and which is played in heaven, the world, and hell.

The Beloved Returns

During his work on Joseph and his Brothers, Thomas Mann stood inwardly very close to Goethe. This is the only explanation for the fact that when he paused after the conclusion of the third large volume, he began to write the Goethe novel The Beloved Returns, a work of almost four hundred pages, and completed it. As early as 1911 at the time of the short story Death in Venice, he had already planned to treat the seventy-three-year-old man's courtship of the nineteen-year-old Ulrike von Levetzow in a narrative. In one of his essays, Mann calls admiration a chief source of poetic creativity. The admiration for a masterpiece fills the soul of the poet and forces him to write in order to free himself from the overpowering impression. When he wrote this novel, the phenomenon of Goethe, which had become a model for his own conduct of life, had already engaged his attention with constantly increasing interest for almost two decades. Goethe could become the subject for such a work as soon as he found the motif in Goethe's life which could serve as the opposite pole in an antithesis, such as he always needed in order to develop the artistic interplay of pathos and irony.

Mann found it in a visit which the sixty-three-year-old widow of the privy counselor, Charlotte Kestner née Buff, made to Weimar in September and October of 1816. She had presented her husband with eleven children of whom nine were living. During her sixteen years of widowhood, she had had much time to fret about the fate which had allowed her to meet the stormy young Goethe in 1772 and then had burdened her with the world-wide fame of the Werther book. Even after forty-four years it presented her with torturing questions: why did the young Goethe storm her heart which had belonged to another for years? Why did he expose to the world so nakedly and without consideration the truth of the experience shared by the three of them, mixed with a lot of strange fiction? Then why did he not bother with her and her family again for four decades? To be sure, she is visiting a younger sister who is married to the privy counsellor Riedel in Weimar. But that is only a pretext. She longs to talk this out with the friend of her youth and to quiet her still young and deeply disturbed heart. She has taken along a dress like the one with the rose colored bows with one missing (the one Kestner had given to his friend at that time), so that it would lead Goethe back lightly to the period of his youth. Her oldest daughter, who keeps house for a widowed brother with children, resignedly fulfilling her duties, no longer young, puritanically minded, looks at this endeavor of her mother very critically and fears that she will experience a severe disappointment. She is right. The mother, however, lives in growing anticipation up to the reunion.

In this novel there is no tense exterior plot. The first six of its nine chapters present the widow's experiences before she sees Goethe again. After she has entered her personal history in the black register of the Hotel Elephant in chalk on the twenty-second of September in the morning shortly after 8 o'clock, the news of her arrival spreads quickly in the little city and toward noon a crowd is already besieging the house in order to see "Werther's Lotte." The waiter Mager vents his emotions in a long reverential conversation which expresses representatively the feelings of the Weimaraners. She sends her daughter in advance to the relatives, writes a few lines to Goethe, and lies down to rest after the taxing ride in the post carriage. But only after thinking about that time long ago, does she fall asleep. After awakening, she dresses and starts to go out. For a while, she cannot; one visit after the other detains her and chains her down for many hours.

First comes a young Irish artiste who is hunting for sensations throughout Europe and has already captured many great personalities in her sketchbook. Charlotte is proud of her renown, wears it with dignity, and grants Miss Rose Cuzzle a sitting.

Then Dr. Riemer appears, classical philologist, thirteen years in Weimar, one of Goethe's secretaries, also active for four years in the city school, married, living in his own home. His bovine eyes, his peevish mouth, and the complaining expression of his face are emphasized again and again. The two-hour conversation with him forces tears into the eyes of the aging woman a number of times. Riemer has declined a call to the University of Rostock. He wants to remain in Weimar and continue to enjoy the great good fortune of frequent companionship with Goethe. He admires the man and his work tremendously, but for the deeply shocked woman he brings to life the wretched, hard, inconsiderate aspects of the great man, who accepts indifferently the sacrifice of Riemer's personal career, often using him for ordinary copying services and not bothering about the well-being of the admiring helper. It is not stated, but apparently even the pay is so slight that in order to be able to marry he has been forced to take on a teaching assignment. The visitor from Hanover feels a fated kinship to this man, reports to him in detail her tormenting thoughts, but probably suspects already what awaits her and is very disturbed.

It gets even worse. Adele Schopenhauer, the sister of the philosopher, a young writer, belonging to the best society of Weimar, follows Dr. Riemer. She too is not lacking in admiration for the aging master. But she and her circle prefer reading the young writers of their own time, which she has to keep secret from him since he does not tolerate any other gods alongside himself. She speaks quite rebelliously of the tyranny which he exercises in the salon of Frau von Pogwisch. She also speaks scathingly of the vulgar Christiane Vulpius and her disreputable conduct, and of the son August, who intentionally appears dry, sober, of merely practical gifts because intellectually he is not able to compete with his father. In all other respects, he is completely subservient to him, obeying him in everything without a will of his own; and, therefore, in even greater measure than Dr. Riemer, August has renounced a life of his own in order to serve Goethe. Without any character of his own, August inclines to drinking and debauchery, and maintains a relationship with the willing wife of a non-commissioned officer in the little town.

Two chapters are completely devoted to Adele's visit. In the fifth chapter, she explains what she has said about the son through an exciting and fascinating narrative which at the same time illuminates an additional depressing aspect of Goethe's attitude. She is intimately acquainted with Ottilie von Pogwisch, a Prussian noblewoman who secretly cultivates relationships with the freedom-loving enemies of Napoloen. Goethe is an admirer of the Kaiser and of French culture, and also naturally his son August. Ottilie is the type of woman whom Goethe finds very pleasing. He wishes that August would marry her; but not until after the death of Christiane Vulpius, who was never recognized socially, does the engagement come about. Ottilie has deep sympathy with the unhappy son of the great father and thinks she can save him. As a result of opposite political inclinations, there is at one time a breach between the two of them. It is the time of the wars of freedom against French domination. Weimar is occupied by the French. Once, an independent Prussian unit succeeds in conquering the city for a few days, but the French gain it back again quickly. On a walk in the park, the two women discover a handsome wounded man in the bushes who begs them for help in a joking tone of voice. They hurry back to the city and make arrangements for him to find bed and board in a remote chamber of the castle. Both of them are mad about this young student, Ferdinand Heinke. The ugly Adele has very little hope for herself and is very happy that Ottilie now really gets to know love. To be sure, a union with this middle-class man can by no means be considered, but she hopes that Ottilie will now finally become free of August, because she is convinced that he will make Ottilie unhappy. That is the reason she reports this whole story. She begs Charlotte to make her influence felt in order to prevent this hopeless marriage. Charlotte rejects this unreasonable demand because, according to the story, all the circumstances are unfavorable. It turns out in fact that Heinke has a loving bride in Silesia. Goethe himself, in a most charming manner, had encouraged Ottilie during a meeting, and August had approached her again after the breach.

After Adele, August von Goethe himself enters the room as an envoy of his father. With this, the illumination of Goethe's powerful personality takes a decisive turn. For his son proves to be not at all dry and sober but rather speaks with great warmth of his father and not without enthusiasm for his writings. He is so uncontrolled in his anger when he speaks about the treatment of his late mother, his father, and even himself at the hands of the Weimar society that Charlotte has to calm him down in motherly fashion. The conversation becomes confidential when she finds the opportunity to ask him whether Ottilie really loves him and wants to marry him for his own sake or for the sake of his famous father, but she does not have the heart to advise him against it. Finally, August carries out his mission of inviting her and the daughter on September 25 for a luncheon with a small circle. In the meanwhile, the relatives have already been asking questions. Now Charlotte can finally hurry to them and give them a report, which quickly gains her forgiveness for the delay. For all these long conversations were revolving around the friend of her youth, for whom her visit is intended.

It is a bold venture to write a Goethe novel. There are all too many hack writers who want to raise themselves up by using famous personalities, even if the venture should not turn out to be exactly a successful speculation. This artistic attempt of Mann reaches its bold highpoint in the seventh chapter with Goethe's extensive monologue. It begins with the retelling of a dream:

Alas, that it should vanish! That my bright vision of the depth must so soon be gone again—as though the whim of a genie gave it and as suddenly snatched it away—it fades into nothing; I emerge. So lovely it was! And now what? Where are we? Jena? Berka? Tennstädt? No, this is the Weimar coverlet, the silken one, here the familiar hangings, the bell-pull. What, what? Here's a brave showing, forsooth! Good for you, old man! Be not dismayed, blithe oldster that thou art! No wonder, either, after all: What glorious limbs, how the goddess' bosom, fine resilient flesh, lay pressed into the shoulder of her handsome huntsman! How chin nestled to neck and slumber-rosy cheek, ambrosial little hand twined around the wrist of the glowing vigorous arm clasping her in its strong embrace! How little nose and mouth sought the breath from his dream-relaxed lips! And Cupid there beside them, half angered, half triumphant, swinging his bow. Halt there, Halloo! While on the other side the bright-eyed beagles gazed and gamboled! At sight of that splendid picture, how your heart leaped in your breast! But whence? Aha, I have it, of course, the l'Orbetto, the Turchi, from the Dresden Gallery, Venus and Adonis. (BR, 281)

In this monologue, the overwhelming grandeur of Goethe becomes truly tangible. He fills every minute of his life with feeling, thinking, planning, and action, ten-fold compressed and intensified, with an heightened productivity in highly varied areas. From the very beginning, Mann is convinced of the questionableness, of the dichotomy, of the "inhumaneness" of art. For this reason, in Goethe's portrait, there is no lack at all of hard, frightening traits, such as Charlotte Kestner, Dr. Riemer, and Adele Schopenhauer experience and complain of. The most important example is Goethe's relationship to Schiller. With the same lack of compassion that we find in the conversations about Goethe, he himself speaks about his friend, who died in 1805. Basically, Goethe did not like Schiller. But that does not prevent him from speaking tirelessly, again and again in admiration and reverence about his character, his immortal artistic achievement, and his intellectually stimulating friendship; for example, in the following words about the Faust poem:

> Yes, time one must have. Time is mercy—a kindly, unassuming boon, to him who will honor it and fill it diligently. Unbeknown she does her work, quietly she brings demonic intervention. I wait, and time encircles me. Doubtless she would perform her task more swiftly, were he still here. Yes, who can I talk to about the Faust, now that the man has taken leave of time? Knew all my problems, all the impossibilities, all the ways and means as well. Immensely quick-witted he was, lively, flexible, had a keen appreciation of the great joke, and emancipation from prosy solemnity. After Helena had come in, did me good to have him praise my distillation of ghost and gargoyle into the classically beautiful and tragic; thought the union of the high and the grotesque, the pure and fantastic might well produce a poetic tragelaph not to be despised. He saw Helena before he died, heard her first trimeters, his noble mind was impressed—that ought to cheer me on. Knew her, as well as did Chiron the rover, from whom I inquired of her. Smiled as he listened and heard how I had managed to imbue each word with the classic spirit:
> Much have I witnessed, e'en tho' the ringlets
> Youthfully cluster over my temples,
> .....
> Through all the clamor of warriors thronging
> Thick in their dust-clouds, heard I the frightful
> Voices of discord, gods in their anger
> Brazenly rising, ring through the field,
> Rampartwards!

He smiled and nodded. "Capital!" said he. That much had his sanction, so far my mind is at rest, it need not be changed, he found it capital—smiled, so that I had to smile too, by reading turned to smiles. Not German here either, smiling at excellence—no German does so. They put on a grim face, not knowing culture is parody—love is parody. He left me behind, confident I should find my way through, discover the right hoop to bind in all the multifarious matter of my design. He saw all that. Knew Faust had to be brought into contact with active life—easier said than done. (BR, 287-8)

The compressed fullness of this monologue cannot be reproduced in abbreviated form. Two subsequent passages may offer further testimony to the intensity of these confessions:

But what a wonderful thing it is about this fall, growing old! A blessed invention of the everlasting Goodness—man fits into his circumstances and they into him, so that he is at one with them and they are his as he is theirs. You get old, you get to be an old man, and look down with contempt, albeit with benevolence, on youth, on the young fry about you. Would you care to be young again, the young cockerel you once were? Wrote the Werther, did the young cockerel, with absurd facility, that was certainly something, at his years. But to go on living, to get old—there is the rub. All the heroism lies in enduring, in willing to live on and not die. And greatness only comes with age. A young man can be a genius, but he cannot be great. Greatness comes only with the weight, endurance, power, mental equipment of age. Mind and power are products of age, they are what make up greatness. Love too comes only then; what is any youthful love beside the spiritual and intellectual strength of love in age? What a callow, green-sickly thing is the love of youth, beside the head-turning flattery paid to lovely adolescence singled out by maturity and greatness —her tenderness exalted and adorned by the force of his mighty emotions! What beside the glowing bliss of age when the love of youth confers on it the boon of new life? Eternal Goodness, I thank thee! Life forever fairer, richer, more instinct with joy and meaning, hence forever more! (BR, 292).

Two-and-twenty years I have had these rooms, and not one single change, save moving the canopy out of the study to make room for my piles of papers. And yes, the first lady-in-waiting, the Egloffstein, gave me the arm-chair here by my bed. Otherwise no change—yet in this unchanging setting, what all has not happened, what a raging storm of labor, effort, birth-pangs, creation, has passed through it! What power to take pains has God given me! That thou honestly hast striven whate'er cometh, God, He knoweth! But time, time always went on over my head. The blood mounts to my temples, always, when I think of it. Two-and-twenty years—something has come of them, we have accomplished something in that time; but it is almost a lifetime, almost the whole life of a man. Hold fast the time! Guard it, watch over it, every hour, every minute! Unregarded it slips away, like a lizard, smooth, slippery, faithless, a pixy-wife. Hold every moment sacred. Give to each clarity and meaning, to each the weight of thine awareness, to each its true and due fulfillment. Keep book of the day, account its each and every use. **Le temps est le seul dont l'avarice soit louable.** (BR, 296-7)

The general admiration of all for Goethe, even the intercession of the son for his father, finds an intensification here.

Three times the monologue is interrupted by conversations with the butler Carl, the copyist John, and the son, in which new aspects of the all-embracing intellectual world of Goethe become visible. For the psychological tension of the novel, Goethe's way of reacting to Charlotte Kestner's visit and her letter are most important. After he has read her lines, he speaks for a long time with August about an especially beautiful crystal which he received from Frankfurt as a present, then about a court festival for which he sketches extemporaneously a great, elaborate masked procession (which is then used in the second part of **Faust**), and has him read a mischievous verse which he would like to send Lotte as an answer if it were proper. Then as usual he decides upon an invitation to lunch. They continue to talk for a while about the case because it excites so much attention in Weimar. "A painful, indeed gruesome matter. The past is in league with stupidity against me to stir up trouble and strife. Couldn't the old lady pass it up and spare me?" Then the reception is set for September 25, and the guest list determined so that sixteen people will come for the meal. Goethe resolves to preserve the proper moderation and the right distance. How right the daughter was with her warning! How was Goethe, a creative person, supposed to retain an emotional experience for forty-four years dating from the year 1772 which had been elevated to the permanence of art two years later in the Werther book? Since that time it had been deluged in the great man's mind by countless new, emotionally moving experiences which were also transformed into poetry, just as in the last two years the love for Marianne von Willemer enriched the **West-Eastern Divan**, indeed even with her own verses of equal quality. Even Ottilie von Pogwisch warms his aging heart. No, Goethe was not able to discuss the excitement and tension of his youthful love, nor to answer her querulous questions, nor to reconcile her with her fate. He wanted to keep her away from himself with a little friendly politeness.

Thus the noonday party at Goethe's house depicted in the eighth chapter was a great disappointment for Charlotte Kestner, indeed a depressing and frightening occasion. To be sure, the master of the house sits between her and her sister and does not hesitate to bestow his favors on her. But otherwise he consciously directs his words to the whole table. The fact that he alone speaks for several hours, is tormenting even for the readers of the novel. They have all been invited as listeners, and they are permitted to admire him, to laugh with approval whenever he recites humorous incidents, but no one is permitted to contribute anything of his own to the conversation. After the outstanding meal, at which Goethe drinks a lot, he shows all kinds of little things from his rich collections and explains them. As one can oftentimes tell from his facial expression, he makes a very great effort to entertain his guests enchantingly and with great variety, but he does it not only to keep the girl friend of his youth at a distance, but all the others as well, an unbearable and wretched procedure quite in conflict with customary social usage.

The courtly lady remains until the middle of October in Weimar, respected in the streets of the city and welcomed in the parties of the families with whom she was together at the Frauenplan. Goethe does not see her again. He writes her another note in which he places his loge in the theatre and his double-yoked carriage at her disposal. She makes use of this offer. When she climbs into the carriage after the performance, there is a surprise. Goethe is sitting in the corner. She is permitted to tell him everything that is on her heart. He begs her for forgiveness and tries to make clear to her that the life of the creative person is itself one of suffering and is indeed a sacrifice. She agrees with him and is reconciled. But this conclusion of the novel is only a vision of Charlotte's, a wish-image created by Thomas Mann.

It is doubtless difficult, if not impossible, to separate poetry and truth precisely from each other in this work. In any case, it is thoroughly wrong to call the novel a secret self-portrayal of Thomas Mann, because it conceals the problem. He has carried out very thorough studies for this artistic work and certainly makes an honest effort at objectivity. According to his own pronouncement, Goethe's monologue is a mosaic of diaries, letters, and conversations, and whatever has been added bears the stamp of this spirit. Many words and phrases which are unusual today and even the orthography of some words give testimony to his efforts to approximate Goethe's time very closely. The author of the work has intentionally not deviated from the truth as he discovered it. But a far-reaching poetic transformation was necessary to create the vivid coherent scenes of the novel. None of them really happened precisely as described.

No poet of the twentieth century can transport himself completely back to the manner of feeling and thinking of the year 1816. The work has a slant just as strongly subjective as painted portraits of our age. In all conversations—they fill most of the pages of the novel—the people carry on a psychological self-analysis which was still strange at that time and which Goethe himself did not practice. One detail may make it clear that Thomas Mann involuntarily carries over much that derives from his own experience to Goethe. Mann studied huge scientific areas thoroughly in order to lend his writings intellectual depth. Goethe did this also; for example, in the West-Eastern Divan, to which the notes give ample testimony. But he also studied many sciences for their own sake. This is demonstrated in his theory of color, by his many hundreds of experiments, in biology with his discovery of the intermaxillary bone, and in his extensive collections which we see even

today in Weimar. For him the scientific studies are not useless by-products which can be thrown away whenever the poem
in concluded.

In this and similar fashion, of course, the many subjective
elements in this novel can be verified. Nevertheless, the
transference of Mann's own characteristics to purely invented
figures, though pronounced, never attains real identity and
does not justify attributing to Mann "secret self portrayals"
(Jonas Lesser). In The Beloved Returns, we are dealing with
a subjectively colored picture of the aging Goethe such as we
have never had up to now in such vividly compressed form.
The risk taken by Thomas Mann, who had no desire to create
a transfigured image, seems to me successful. Against this
background of deep shadow which Goethe casts on his surroundings, his figure stands out all the more powerfully.

The Transposed Heads

In the seventh chapter of The Beloved Returns Goethe speaks
among other things about his "Legende" in the trilogy Paria, at
that time still unwritten, which illustrates the uncanny selec-
tive power of beauty and which ends with a report of the trans-
position of the heads of two women. Here Thomas Mann found
the inspiration to take up and reproduce another Indian legend
(The Transposed Heads). He even wrote this before he resumed
his work on the biblical novel. The story of the sensuous Sita,
her intellectually trained husband Schridaman, and his physically handsome friend Nanda is in itself dark, bloody, and
frightening, but the narrator has invested it with so much
humor without disturbing the ethical seriousness of its contents, that it is cheering to read. The close friendship between
the two young men rests on the fact that the intellect longs for
beauty, and beauty for intellect. The merchant Schridaman
belongs to a Brahman sect, is schooled in Indian wisdom, and
always knows how to apply it so beautifully in clever words
that Nanda, the smith and shepherd, a simple child of the people, often cries when he listens to him, and admires him very
much. On a journey together, they rest close by a quiet sacred
bathing beach on a little river in the Ganges system; and, after they have conducted their religious practices, they eat and
rest in the grass. The intellectual young man lies back, looks

up into the heavens, and relates his observations to it; the other one prefers to squat down and look around the world about him. Therefore, he is first to catch sight of the naked girl on the steps which lead down to the water. The narrator knows how to describe the charms of her beautiful body for us:

> A young girl stood at the lonely shrine, about to perform the ritual of the bath. She had laid her sari and bodice on the steps and stood there quite nude, save only for some beads around her neck, her swaying ear-rings, and a white ribbon around her thick hair. The loveliness of her body was dazzling. Made of Maya it seemed, and of the most enchanting tint, neither too dark nor too pale, and more like a bronze with golden lights. Gloriously formed she was, after the thoughts of Brahma, with the sweetest childish shoulders, and hips deliciously curved making a spacious pelvic cavity, with maidenly firm, budlike breasts and splendidly spreading buttocks that narrowed above to the smallest, most tender back. How supplely it curved, as she raised her slender arms and clasped her hands at the back of her neck, so that the tender arm pits showed darkly! In all this the most striking thing, the most adequately representative of Brahma's thoughts—yet, without prejudice to the dazzling sweetness of the breasts, which must infallibly win over any soul to the life of sense—was the conjunction of this magnificent rear with the slimness and pliant suppleness of a back of elfin delicacy. By way of emphasis was the other contrast, between the splendid swing of the hips— this of itself worthy of a whole paean of praise—and the dainty attenuation around the waist. (SL, II, 225)

The two friends are both enraptured. Nanda expresses his emotions coarsely and jokingly, but Schridaman explains to him that one must penetrate through the beautiful appearance to the being of the soul, a speech to which his friend listens with tears in his eyes. He knows the girl. She is from the nearby village where at times he used to be permitted to swing her up high into the sun when she was chosen at the big folk festival in honor of the giver of light.

They separate for three days. When they meet again, Schridaman is very sick, can neither eat nor sleep, and begs

Nanda to erect a funereal hut for him. Nanda wants to promise to burn himself up with Schridaman but would like to know
what sickness he is talking about. After a lot of beating around
the bush, the sick man confesses that he is hopelessly in love
with Sita (that is, the furrow). Thereupon Nanda laughs at him
and advises his wise friend that certainly nothing stands in the
way of sowing in this furrow. She is a respectable, well-
brought up child, as yet not promised to another. And he declares himself ready to woo her for his friend. Sita is not
asked. Nanda brings it about that the parents on both sides
negotiate with one another, and he is inexhaustible as mediator
and festival arranger so that his friend is soon married with
the desired girl. Six months later, the three of them find
themselves on a common journey to visit the pregnant Sita's
parents. Nanda steers the cart in which the couple is sitting.
The mood is depressed and sad. Nobody utters a word. Their
relationship to one another has disintegrated. Since they are
traveling during the night because of the heat, they lose their
way because of their emotional condition. Nanda misses the
right path which leads from the road to the village. They end
up in a gorge where there is a temple to the all-mother Kâlî.
Schridaman says he wants to go in for a moment. But at the
frightening sight of the image of the god-head he seizes the
sacrificial sword and cuts off his head. After a lengthy wait
which is not shortened by any intimate conversation between
Sita and Nanda, she begs her friend to fetch Schridaman, so
that he does not cause further delay by his prayer.

It is getting warmer and warmer. Nanda climbs down into
the sanctuary and soon sees the sacrifice. The observer understands that his friend has done away with himself in order
to clear the field for him and his wife. Nanda does not want to
accept this sacrifice in any case but follows the law of friendship, releases the sword from the hand of the dead person, and
kills himself too. Outside Sita waits impatiently, for it is becoming more and more uncomfortable. She thinks that the two
are quarreling or even battling with one another. Finally she
too climbs down into the terrible depth. When she sees what
the two have done, she falls unconscious. Then she wails and
mourns piteously. She is not able to use the heavy sword to
kill herself and the seed of life in her body. She hurries into
the open in order to hang herself on a tree with a vine.

Suddenly, however, she hears the grating voice of the goddess, who upbraids her as a "stupid goat, turkey hen, foolish girl" and threatens to box her ears. That is the way mother Elba in Wolfgang Borchert's The Man Outside mocks the returning soldier too who wants to drown himself and casts him back on the bank. Then Kâlî demands of Sita a true report.

Sita explains that she was still a cool maiden when Nanda swung her into the sun and she thanked him merely with a little rap on the nose. It began when he wooed her for his friend. She obeyed her parents to be sure, loved and honored her clever husband, and experienced with him what made her into a woman and mother. At the beginning he was very happy. But soon he noticed that in his arms she longed for Nanda. She admired the finely featured, intelligent head of her husband but his weak, powerless body was unable to make her truly happy. Thus had fate hung over all three of them. For her sake, her husband would have taken his life, as would Nanda for his friend's sake. The goddess reproved her harshly for this fresh speech. Without the transport which the sight of her image created in the blood-dripping sanctuary, both of them would still be alive. But she does not want to permit her noble motives to go unobserved. Now she gives the mother-to-be precise instructions as to how she can bring the men back to life and warns her not to reverse the heads on them and to place the face at the back of the neck.

Just as Thomas Mann immersed himself in the world of his age in the Joseph novel, he did the same here too, fitting religion, morals, and customs into Indian philosophy, which was already known to him through Schopenhauer, but without critical observations. His irony is only noticeable peripherally; for example, in the treatment of the hermit.

Sita hurries back again therefore and does what the zealous goddess warned her not to do, probably intentionally, since she is also called the "goddess of disorder." She places the wrong heads on the bodies of the men. Laughing and crying with happiness, the three reunited people embrace one another; but now, when the question must be answered as to whom Sita belongs, the friendship splits up and each of them claims her. Nanda maintains rightfully that his body has created the child to be. Schridaman just as righteously, on the other hand, claims that the head is the most important thing for the ego of man. Nanda has found a hermit at one time in order to receive instruction, and now he proposes to travel to him so they can yield to his decision.

When Thomas Mann read this narrative aloud in his family circle, the listeners laughed heartily at the next section. The Indian hermits who observe their vows religiously live in stringent asceticism. The one whom the three look up is standing up to his neck in water, he is only skin and bones, and offers them berries while he is eating roots. His supplies are stored in a hollow tree in which he does not live. He berates them for intruding into his human vacuum with their bodily vapors and disturbing him. But the ascetic has to prove again and again his resistance to the blandishments of life. This is also a form of asceticism. Behind this sophistry he conceals his curiosity about their story and his pleasure at the sight of the attractive Sita. He indulges in an obscene description of her body.

> Trust me, your nearness and the fumes of life you give out lie heavy on my chest and bring an unpleasant flush to my cheek, as you could see were it not for their seemly coating of ashes. But I am ready to bear with you and your vapors, particularly since I have observed from the first that among the three of you is a woman grown, whom the senses find glorious; slender as a vine, with soft thighs and full breasts, oh yea, oh fie! Her navel is beauteous, her face lovely with partridge-eyes, and her breasts, I repeat, are full and upstanding. Good day, O woman! When men look upon you, do not the hairs of their bodies rise up for lust? And the troubles of the three of you, are they not all due to you, you snare and allurement? Hail! I should most likely have sent these young men to the devil, but since you are with them, my dear, pray stay, as long as you like! (Sl, II, 265)

He even celebrates the sensuousness of sexual life in a rhymed hymn! Apparently the ascetic life had not purified him at all or made him impervious to the power of seduction by any beautiful female being. He even becomes confused in his advice: First he promises Sita to the Nanda head, but then finally to the Schridaman head. The couple departs in ecstasy, and

Nanda becomes a hermit.

It had not been completely erroneous that Sita had united Schridaman's head with the body of Nanda after she had longed to be in her husband's arms. Now she has both, the finely featured head and the powerful body. Even her husband is happy that he can now make her happy. But what she did intentionally was still an error. In no way does Schridaman alter his life's pattern, and after some time the body adapts itself to the head. It "refines" itself. And the head adapts to the strange body. It loses its fineness just as its spirit also loses the melancholy with which it longed for the beauty of Sita and Nanda. Thus, it comes about that after four years, when her husband has gone on a trip, Sita sets out with her son and journeys to Nanda with the Schridaman body, in which the opposite transformation has taken place: his head has become more delicate, his body more powerful. They are only able to spend a single night together. Early the next morning, Schridaman has already arrived on his riding ox and is waiting until they arise. He is not angered with them because he understands the fate which has dominated them and bows to it. On the trip he has been reflecting for all of them and has made a decision. He and Nanda must kill each other in a duel. Both of them agree with him without delay. Sita wants to erect the funeral pyre for the three and burn herself with them. In no case can polyandry be considered for higher beings. For the sake of their son's honor, all three of them must go to their death together.

The cremation of the two brave man and the proud Sita becomes a great folk festival. A monumental obelisk is erected for her. She becomes famous, and her handsome son is cherished and cared for and advanced. He becomes the reader for the King of Benares.

We understand at this point that Thomas Mann often calls his writings "jokes" or "spoofs." The legend of The Transposed Heads is an example of the wonderful mixture of pathos and irony of which he is a master. It is one of his most successful and beautiful narratives.

The Tables of the Law

The narrative The Tables of the Law first originated in 1943 after the conclusion of the Joseph novel. One might assume that it fell into Thomas Mann's lap like an additional mature fruit as a result of his Old Testament studies. But that is not the way things stand at all. When he was describing the origin of monotheism among the patriarchs of the Old Testament, he was very little interested in Moses and the prophets of the later period who are much more significant for the development of the Jewish belief as the basis of the three religions of humanity than are Abraham, Isaac, Jacob, and Joseph. In 1943, the American A. L. Robinson asked Thomas Mann to write an introduction for him to his planned anthology The Ten Commandments: Ten Short Novels of Hitler's War Against the Moral Code, for which ten known writers of various countries were each composing a contribution; thereupon Mann wrote this narrative in which the origin of the whole decalogue is described logically. To some extent one can tell by looking at it that the motif did not move his creative powers directly but that he was dutifully fulfilling a demand of the day of political significance.

From the Joseph novel we know that Thomas Mann liked to practice biblical criticism and that he secularizes and humanizes the theological representation of the Bible, in which, for the most part, a passive attitude is accorded God, the director of our destinies. Here too it is not a question of a God-narrative but of a Moses-narrative.

In the introduction, the narrator reports that Moses became acquainted among the gods of the Midianites with one who was invisible and moved him so powerfully that he was shaken by musings, visions, and revelations, which in fact at one time were compressed into an hallucination in which the task was thrust upon him to proclaim the invisible god and to lead the Hebrews out of Egypt. That would be a rediscovery of God, since Abraham had already discovered him (according to the Joseph novel) whereas the text of the Bible leaves no doubt that the Hebrews in Egypt had preserved the tradition of their forefathers. In it Moses is the great lawgiver of the Jewish people, but not the first who cements a bond with the invisible God.

Thomas Mann transforms Moses into the illegitimate son of a daughter of the pharaoh, just as the fanatics of the "Aryan" race transformed Jesus into the son of a Roman captain. Since even today among orthodox Jews the mother is decisive for the admissibility of the child to Judaism, Moses accordingly would not be a Jew, but an Egyptian. As the leader of his people chosen by God, Moses exploits thoroughly his relationship with the pharaoh. All the miracles of the Lord about which the Bible reports are rationally reinterpreted. The narrator explains nine plagues as natural phenomena and hence without effect. For the tenth, however, he lets Joshua worry about the military support of Moses. Joshua, who has trained storm troop units and let them carry out the nightly deeds of murder, is the humanized "avenging angel of the Lord." This is quite a vicious interpretation, whereas the taking along of the silver and gold tools of the Egyptians corresponds to the text of the Bible. Later, Joshua leads the battle for the Oasis Kadesch and in it exercises bloody police force against those who are instigating the breaking of Moses' laws and commandments, especially in the heathen folk festival in honor of the Golden Calf. Joshua is the practical person with clear head and firm hand at the side of the spiritual Moses.

Even in Mann's narrative, the story of the origin of the ten commandments, as the title announces, is the main thing. For him also is Moses regarded as the lawgiver, as the creative spirit, who wants to "heal" his people under monstrous difficulties, and wants to lead them to a new morality. The people are represented as vacillating, repulsive, crude, and licentious, symbolically like a crude stone which has to be hewn, a block of wood which has to be carved properly, whereas the beginnings of a moral order have already become visible in connection with Jacob in the novel and are preserved in Joseph. Moses groans under his work, complains and wails to God, and would like to cast off the burden. But even if God in his anger wants to destroy the whole race, he defends them and begins anew because he takes great pleasure in his creative work for the education toward humanity. Even Moses himself and his closest co-workers are depicted as quite barbaric with great weaknesses and in fact quarrel with one another. The didactic achievement of the lawgiver Moses appears all the more admirable. Even in the forty days solitude on the fire-spewing Mount Horeb, Mann ascribes to him the invention of letters which are not picture language for the words, but reproduce the consonants that are useful for all languages. They are the appropriate expression for the words of the invisible God, the Lord of all peoples, and his ten commandments are the ABC of human decency for all mankind.

In The Transposed Heads, Thomas Mann uses several coarse everyday expressions here and there, but the tone is otherwise pathetic, hymnic, or humorous. Here the total language is larded with coarse words which characterize the all-too-human event in an appropriate manner. Despite the serious subject, the representation is ironic throughout and is never elevated to a lofty style.

The whole work drives toward its conclusion, with the great curse which Moses flings at the man who rejects the eternal validity of the law on the two tablets, and he ends with the words:

> And the Lord says, I shall raise my foot and shall trample him into the mire, to the bottom of the earth shall I cast the blasphemer, 112 fathoms deep. And man and beast shall describe an arch around the spot into which I have cast him; and the birds of the heavens, high in their flight, shall shun the place so that they need not fly over it. And he who shall speak his name, he shall spit towards the four corners of the earth and shall wipe his mouth and say, "Forfend!" that the earth again may be the earth, a vale of want, yes, but not a sty of depravity. To that say ye Amen! (SL, II, 136)

According to its title, this American anthology was directed against Hitler. His name does not occur in the separately printed German version of the narrative. But no one doubts that the great curse is coined for him. In it Thomas Mann expressed without restraint his deep revulsion at the dismal moral depth of the Lord of the Third Reich.

Would it not be advisable to classify this commissioned work which was written for war propaganda against the Third Reich among the political manifestos? As poetry it seems to me uninspired, less than satisfactory, and below the level of most of the other works by Thomas Mann.

6. POLITICAL MORALITY

During the quarter of a century from 1918 to 1943, in which the artistic work of Thomas Mann ripened into the humanitarian epic Joseph and his Brothers, he also underwent a fantastic political development, from the unpolitical observer of historical events to the militant humanist. The great confessional book was concluded around the end of 1917 and appeared in the fall of 1918. On January 3 of the same year, he rejected still another attempt at reconciliation on the part of his brother; and, in the Song of the Little Child in 1919, echoes of the struggle against the enemies of the Kaiser's Germany are still found. He had equated the politicalization with the democratization of the German people and thus created for himself his own narrow concept of politics, as if previously there had been no politics in Germany at all. It was quite some time before he could take a public position toward the new situation in Germany. Not until October 10, 1922, in his lecture in the Beethoven Room in Berlin, The German Republic, did he expressly espouse the new form of statehood. Before this, on January 31, 1922, he had sent flowers to his gravely ill brother, with some conciliatory lines. In the fifth edition of the Reflections in 1922, he deleted several violent attacks against him.

Many things worked conjointly to produce this turn in Thomas Mann's political attitude. In the Reflections it already had become clear that he considered the democratization of Germany as unavoidable, and thus he later designated the book as a defensive skirmish. The critical letters of the astute Paul Amann (cf. under IV) had their subsequent effect. In the fifth edition of the Reflections, he also deleted a number of passages directed against Romain Rolland, whom Amann admired. Among other things, Mann himself cites his turn toward Nietzsche's affirmation of life. Still, we would have to

regard as stronger the influence of Goethe, of whom Mann was
not so conscious in this context since he considered him apolitical. The decisive ballot, however, was cast in these years
by the visual evidence of the political life in Germany. About
this, Mann says in the lecture My Times, 1950: "It [the book]
was hardly finished, 1918, when I released myself from it—a
release which was made easy for me in every way: through
the dull rejection of the book on the part of the German conservatives, for whom it was much too European and too liberal; through certain personal contacts with these circles in
their political and intellectual reality, which frightened me to
the marrow of my bones; and through the rise of that wave of
revolutionary obscurantism in the intellectual and scientific
spheres—from my point of view a thoroughly disturbing movement which pitted nationality against humanity and treated it
as settling slag, in short, the rise of Fascism."

Mann's surprising allegiance to the German Republic excited great attention all over the world. Again, as after the appearance of the Reflections, he stood in the middle of public
life and remained effective in it. What did he want to do? What
did he do? Initially he joined the International Writers PEN
Club and took part in their meetings and congresses all over
Europe. Much later, as an eager member, he belonged to a
committee for intellectual cooperation of the peoples' unions
belonging to UNESCO. He wanted to work against war, and for
peaceful understanding among all peoples. Thus in Munich he
also joined the Rotary Club, lectured to the local group, and
visited Rotarians at Stockholm, Copenhagen, and The Hague on
his travels. When the Prussian Academy of Poets was established, he joined it. Although as an individualist little inclined
to such organizations, it now seemed to him necessary to co-
operate with them. He never joined a political party, but he
used every opportunity to express himself publicly on political
questions. From 1924 on, he confesses his sympathy for social democracy because it proved to be friendly to culture. His
struggle against enemy propaganda and against the civilization
hack in the Reflections was above all a defense of the "unpolitical" German culture which seemed to him to be in danger.
But if the Republic protected and advanced this culture while
its enemies fought against it with barbaric means, he belonged
on the side of the new state. Therefore, as he said in the

preface to the independent edition of his **German Republic** speech in 1923, he saw in his political turn-about no change of mind at all. Culture and humanity always remained for him the chief concern.

When he was invited to Paris for a lecture in 1926, it was surely a political occasion too, since the acceptance of Germany into the League of Nations was pending. After his return, he published his **Parisian Account,** in order to counteract malicious misinterpretations. His lecture was again an allegiance to the German unpolitical culture which might require supplementation through western democracy for the sake of the peaceful development of Europe. Together with many other leading personalities on both sides of the Rhine, he saw that, above all, the "inherited hostility" between Germany and France must be overcome. Deeply moved, he experienced in Paris how magnificently the French received him as an intellectual emissary and how much penetrating understanding they showed for his works.

It should be added that, in the figure of Settembrini in **The Magic Mountain,** he took the civilization hack seriously whom he had formerly treated so scornfully, and treated him justly; in fact, raised him to the mouthpiece for his friendly leanings toward man and the future, a sign of the fact that he had inwardly approached his brother Heinrich to a great extent.

He was no longer the German conservative patrician's son and romantic individualistic poet of the time before 1914 but a good European who worked in Germany for the balance between left and right, and abroad for understanding—the humanist who was concerned for humanity in all relationships. When the Nobel Prize was awarded to him in 1929 he gave a political turn to his thanks in Stockholm by accepting it as an honor for his people, who were extremely receptive to such a sign of recognition after their defeat.

During this decade, Thomas Mann followed with great care the intellectual currents which were directed against the primacy of reason, against idealism and ethics, and which made even intellectuals receptive to radical right political movements. The headquarters for the National Socialist Workers Party was in Munich, where he lived. In the novel **Success,** Lion Feuchtwanger described the favorable atmosphere of that time in Bavaria. To be sure, Hitler's revolt failed in 1923, out that merely delayed his rise in Germany. Most people did not read his book **Mein Kampf**, which was written in miserable German,and which contained in the last three chapters his political program to make Germany into a world power of the rank of the United States, of the British Empire, and of the Soviet Union. People underestimated his demagogic capacity to incite masses to fanaticism,to sweep the intellectuals along through his appeal to their nationalistic instincts,and to outwit and defeat his political enemies who thought they were so superior to the uneducated upstart. Thomas Mann was outraged above all at the lack of culture, the immorality, the deceit and brutality of National Socialism; and he opposed it as early as 1924. When, in September 1930, Hitler's Party with 130 uniformed delegates moved into the German Parliament, Thomas Mann delivered on October 17, again in the Beethoven Auditorium in Berlin, his address **Appeal to Reason,** in which he entreated the citizenry to join up with the culturally friendly Social Democrats to repulse the completely un-German, barbaric attack of the National Socialists on a humane Germany. The National Socialist Youth, among them, Arnold Bronnen, tried to disturb the speaker, who, however, stood fast and after the lecture was brought to safety through a side exit. But Mann's warning disappeared in the witch's kettle of the political struggle.

Hitler was never a genuine revolutionary but always adhered to the powerful groups in the state, to the national guard, the large landowners, and heavy industry, which misused the national idea and regarded it as a tool for their fight to maintain their position of power. He would never have come to power without their support, without the merging of the National Socialists with the German Nationals in the Habsburg Front of 1932. The word of Thomas Mann was naturally ineffective against these powerful interest groups.

In 1933, politics, which up to that time had been only an interest along with his artistic work,became his sole occupation. It reached unexpectedly with a heavy hand into his personal life and suddenly made him homeless and without possessions. On February 10, 1933 in Munich he gave his lecture **Sufferings and Greatness of Richard Wagner** and on the next day traveled abroad in order to repeat it in German in Amsterdam and in French in Brussels and Paris and then to recover in Switzerland as he had done so often before. In this lecture he had raised an objection, in passing, against distortion and misuse of the art of Richard Wagner in the politics of the day. The response in the National Socialist Press was so vicious that Mann's children and friends advised him urgently against returning.

After some moving around, he settled in Küsnacht on Lake Zürich and conducted himself for several years watchfully and calmly in the face of the Third Reich for the sake of his books, as he explained in his letters, which were still appearing in Berlin in the S. Fischer Press and which might bring countless readers strength and consolation. He did not take part in the journal "Die Sammlung," which Klaus Mann published in Amsterdam in 1935-36 and in which literary Europe collaborated.

A large group of printed accessible letters fall into this period of public silence besides the diaries from the years 1933-1934, which he had printed in 1946 in Los Angeles under the title **Sufferings from Germany.** In his testimony it is clear that he never wavered in his sharp condemnation of National Socialism. In fact, for a long time he cherished the plan of interrupting his artistic work again as in 1914 and of writing a great polemic work, but he finally gave it up. It seems to me quite idle to add "unfortunately," or "fortunately." In any case, he stuck to his biblical novel.

An essay by Eduard Korrodi in the **Neue Züricher Zeitung** of January 26, 1936, which challenged him to separate himself from the rest of the emigrants, Mann answered with a sharp letter which appeared on February 3 in the same section and brought on the breach between him and those in power in Berlin. At first nothing happened because of the Olympics in Berlin. But in the fall of 1936, he lost his citizenship, as Erika, Heinrich, and Klaus Mann already had before him. Then when the Dean of the Philosophical Faculty in Bonn retracted the honorary doctor's degree awarded to him earlier in a letter of December 19, he wrote the reply at the end of 1936 which was translated into all important languages, smuggled into the Third Reich in a camouflaged miniature edition, and distributed in thousands upon thousands of copies. In this he states among other things:

I could never have dreamed, it could never have been prophesied of me at my cradle, that I should spend my later years as an émigré, expropriated, outlawed, and committed to inevitable political protest.... I could not have lived or worked, I should have suffocated, had I not been able now and again to cleanse my heart, so to speak, to give from time to time free vent to my abysmal disgust at what was happening at home—the contemptible words and still more contemptible deeds.... They have the incredible effrontery to confuse themselves with Germany! When, after all, perhaps the moment is not far off when it will be of supreme importance to the German people, not to be confused with them.

He closes with the fervent prayer: "God help our darkened and desecrated country and teach it to make its peace with the world and with itself!" (OD, 107, 108, 110, 113). The whole political manifesto, born of the passionate pathos of a deeply disturbed soul, was written in the grand style of the sentences cited, one of the most important testimonies of genuine humanity from this period.

In 1938 the anthology Europe, Beware! appeared together with the political manifestos of Mann since 1930. With it he joined the humanistic front which had formed among the German refugees intellectually active in all parts of the world to rescue Germany. They were certainly not unaware of the great German heritage from the age of humanism when they fled the Third Reich. Among them there were many groups and many oppositions. But this heritage was revealed in the face of events in the Third Reich. There all culture was subordinated to the march towards world domination. The Second World War was systematically prepared as announced in Mein Kampf. The refugees warned the world of Adolf Hitler's plans. For this reason many of their books have the word "Europe" in their title. But only a few of the responsible statesmen read what these poor refugees were writing. They did not even read Hitler's Mein Kampf.

When Thomas Mann was deprived of his citizenship by the Third Reich, Czechoslovakia under Theodor Masaryk and Eduard Benesch immediately granted him citizenship. But staying in Europe became too unsafe. Three times in the thirties Thomas Mann had visited the United States, delivering lectures on the political situation. From 1933 to 1938 fifteen of his works were published there in translation. When he decided in 1938 definitely to emigrate to America, he was received with honors. He began to deliver lectures at Princeton University, where Albert Einstein was also working, and this lasted until 1941. He then had a house built in Pacific Palisades in California and thus again found a quiet place to work. However, every demand of the day to take part in public life found him ready and willing. He never fell back again into "apolitical observations." In 1939, he wrote his lecture The Problem of Freedom, which no longer dealt with the inner freedom but with political freedom. He took it along with him to the meeting of the PEN Congress in Stockholm. In the middle of the dinner, which Frederik Ström, President of the City Parliament, was giving in honor of the PEN guest, news of the outbreak of war interrupted. The convention was cancelled. During the Second World War, the United States became the refuge for those fleeing from all areas brought under Hitler's terror.

It is understandable that this individualistic artist hesitated a bit in plunging again and again into the political struggle of the day. One of his essays in the Neues Tagebuch of Leopold Schwarzschild in Paris, 1939, is entitled Compulsion Politics. Still even the artist must become a fighter when the basis for human morality and the elemental human rights are threatened. But at times the feeling overcame him that he was moving about on dangerous ground, on a territory which in the final analysis always was foreign to him. This was very much justified, for all his life long he remained at base an apolitically thinking intellect who did not always include in his observations the elementary driving forces of historical happenings, the struggles of vested interests for riches and power, for raw materials, labor and markets with their total raw force. In 1922, when he delivered The German Republic to a hostile public, to students who scraped their feet, he spoke over their heads to Gerhard Hauptmann and summoned aid from two dead poets—the profound romanticist Novalis and the wildly enthusiastic singer of democracy and brotherhood Walt Whitman. In 1927, in Warsaw at a luncheon of the PEN Club, he had expressed the idea that writers could prevent a coming war if they would make their moral protests valid. When, in 1930, he advised the citizenry to join up with the Social Democrats, he did not consider that the contrast between employers and employees in the struggle for the worker's yield or between profit on the one hand and subsistence on the other, dominated the groups and kept them apart. A realistic politician would never have written a letter to the National Socialist Ministry of Interior in order to seek portions of his confiscated property in Munich. It was besides unsuccessful. In the Neues Tagebuch, Mann wrote in 1939 a contribution entitled **Brother Hitler** in which he represented the dictator ironically as an artist who has fallen upon bad days just as the confidence man is "a kind of artistic person." Had this been found in his posthumous papers, one might have read this witty brain storm perhaps with a smile. But in the political situation of that time, it excited a general shaking of heads. Many more examples might be presented. Many romantically inclined observers, for example Ferdinand Lion, reproached the poet for descending at all from the heights of his pure art into the political arena. Unfortunately, that still corresponds to the concepts of broad circles of the intellectual citizenry who cherish their culture and their inner freedom but at the same time lose the soil under their feet. How can we justify not worrying about politics when they determine our fate—our daily life in peaceful times —and in stormy times drive us to the human slaughterhouse of war or into the misery of exile. Thomas Mann followed his conscience.

If we examine his political manifestos, we see that he was always a fighter for humanity, for culture, morality, and human dignity. Mankind urgently needs such personalities of high rank and good will who constantly hold up their moral demands to the politicians. In the long run, human relations on earth can only be put into a somewhat sensible order if so much ethical guidance is built into them that humanity gains a certain validity. People from everywhere honor and pay homage to Thomas Mann for the fact that he became an artist and a fighter, that he ripened to political morality beyond his profession under the hard blows of fate in his time, regardless of the outcome.

III

THE RETURN OF THE WORLD CITIZEN

7. THE RETURN

Soon after the National Socialist reign of terror had collapsed in the spring of 1945, Thomas Mann, in a letter from Walter von Molo which appeared simultaneously in the press, received the urgent request to return to Germany and help his people by word and deed. In his charged answer, the seventy-year old writer rejected this, not curtly and arrogantly, but graciously. He confessed at the same time his indissoluble union with the German language and culture and added consoling words about the future of Germany, even promising future visits to Europe and to his homeland. He had never really completely overcome his estrangement from his own people, who had followed such questionable leaders for twelve long years. Hence, he never lived or worked again in Germany. In 1945, there could be no talk of forgetting and forgiving all that had happened and of a reconciliation in his returning.

There is an overwhelming plethora of testimony, nevertheless, that Thomas Mann never ceased to include his homeland in his painful thoughts from the time he left Germany in 1933 to remain abroad. In Los Angeles, there appeared in 1946 as a private printing of the Pacific Press Sufferings from Germany, Diary Leaves from the Years 1933 and 1934, that is to say, a work from his first period of estrangement, edited somewhat for print but still a creditable testimony to his disturbance in the face of the terrible happenings in his homeland. In the letter to von Molo, Mann mentions the lecture Germany and the Germans, which he delivered in June 1945 at the Library of Congress in Washington. Thus shortly after the end of the war, he dared to put in a good word for the Germans whose political immaturity is the opposite side of the coin to their musicality. Between these two declarations, there are countless others which bear witness to his constant worry about the unhappy fate of Germany.

Mann's deep roots in German language and culture surfaced when he interrupted his work on the biblical novel in order to create his vivid Goethe portrait. After this, he seized upon an idea which he had already set down briefly in the year 1901—

to write a work about the German Faustian figure for whom music is the content of his life and significant expression of his inward being. **Buddenbrooks**, as he often explained, was the novel about his birthplace Lübeck, **The Magic Mountain** a European book, **Joseph and his Brothers** a work on humanity. With **Doctor Faustus** he is returning, enriched by the experience of his years, to his point of departure. With this work, therefore, Thomas Mann returned home from his period of mythical thinking, of the Jewish patriarchs and of the Pharaoh Ikhnaton—from Palestine and Egypt to the present and most recent past and to Germany. At the same time he was returning to the prime motif of his early period, the questionability of art and, in the shadow of the Second World War, to the pessimistic world view of Schopenhauer. It is a return forced by nostalgia into the heavy, rich, memory-laden German atmosphere, to German music and German religion, permeated by historical events.

And this German world does not let Thomas Mann go so quickly again. Right after the musical novel he writes his version of the story of Pope Gregory, which faithfully follows the plot of Hartman von Aue's epic **Gregorius.** The short story **The Black Swan** relates the fate of a Rhenish woman. Even the confidence man, Felix Krull, is from the Rhineland but his "occupation", to be sure, leads him quickly out into the world and into the life of the international social set where his art thrives. This parody on the Bildungsroman deals with an "artist," and thus is closely related to the great musical novel.

The poet Thomas Mann returned home and brought his life's work to full circle. This work always included Germany and, in accordance with his innermost nature, remained unmistakably German no matter how much of the great world around him his nature embraced.

8. LATER WRITINGS

Doctor Faustus

Thomas Mann's The Origin of Doctor Faustus, 1947, written down after the conclusion of Doctor Faustus, gives such a welcome insight into his workshop and about how he himself conceived of his work that one would do well to read this account along with the novel.

It contains all sorts of personal material. During the years around Mann's seventieth birthday, from 1943 to 1947, his health showed a declining curve which reached its low point with a lung infection and operation in Chicago from the end of March to the end of May 1946, whose disturbing after-effects could be detected for a long time. He writes that his zealous participation in world events with Germany as the exciting focal point, and the corrosive efforts surrounding "the terrible book" belong among the causes of the illness and that his rapid recovery made possible his completing the work. He often talks lovingly of his children and grandchildren, but he writes of them in detail only when he is dealing with their relation to the incipient work. The darling grandson Frido enters into **Doctor Faustus** as the heavenly messenger "Echo." Erika is permitted to shorten the manuscript. The personal element is subordinated to the factual.

Among the interruptions in his work must be counted the "demands of the day"—at least 65 lectures, congratulatory wishes, elegies, political manifestos and such, among them twenty radio broadcasts to Germany, two lengthy lecture tours, and two difficult essays on German problems, which robbed him of an unusually large amount of time.

The social amenities and correspondence also loom quite large. Almost 150 names are mentioned, chiefly of well-known personalities—poets, musicians, actors, and scientists who are sometimes characterized at length. But this work is in general contributory to his art. Thomas Mann imparts his plans to literary people and musicians of his acquaintance and discusses related problems with them. He reads part of the work aloud in intimate circles and rejoices over the moving effect and the cheering agreement. He introduces Arnold Schönberg's twelve tone scale into his novel, and Theodor Wiesengrund-Adorno becomes his adviser in musical questions. There are frequent reports of musical evenings at home and public concerts. His musical novel determines to a large extent his social life.

The scope of his reading is astonishing. Thomas Mann mentions one hundred and thirty-five works, and among them are many in several volumes. Many of them contribute materials and quotations—for example, two dozen books about music and musicians. Others serve as support during the narration; for example, novels of Conrad, Gotthelf, Keller, and Stifter. These writings are described and criticized. Mann reads Franz Werfel's **Star of the Unborn** twice and plans a lecture on it, but nothing ever comes of this plan. He compares Hermann Hesse's **Magister Ludi** with his own work, since the relationship is striking; but he then underscores the contrast: "Mine, probably more precise, sharper, more acute, or dramatic, because it is more dialectic, closer to reality and more directly moving. His more tender, more enthusiastic, more intricate, more romantic, and more overdrawn in a lofty sense."

Oftentimes he speaks of his own obsession with work. When he has concluded **Joseph and his Brothers** after 16 years, he regards the "weightless" condition as "questionable"; and two days later, on 15 March 1943, he begins to plan the new work, which he concludes after three years and ten months on 29 January 1947.

For a long time the poet has doubts about the success of **Doctor Faustus**, which places such unheard of demands on him; the response after public readings helps him over these conditions. "The worry about the disintegration of the book" returns frequently. He confesses: ... "I had a horror of making a mess of an important matter," and was really afraid to the point of desperation of doing it.

The narrative's theme excites him to an unusual degree. "Like nothing else, it ate at me and challenged my innermost powers." With the resumption of the plan, which after all was 42 years old, "an emotional excitement goes hand in hand, if not to say a turbulence, which makes it very clear to me how an aura of living feeling, an evanescent cloak of biographical mood surrounded the bare and vague thematic core from the very beginning...." He calls his work **Confession and Sacrifice** and writes that he had loved none of his other figures, with the exception perhaps of Hanno Buddenbrook, to such an extent as Adrian Leverkühn. "How much Faustus contains of my life's attitude! A radical confession basically."

Alongside this stand factual characterizations of the novel. It has "preserved a peculiar power of radiation from the moment of its appearance ... a certain vitally charged quality."

He calls it his "wildest book." In his youth it was planned as a final work of his old age, as his **Parsifal**, which, as in the case of Wagner, was to come at the end. He sees an inner relationship between the swindler material and the Faust material, "resting on a motif of loneliness—in the latter case, tragic/mystic, in the former humorously criminal." At the beginning of May 1943, the work had already taken over his life." It deals with the flight from the difficulties of the cultural crisis to the devil's pact, the thirst of a proud intellect, threatened by sterility, seeking release at any price and the parallel between decadent euphoria with the Fascistic mob hysteria leading to collapse. "To exhibit the demonic element by means of a classically undemonic medium, to commission a humanistically pious and slick, delightfully frightened soul was in itself a comical idea." "May Heaven grant that a little artistic play and joking, irony, travesty, sublime comedy might be permitted to participate even in things which are radically serious, threatening, and surrounded by a mood of sacrifice in some manner." Through the narrator, Mann gained the possibility "of allowing the narrative to play on a double level, of intertwining polyphonically the experiences which shake the writer even as he is writing with those about which he is reporting."

The realization of the life's story and of the musical creativity of the fictitious composer demanded a ruthless montage of "factual, historical, personal, even literary events....This montage technique, which continually estranged me and even gave me pause, belongs to the conception or to the 'idea' of the book."

On 23 May 1943, when Thomas Mann began to write, the plot of the novel—planned already in his mind—lay before him. He worked "with his motif-complex in toto," gave "to the beginnings the depth perspective of the whole immediately," and was able "to act the biographer, excitedly overcome by his subject, constantly pushed to anticipate subsequent events and then losing himself. How necessary the mask and game were in the face of the seriousness of my task. As much fun as possible, imitation of the biographer, self-mockery to cut the pathos—as much as at all possible of these!" Here it becomes especially clear that irony is only an artistic device to dampen the pathos.

The music in the novel is also "only foreground and representation, only paradigms for more general things, only means to express the situation of art, culture, of the intellect—indeed, of man himself in our thoroughly critical ethics." To Leonhard Frank, Mann said: "Leverkühn is, so to speak, an ideal figure, a 'hero of our time,' a man who bears the suffering of the epic."

As an introduction to the work, this account of its origin can preserve the reader from all kinds of misinterpretations.

The most striking thing in Mann's comments about **Doctor Faustus** is what he writes about the montage technique. A Swedish literary historian has chosen to investigate the significance of these words as the main theme of her doctoral dissertation: Gunilla Bergsten, **Thomas Mann's Doctor Faustus: Investigations of the Sources and Structure of the Novel**, Uppsala, 1963. Even for those who think they know the working methods of this poet, what she has discovered is surprisingly copious and quite varied. The thesis discusses all sorts of personal experiences—for example, the fates of his two sisters, the contradictions and suggestions of relatives and friends—among them, Theodor Adorno's ideas on music and also some literal or easily varied quotations from Mann's own writings and those of others which are not made recognizable through quotation marks. As an appendage, she adds her "Index of quotations in the various chapters of the novel." This deals with approximately forty different works. Hundreds of passages which we read as prose of Thomas Mann are literally taken from other books—for example, from the **Gesta Romanorum**, Luther's letters, the chapbook of Dr. Faustus, Grimmelshausen's **Simplicissimus**, P. Bekker's **Musical History**, the memoirs of Stravinsky, Adorno's **Philosophy of the New Music**, and more of the same. Completeness is not her goal, nor is it to be obtained. Beyond this Mrs. Bergsten occupies herself with the structure of the work also, revealing various temporal levels, as, in its historical flashbacks, the novel reaches back into the past, above all into the sixteenth century; so that there is occasion for musical and theological, historical and philosophical investigation. The results of Mrs. Bergsten's work are indispensable to the Thomas Mann scholar. But I can imagine that the opponents of his work think to themselves: "After all we have always maintained this. Everything in this writer is montage, combined, constructed, calculated, contrived, none of it truly creative poetry." To be sure, everything that Mrs. Bergsten digs out of this work is technical montage and intellectual structure and abstraction, to a certain extent the "bony skeleton." She has accomplished a limited scientific task; her presentation requires a supplement which depicts "the living thriving flesh" which the poet has spread over the skeleton.

The descriptions of landscape and place in this novel are somewhat sparse, except when Adrian Leverkühn spends some time in these milieus. Once a winter trip into the Bavarian Alps is described: "It came about naturally and properly that after Adrian's arrival the landscape outside began to elevate itself into a more important sphere and the snowed-in world aloft began to look in, albeit from a distance. The Bavarian Alps reveal no giants of the loftiest rank among their elevations, but still in its pure garment of snow it was a bold and impressive winter splendor, alternating between wooded gorge and vast expanse, into which we rode." That is all. On the other hand, he describes thoroughly the Buchel estate in the village of Oberweiler near Weissenfels, where Adrian comes into the world; the city of Kaisersaschern, where he attends school and enters into the musical world; and the estate of Pfeiffering near Waldshut, where he lives for almost two decades up to his intellectual break-down. Even in this case, however, more attention is devoted to character description.

Thomas Mann likes to bring the human atmosphere alive through little living vignettes, as in his illustrating the medieval attitude of Kaisersaschern by means of its queer people, among them old women: the most popular, most teased and feared was 'Cellar Liese' ..., an old lady whose garb had adapted itself to the preconceived public notion to such a degree that an archaic horror could overcome even those who were not completely set on meeting her, especially if the young people were after her and she drove them into flight with her screaming curses, even though there was definitely nothing wrong with her." (This is literally taken over from Lübeck as an Intellectual Form of Life.) We stumble upon such "living vignettes" en masse in the main plot and in the minor episodes.

External descriptions of things are rare. The big exception

is the store of musical instruments in the house of Adrian's uncle Nikolaus Leverkühn at Parochialstrasse 15 which is also described.

> There hung behind glass, or lay bedded in receptacles which like mummy vases were made in the shape of their occupants, the charming violins, varnished, some yellower and some browner, their slender bows with silver wire round the nut fixed into the lid of the case; Italian ones, the pure, beautiful shapes of which would tell the connoisseur that they came from Cremona; also, Tirolese, Dutch, Saxon, Mittenwald fiddles, and some from Leverkühn's own workshop. The melodious cello, which owes its perfect form to Antonio Stradivari, was there in rose; likewise its predecessor, the six stringed viola da gamba, in older works still honored next to it; the viola and that other cousin of the fiddle, the viola alta, were always to be found... There were several specimens of the violone, the giant fiddle, the unwieldy double-bass, capable of majestic recitative, whose pizzicato is more sonorous than the stroke of a kettle-drum, and whose harmonics are a veiled magic of almost unbelievable quality. (DF, 40 f.)

There follow the numerous woodwinds and tympany, castanets, and more of the same. The description runs over more than three pages. Truly, it is not confined to external description but reports on their origin. Sound effects are described, and personal relations of the observers to individual instruments are added. Along with this is the description and explanation of the Italian helper Cimabue. A vivid picture develops from the description. Its breadth is justified because the future composer Adrian soaks up everything eagerly.

But the people are described in far more detail than the surrounding world—the more in detail the closer they stand to Adrian; for example, the father:

> Jonathan Leverkühn was a man of the best German type, such as one seldom sees now in our towns and cities...a cast of features stamped as it were in an earlier age, stored up in the country and come down from the time before the Thirty Years War. ... Unkempt ash-blond

hair fell on a domed brow strongly marked in two distinct
parts, with prominent veins on the temples; it hung un-
fashionably long and thick down his neck and around the
small, well-shaped ears, to mingle with the curling
blond beard that covered the chin and the hollow under
the lip. This lower lip came out rather strong and full
under the short, slightly drooping mustache, with a smile
which made the most charming harmony with the blue
eyes, a little severe, but a little smiling too, their gaze
half absent and half shy. The bridge of the nose was thin
and finely hooked, the unbearded part of the cheeks under
the cheek bones shadowed and even rather gaunt. He
wore his sinewy throat uncovered and had no love for
'city clothes,' which did not suit his looks, particularly
not his hands, those powerful, brown and parched, rather
freckled hands, one of which grasped the crook of his
stick when he went into the village to a town meeting.
(DF, 12)

It had been established that Thomas Mann modelled the parents of Adrian on pictures of Albrecht Dürer. This belongs to
the time level of the sixteenth century, to which we alluded
earlier. But it was the artistic work of Mann which was first
able to create people of flesh and blood in these models. Besides this portrait of Jonathan, there follows further the list
of his readings, as well as his unusual natural experiments
and speculations. This kind of description of human beings
takes up much space in **Doctor Faustus.**
The people come together by twos or in larger groups for
long discussions, which often develop into lively arguments,
with Adrian usually taking part—often, a leading part. Many
intimate conversations take place between him and his friend,
the narrator Serenus Zeitblom. There are heated debates in
the student society Winfried in Halle and in the Kridwiss Circle in Munich. They all originate from Thomas Mann's artistic
workshop. In central position in the novel stands the strongest
testimony to his creative fantasy and linguistic power—Adrian's
dialogue with the devil of over forty pages, which the biographer takes from his friend's copy. The conversations contribute
substantially to the epic breadth of the work.
Further elements of this rich, gaily colored mosaic of the
narrative are among other things the musical lectures of

Kretschmar, the theological lectures of Professor Kumpf and of the instructor Schleppfuss, Adrian's letters—all of this partly in direct speech, and partly in indirect speech—and the countless general and particular observations of Zeitblom, which have to be illuminated a bit more closely—elements which unfold voluminously and expand the work.

The progress of the plot, on the other hand, is presented very briefly. The first meeting with the girl in the brothel in Leipzig, is reported by Adrian to a friend on one page, buried in a letter of eight pages, which talks about quite different things. Zeitblom's commentary on this fills several pages. The visit in which Adrian contracts the fateful disease is related just as tersely. In **Doctor Faustus** as in most of the novels by Thomas Mann, the emphasis lies in psychological description of people and the intepretation of their life's problems, not on sensational plot.

This listing of the various elements of Mann's art of narration leaves the main points still unsaid; namely, that these elements are all subordinated and fitted into the main theme, the "life of the German composer Adrian Leverkühn." To be sure, a powerful time-perspective back into the past is built into this novel. Adrian after all identifies himself with Dr. Faustus and weaves himself completely into the sixteenth century. But however many theological traits and musical and political historical features are woven into the novel, as in the selection of names, its actual subject is still Adrian's lifetime from 1885 to 1940, his biography, his intellectual and musical development, his deeply tragic fate, which we follow excitedly, tensely, and completely fascinated. For this configuration Thomas Mann has used all sorts of sources, the Faust chapbook, the life of Nietzsche, the creative achievement of the composer Schönberg, his own artistic career; but all of them fuse into the life history of this highly gifted and heavily burdened musician from the time of his boyhood up to his intellectual breakdown—a fictitious biography which is the completely unique property of the poet.

When he conceives the idea for this work prior to the First World War, the contrast between the intellectually possessed artist and the naive life was the central, richly varied theme of his narrative—the inhumanity of art. It returns here in an intensified form. Characteristic of Adrian is his laughing in the face of phenomena which warm-hearted people admire and love. He places intellectual interests higher than love. His inner superiority expresses itself in a reticence which makes him lonely. He hardly lets anyone get close to him. He radiates coolness and almost always rejects signs and expressions of intimacy. He consciously sends to his death the violinist Rudi Schwerthfeger who forces himself upon him and wrests proof of friendship from him. To be sure, he would like to love, but it is denied him; for his life, as that of every great artist, is filled with an obsession for work. He seeks out the sickness which grants him the creative intuition. The devil projects externally what inherited disposition and fate is—he radiates icy coldness. Here the description of human beings reaches its high point.

Thomas Mann's own relationship to religion cannot be determined from this novel. Zeitblom, the narrator, does not believe in the devil who is a part of Adrian's hallucinations; but the musician is undoubtedly a religious believer in God. His friend had already discovered this during his school years. Adrian says to him about mathematics: "In the final analysis, the finest thing of all is to regard relationships of order. Order is everything. Romans 13. 'The powers that be are ordained of God.'" Zeitblom adds to this: "He reddened and I looked at him in astonishment. It turned out that he was religious." Without belief in God, Adrian's pact with the devil is impossible; and just as impossible is his hope for grace, which is based on the fact that he does not subscribe to the pact for gain or enjoyment but for the sake of his creative work. Adrian must be a believer as Faust was in the sixteenth century. But it is not proper to characterize Leverkühn as a grail-seeker, as Hermann Stresau does, although Mann calls this novel as a final work his **Parsifal**; the goal to which the musician sacrifices his life's fortune is not religious; it is undoubtedly the new creative music. It is just as unlikely that the characters in Mann's novels are seeking the grail. Disregarding the swindler Felix Krull and Pope Gregory completely, Prince Karl-Heinrich, Hans Castorp, and Joseph find an intellectual formula through their experiences along life's path which makes it possible for them to overcome their inner difficulties and to prove themselves as contemporaries in their surroundings, an ethic of affirmation directed toward life.

The life of the composer Leverkühn is depicted as a laborious, difficult path to a new art. In this novel the broadest scope is allotted to music, the musical instruments, music history, observations about music in general and about works of particular composers, and then above all the musical experiences of Adrian from his canon-singing under the direction of the stable maid—"Hanne with flapping bosoms and bare feet eternally covered with dung,"—through the vivid picture of Kretschmar's lectures and his instruction in Kaisersaschern, later in Leipzig, up to Adrian's own compositions. No matter how much of this originates from foreign sources or whatever Mann has taken over from specialists, an incredibly large amount of this copious treatment of music he invented and did invest with its literary form.

This is above all true of Adrian's musical creations. It was difficult to find an unoccupied place for this composer and his works within modern music. For the writer Thomas Mann, it is characteristic that these fictitious musical compositions are set almost exclusively to literary texts. After much stylistic practice which Adrian performs under the direction of Kretschmar in Leipzig and in which often his own contribution to the suppression of traditional banalities makes itself felt, Adrian first puts songs and epic fragments to music according to an anthology which, expressed in German, "embraced Provencal and Catalonian lyrics of the twelfth and thirteenth centuries, Italian poetry, visionary highpoints of the **Divine** Comedy, then Spanish and Portuguese things." Afterwards he turns to the opera and takes Shakespeare's **Love's Labor Lost** as a libretto. There follow settings for English poems by William Blake and John Keats. From an old story book **Gesta Romanorum**, he then takes motifs from a suite of grotesques which he calls "cosmic music" and wants to have played by marionettes, in which case he is picking up the threads from the essay by Heinrich von Kleist. The violin concerto which he writes at Rudi Schwerthfeger's urging, a parodistic "apotheosis of salon music," is to be regarded as an intermezzo. His next composition picks up the theme of the Apocalypse from Albrecht Dürer's woodcarvings. Then in quick succession Adrian composes a series of chamber music pieces and, in addition, puts Ariel's songs from The Tempest to music. The title of his last work is taken from the chapbook **Dr. Fausti Weheklag.**

All these musical works are described with professional skill and in great detail. By means of these, the narrator Zeitblom illustrates the musical development and the striving of his friend to overcome the banal tradition threatening the critical artist with sterility through strict composition and adherence to tradition, and his striving to break through to the most elemental means of expression. The devil's sickness brings horrible suffering to Adrian, long unfruitful periods but others as well full of inspiration to creative activity. This is related to Mann's conception of the questionability and "inhumanity" of his own art, but he places the nature of music in very close relationship to the dark forces which are incorporated in the devil. There are, indeed, broad musical areas which lead us into a purely spiritual and intellectual world. Zeitblom even speaks of some creations of Leverkühn as if they were free of demonic elements. But the "Apocalypsus cum figuris" is presented as a negative counterpart to Beethoven's Ninth Symphony and offers instead of the Ode to Joy a hellish laughter. In Doctor Faustus' Lament, Adrian confesses his sinful life like the magician in the chapbook before he collapses into insanity.

As an example I shall add here a mocking phrase in reference to Wagner: In The Origin of Doctor Faustus it is said of the fourteenth chapter: "This offers the correspondence between Adrian and Kretschmar and, in Adrian's letter, the undeclared imitation of the Prelude to the third act of Meistersinger, in which I took pleasure." In the novel we read:

> It goes like this, when it is beautiful: The cellos intone by themselves, a pensive, melancholy theme, which questions the folly of the world, the wherefore of all the struggle and striving, pursuing and plaguing—all highly expressive and decorously philosophical. The cellos enlarge upon this riddle awhile, head-shaking, deploring, and at a certain point in their remarks, a well-chosen point, the chorus of wind instruments enters with a deep full breath that makes your shoulders rise and fall, in a choral hymn, movingly solemn, richly harmonized, and produced with all the muted dignity and mildly restrained power of the brass. Thus the sonorous melody presses on up to nearly the height of a climax, which, in accordance with the law of economy, it avoids at first, gives

way, leaves open, sinks away, postpones, most beautifully lingers; then withdraws and gives place to another
theme, a songlike, simple one, now jesting, now grave,
now popular, apparently brisk and robust by nature, but
sly as you make them, and for someone with some subtle
cleverness in the art of thematic analysis and transformation it proves itself amazingly pregnant and capable
of utter refinement. For a while this little song is managed and deployed, cleverly and charmingly, it is taken
apart, looked at in detail, varied, out of it a delightful
figure in the middle registers led up into the most enchanting heights of fiddles and flutes, lulls itself there a
little, and when it is at its most artful, then the mild
brass has again the word with a previous choral hymn
and comes into the foreground. The brass does not start
from the beginning as it did the first time, but as though
its melody had already been there for a while; and it
continues, solemnly, to that climax from which it wisely
refrained the first time, in order that the surging feeling,
the Ah-effect, might be the greater. Now it gloriously
bestrides its theme, mounting unchecked, with weighty
support from the passing notes on the tuba, and then,
looking back, as it were, with dignified satisfaction on
the finished achievement, sings itself decorously to the
end.

Dear friend, why do I have to laugh? Can a man employ
the traditional or sanctify the trick with greater genius?
Can one with shrewder sense achieve the beautiful? And
I, abandoned wretch, I have to laugh, particularly at the
grunting supporting notes of the bombardone, bum, bum,
bum, bang! I may have tears in my eyes at the same
time, but the desire to laugh is irresistible—I have always had to laugh, most damnably at the most mysterious
and impressive phenomena. I fled from this exaggerated
sense of the comic into theology, in the hope that it would
give relief to the tickling, only to find there too a perfect
legion of ludicrous absurdities. Why does almost everything seem to me like its own parody? Why must I think
that almost all, no, all the methods in conventions of art
today are good for parody only? (DF, 133-4)

The description of one of the late compositions of Leverkühn is naturally much more difficult since no model for the "Apocalypsus cum figuris" exists. First comes a description of the composer at the time of the work's origin:

> Obviously, and admittedly this man lived at the time in a state of tension so high as to be anything but agreeable. It was more like a constant tyranny: the meteoric occurrence and definition of a compositional problem (over which he had heretofore always lingered) was almost simultaneous with its lightning-like solution... I see him suddenly stiffen from a relaxed posture, his eyes in fixed focus, expectant, his lips part and—unwelcome sight to me—the flickering red rise in his cheeks. What was that? Was it one of those melodic illuminations to which he was, I might almost say, exposed and with which powers whereof I refused to know aught kept their pact with him? Was it one of those so mightily plastic themes in which the apocalyptic work abounds, rising to his mind, there it wants to be checked and chilled, to be bridled and bitted and made to take its proper place in the whole structure? I see him ... move to his table, open the folder of orchestral drafts ... read to himself, where perhaps was sketched that frightful chorus of humanity fleeing before the four horsemen, stumbling, falling, overridden; or there was noted down the awful scream given to the mocking, bleating bassoon, the "Wail of the Bird"; or perhaps that song and answer, like an antiphony, which on first hearing so gripped my heart—the harsh choral fugue to the words of Jeremiah: "Wherefore doth a living man complain...."
>
> I call the piece a fugue, and it gives that impression yet the theme is not faithfully repeated but rather develops with the development of the whole, so that the style is loosened and in a way reduced ad absurdum, to which the artist seems to submit himself.... (DF, 359 f.)

It is the breakthrough to a new parodistically colored music. Then follows the description of the work:

> You have there ensembles which begin as speaking choruses and only by stages, by the way of the most extraordinary transitions, turn into the richest vocal music;

then courses which pass through all the stages from
graded whisperings, antiphonal speech, and humming up
to the most polyphonic song—accompanied by sounds which
begin as mere noise, like tomtoms and thundering gongs,
savage, fanatical, ritual, and end by arriving at the
purest music.... (DF, 373)

Stuck there, so to speak, in naturalistic atavism, a barbaric rudiment from pre-musical days, is the gliding
voice, the glissando, a device to be used with the greatest restraint on profoundly cultural grounds ... what I
have in mind is Leverkühn's preference for the glissando
... exceptionally frequent use of it ... at least in this
work ... In the place where the four voices of the altar
order the letting loose of the four avenging angels who
mow down rider and steed, Emperor and Pope, and a
third of mankind, how terrifying is the effect of the trom-
bone glissandos which here represent the theme" This
destructive sliding through the seven positions of the instrument! The theme represented by howling—what horror! And what acoustic panic results from the repeated
drum-glissandos ... but most shattering of all is the
application of the glissandos to the human voice, which
after all was the first target in organizing the tonic material and ridding the song of its primitive howling over
several notes: the return, in short, to this primitive
stage, as the chorus of the Apocalypse does it in the form
of frightfully shrieking human voices at the opening of
the seventh seal, when the sun became black and the
moon became as blood and the ships are overturned. (D
F, 374 f.)

And then:

... the memory of that pandemonium of laughter, of hellish merriment which, brief but horrible, forms the end
of the first part of the Apocalypse ... the same fear, the
same shrinking and misgiving awkwardness I feel at this
gehennas gaudium, sweeping through fifty bars beginning
with the chuckle of a single voice and rapidly gaining
ground, embracing choir and orchestra, frightfully swell-
ing in rhythmic upheavals and contrary motions to a
fortissimo tutti, an overhwelming, sardonically yelling,

screeching, bawling, bleating, howling, piping, whinny-
ing salvo, the mocking, exulting laughter of the Pit.... .

For this hellish laughter at the end of the first part has
its pendant in the truly extraordinary chorus of children
which, accompanied by a chamber orchestra, opens the
second part: a piece of cosmic music of the spheres,
icily clear, glassily transparent, of brittle dissonances
indeed, but with all of an—I would like to say—inaccessibly
unearthly and alien beauty of sound, filling the heart with
longing without hope.... And this piece... is in its musical essence, for him who has ears to hear and eyes to
see, the devil's laughter all over again.... The passages
of horror just before heard are given, indeed, to the indescribable children's chorus at quite a different pitch,
an unchanged orchestration and rhythm; but in the sear-
ing susurrant tones of spheres and angels there is not one
note which does not occur, with rigid correspondence, in
the hellish laughter.

That is Adrian Leverkühn. Utterly. That is the music
he represents. (DF, 378 f.)

Here we have one of the most impressive examples of Mann's
verbal musical descriptions.

To be sure, Thomas Mann had incorporated musical descriptions into his narratives before. If we compare his poetic
reproduction of music with that of other poets—for example,
Wilhelm Wackenroder, E.T.A. Hoffman, Jacob Wassermann,
or foreign writers like August Strindberg, Selma Lagerlöff,
Romain Rolland—Mann's special accomplishment, his deepening and enriching of the meaning of the music, appears all the
brighter. This description of music also belongs to the romantic tradition.

In The Origin of Doctor Faustus Thomas Mann says: "I
certainly felt that my book itself would have to be what it
treated; that is, constructive music." At the same time we
recall that he designates music as "foreground." It concerns
the problem of the artist in his critical period. Neither the
horrible end nor the career of Adrian corresponds after all to
that of the poet, but the artistic necessity is the same, and it
is supposed to be solved in this novel with the same artistic
means. The densely tied net of hundreds and hundreds of individual relationships which draw together all the motifs of the

work into a solid whole corresponds to the tight construction of the composer. But what can we compare with the break-through, the return to elementary means of expression?

Between himself and the motif of the novel and between himself and his readers, Mann places the narrator Serenus Zeitblom, a Catholic philologist whom he certainly invests with much of himself, as in Zeitblom's attitude toward the history of the times, toward the war of 1914/18, to the Third Reich and its world war; but Mann moves the narrator away from himself and gives him the stamp of an independent figure. Zeitblom accompanies his work on the novel, all the happen-ings, in which he is for the most part participating and which he describes, such as the life story of his friend Adrian, with very detailed observations which considerably increase the scope of the work. Just as before with Felix Krull, Mann rep-resents Zeitblom as a dilettante writer who, completely counter to the spirit of creative activity, constantly reflects about his intentions, among other things about his own inadequacy and defectiveness of execution. His dilettantism is revealed in the fact that he speaks incessantly of the emotions which dominate him during writing and cause his hand to tremble. A few pas-sages from the first chapter may serve as examples:

> I read over the previous lines and cannot help noting in them a certain discomfort, only too indicative of the emotional state in which I sit down today in order to make a beginning with a biographical description ... charac-teristic of an emotional condition in which a palpitating impulse to communicate and a profound distrust of my own adequacy become mixed in a most distressing man-ner. (DF, 3)

He discusses the word "genius" and says:

> And indeed it is not to be denied, nor has it ever been denied, that the demonic and unreasonable element has a disquieting share on this radiant sphere, that a relation-ship provoking subtle horror always exists between it and the lower realms ... (DF, 4)

He speaks "of an object," which for him "is dear as life and acute." Thereupon follows his confession: "I loved him—with tenderness and terror, with compassion and devoted admira-tion." (DF, 5) He describes the unloveableness of Adrian and concludes: "All about him was coldness—and how do I feel, using this word, which he himself in an uncanny connection, once also set down?" (DF, 6) Use of this word occurred in the conversation with the devil.

Mann made great fun of the dilettantes in **Tonio Kröger**, who think that one can create artistically if only dominated by feelings, yet it is Zeitblom who completes the breakthrough to the elementary lament in this work. He transforms the life story of Adrian Leverkühn into a powerful elegy, a lament for the departed friend to which he adds the hymnic songs of praise of his brilliant tonal creations, as the court singers of the early Middle Ages did with hymns to the heroic deeds of princes in their intensely tragic songs. This melancholy plaintive tone elevates **Doctor Faustus** to tragic writing of the highest rank. It is Thomas Mann's only thoroughly pathetic novel over which the ironic persona of Zeitblom only spreads a transparent veil. The narrator's painfully emotional lament resounds as if it were for the fate of Clarissa Rodde, who takes her life, or for her sister Inez, who shoots her lover Rudi Schwerthfeger when he becomes unfaithful to her, or for the violinist himself to whom Adrian, deeply hurt by his pushiness, intentionally gives the order to woo Marie Godeau for him and causes his destruction, or for the charming heavenly messenger Nepomuk Schneidewein, the child whom Adrian loves and who becomes sick and meets a wretched end, or for his own difficult fate or even more for that of the German people. There are only a few people in this work who are self-sufficient, such as Adrian's parents and the workers on the Pfeiffering Farm. There is no talk at all of a happy turn of fate, of the double blessing from above and below, as in the case of Joseph. The great work is uniform and closed as a result of its dark melancholy. In this respect it is related to the early writings, and above all to **Death in Venice.**

During the work on **Doctor Faustus** Mann wrote, as an introduction to a selection of Dostoevsky's stories, an essay **Dostoevsky—With Limits,** in which he speaks at great length about that writer's and Nietzsche's sickness and glorifies them in hymnic words: "sickness—above all things it depends on who is sick, who mad, who epileptic or paralytic: an average blockhead in whom the sickness is lacking the intellectual and cultural aspect to be sure; or a Nietzsche, a Dostoevsky. In their cases something results from the sickness which is more important and enhancing for life and its development than any kind of a medically approved malady...life is not finicky, and one may well say that sickness which dispenses creative genius, sickness which takes the hurdles on high horse, springs from cliff to cliff in bold exhilaration, is a thousand times preferable to life than health, dragging along on foot." Thomas Mann transferred Nietzsche's syphilitic sickness to his composer Leverkühn. A number of sentences from the Dostoevsky essay recur literally or only slightly varied in Adrian's conversation with the devil. Intuition as a result of inflammation of the brain is one of the central ideas of the work, which Zeitblom expresses once in these words: "It is not otherwise. I owe the insight to a friendship which has given me a great deal of misery and horror but has constantly filled me with pride: genius is a creative form of life's force, deeply experienced in sickness, creating out of it and because of it." This thought has complete validity within the work, but not afterward on calm reconsideration.

After completion of the novel, Mann delivered a lecture in Zurich at the convention of the PEN Club on 2 June 1947 entitled **Nietzsche's Philosophy in the Light of our Experience**, which he mentions in **The Origin of Doctor Faustus**, "the essayistic postlude" to the novel. In it he quotes the famous passage from Nietzsche's **Ecce Homo** on the inspiration, out of which the work **Thus Spake Zarathustra** grew and on which he then passes a very hard judgment: "This faceless and shapeless monster and fugleman Zarathustra with the rose crown of laughter on his unrecognizable head, his 'grow hard!' and his dancer's legs is no creation, he is rhetoric, excited word magic, tortured voice and doubtful prophecy, a phantom of helpless grandeur, often moving, but mostly painful—a mock figure bordering on the ridiculous." To my way of thinking, Mann's criticism is unjust; above all it strikes the lack of solid form in the Zarathustra figure in the frame story which displeases the master of human description; Zarathustra, after all, is not a narrative but a collection of sermons on the man of the future—which also includes ethical demands on the man of the present—and of hymns full of cosmic experience. It is not astonishing that Thomas Mann here subjects that work to ridicule to which the last great compositions of Adrian correspond in the musical novel—both of them products of the sickness? It amounts to a recanting of the thesis that sick genius is "a creative form of the vital force."

We approach an understanding of this contradiction if we make it clear to ourselves that when he seized upon this motif from his youthful period, Thomas Mann, to be sure, was also returning into the melancholy concept of that time, which was renewed and strengthened by the heavy pressure of the Second World War and the unhappy guilt of the German people; but that, guided by his reason, he never completely gave up the legacy of Goethe. With this the question arises as to what relationship the novel bears to Goethe's **Faust**.

Naturally Thomas Mann would never have written his **Doctor Faustus**, if Goethe's **Faust** had not existed. The concept of a Faustian German was taken after all from the first part of the drama in which the young Faust feels himself to be a "superman," roams around in infinity, strives for the eternal, and indentures himself to the Devil in order to find out "what holds the world together in its innermost parts." At the beginning of the second part, the reawakened Faust expresses another leading thought: "Life is contained in the multicolored reflection." He turns completely to earthly phenomena, to the study of nature, Greek antiquity, and practical work for a free people, on free soil which he wrests from the sea and the swamp. And nothing of such "world-piety" has gone into the idea of the Faustian man, which belongs completely to the romantic tradition in which Thomas Mann lived and wrote for so long.

Following Lessing, Goethe does not surrender his Faust to the forces of hell. Because he makes the effort to strive, he is rescued by the heavenly forces and led by Gretchen, the eternal feminine, to the highest of heights. The Faust drama is a flaming protest against the church tradition that represents woman as the pliable tool of the devil to divert man from God and to denigrate love between the sexes.

Thomas Mann confesses openly that his novel has in common with Goethe's **Faust** only the source, the chapbook. This little book is a religiously inspired propaganda piece directed against the new and spreading secular intellectuality. Mann has taken a great deal of material for his work from the chapbook and from other popular and learned Faust literature. A harlot is the devil's mediator. The journey into hell at the conclusion is replaced by horrible madness. Thomas Mann

surely did not want to oppose Goethe. He was driven by a completely different train of thought to this configuration of the
Faust saga. But that alters nothing about the fact that it is not
like Goethe. I call **Doctor Faustus** that work of Mann farthest
removed from Goethe. Mann's world of ideas is not a systematically erected structure; in this novel it is subordinated
completely to the tragic theme.

Thomas Mann makes demonic not only the music and the
life of the genial musician, but also the story of his time.
Throughout the whole work he places the fate of Adrian, who
indentures himself to the devil and grows mad, in parallel
with the fate of the German people who trusted themselves to
the "Seducer," Adolf Hitler, who leads them first into the
moral abyss and then into the political one. What drives
Thomas Mann to this is that the master of the Third Reich fills
him with disgust as the incarnation of all dark and evil forces.
In this novel Mann wants to know nothing of the Other Germany,
nothing of the democratic freedom movement of the first half
of the nineteenth century, of the growing workers' movement,
of the total war between left and right, of the resistance in the
Third Reich. The historian will try to understand the slow political maturation of the German people from its unfortunate
political history. Mann, however, derives the incapability of
shaping their own fate in a democratic order from the Faustian
nature to which musicality and the relationship to hell belong.
This may be valid as a symbolic comparison in a work of art.
Political perception it is not. Not even when Thomas Mann
says so in his lecture **Germany and the Germans** at the Library
of Congress. The image originates in a romantic individuality
and, in the final analysis, in an apolitical poet.

The greatness of a work of art does not depend on the correctness and durability of some of its ideas but on the artistic
configuration of its themes and on its language. Mann gives a
whole series of his figures in **Doctor Faustus** an unusually
personal manner of expression; for example, he gives to
Adrian the language of the Luther period; to the music agent
Feitelberg, a sophisticated German-French power of persua-
sion; and to the little Nepomuk, the words of a child-like
messenger of heaven. The discussions in the Winfried circle in
Halle are interlaced with many abstract expressions from their
studies on which the philologist Zeitblom makes his marginal

notes. For all the individual forms of the narrative which I have treated briefly, Mann creates the appropriate linguistic expression. As we have seen, this is especially true for everything which is related to music. His artistic language unfolds luxuriantly in observation, description, and illumination.

In 1935 Mann entitled a volume of essays **Sufferings and Greatness of the Masters.** From his own painful experience, he knows of the creative artist's obsession to work, of the merciless domination of fantasy which demands so much sacrifice of closeness to life and human warmth. In the Dostoevsky essay cited, he accuses himself of having written about the blessed writers, Tolstoi and Goethe, but not about the cursed ones, Dostoevsky and Nietzsche, the sick geniuses. This neglect is made good in **Doctor Faustus.** By using the age-old Faust book, he has depicted the representative fate of the genial composer Adrian Leverkühn through the melancholy death lament of his friend. It is the only Faust poem which one may mention in the same breath with Goethe's drama. To my way of thinking, it is the most profound and important work of Thomas Mann.

* * * * *

The Holy Sinner

Zeitblom relates the legend of Pope Gregory briefly in **Doctor Faustus**, because Adrian Leverkühn is composing it into a suite whose pieces he takes from the medieval **Gesta Romanorum**. In his novel Thomas Mann then follows the action in Hartmann von Aue's Middle High German verse epic **Gregorius**, adapted from the Old French **Life of St. Gregory**. But Mann leaves the narration to the Irish Benedictine monk Clemens, who is writing in St. Gall at the desk of Notker, without revealing in what age. The monk reflects a great deal about his intention. He asks himself why he does not report the story which he knows so well of a sibling pair who live in chastity with one another and spread the doctrine of Christ, and then answers that in it there is only talk of sanctity, but in the latter, though there is talk of great sin, there is also sanctity and the grace of God. Again and again he interrupts the narrative himself, chides its hero, is always full of sympathy for him, and loves his work very much, since it at least permits him, who is separated from the secular life, to take part in the performance, in the joys and sorrows of mankind. The horrible sins which are committed, he denounces appropriately, but he cannot avoid presenting them in detail, as with the passionate love union of the princely siblings Wiligis and Sybille on the night of their father's death. At first he skips the ardent love confession between Sybille and her son and points with emphasis to the fact that he is excluding it; whereupon he describes it. Thomas Mann furnishes here a study in the psychology of astheticism and takes pleasure in doing so.

What may have attracted the poet of the twentieth century to this medieval legend? Did it excite his imagination or stimulate his desire to create? From Mann's great biblical novel,

we already know that he secularizes and humanizes the pious
myth with all the means of his art. The goal of the Gregorius
legend is to present the sacredness of the Pope and the grace
and wonderful power of God. Thomas Mann's interest, on the
other hand, is directed toward mankind, toward his life and
his problems. Here also he describes the landscape and the
immediate world with a penetration which is foreign to the old
versions of the story. Likewise, he depicts human features,
gestures, and grimaces, and describes the impression the
characters make on their surroundings, as well as their
conversations. He uncovers all the secret events of their innermost selves. It is the same careful, vivid description as
in all Mann's narratives.

Mann's special interest in this material, however, is
indicated in the title [literally "the chosen one"]. It does not
point to sin and sanctity, but rather to the selection by God of
a pope for all Christianity. The premise for this selection is
the unusual birth which creates an exceptionally rich, many-
sided gift. The horrible sin proves to be just as fruitful as
the syphilitic sickness in **Doctor Faustus**.

The royal twins, who live together intimately from the womb,
love one another fervently because both are equally beautiful,
charming, and delightful and feel equal to each other. The
sibling marriages in Egyptian dynasties rest on the same concept of the unique equal birth. In **Blood of the Walsungs**, Mann
had already treated this theme, following Wagner.

From this sibling union, regarded as sinful in the Christian
world, the hero of the novel develops, a man-child of unusual
gifts, a radiant figure. He is differentiated from all men by
the aristocratic fineness and charm of his figure, slender and
willowy with silken hair and eyes of midnight blue. His intellectual ability is even more prepossessing. Accepted into the
monastery at six, he learns reading and writing with great
ease, then theology and law. But when he finds the stories of
knighthood in the monastery library and reads them with great
rapture, he senses that not only the fisher folk with whom he
grew up but also the monks with all their learning are completely foreign to him and will remain so. He keeps his insight
secret, but from that time he knows that he was born to knighthood. He is physically adept; in sports only his foster brother
Flann, the fisherman's son, is his equal. The coarse bumpkin

hates the fine, learned monastery student and challenges him in a fight to the death. Here it is shown for the first time that the concentration of all his energies, his intellectual superiority, decides the battle. Flann falls upon him, shouting with words of rage: "I will cut you to ribbons, I will smash your mug, I will bash in your stomach, I will crush your kidneys, so get ready for me to polish you off!" Grigorss—as he is then called—answers calmly: "Take care of your own kidneys!" Flann remembers this during the long fight. When Grigorss once again aims at his kidneys with his left fist, Flann cleverly avoids him. At the same moment the opponent's right fist with the seal ring thuds into his face and smashes his nose. That is the way the fist fight ends. It has a postlude. Flann goes home. Grigorss follows him in order to make peace with him. The mother, horrified at the bloody face of her son, erupts in wild curses directed at Grigorss and betrays what she has faithfully kept quiet until now, that he was wafted up in a boat, a foundling of doubtful origin. He listens to all this outside the door. It brings on his impulse to depart from the island in the sleeve canal for his trip out into the world.

By intellectual superiority he conquers even the rough warlike suitor of the Duchess Sibylle of Artois-Flanders, King Roger of Arelat, who up to that time had conquered all the knights of the besieged fortress of Bruges by the sea. He intentionally permits him to strike the sword out of his hand in order to take the horses' reins and the sword in an unbreakable grip with his free hand and drag the enemy along with him through the gate into the castle. He says to the Duchess that he has done it because a captured enemy is certainly more preferable to her than a dead one. She calls this statesman-like. King Roger has to redeem his life by a contract which is very favorable for Flanders-Artois.

This victory leads to a new repulsive sin—the marriage between mother and son. They live together for three years ecstatically happy. Sibylle bears a daughter and becomes pregnant for the second time. But a shadow lies over their union. Each is concealing something from the other. The mother soon recognizes her son. He looks all too similar to her brother and beloved who died of over-exertion on the way to the holy land before he reached the harbor of Marseilles. Furthermore, her son wears a splendid garment of silk, which she gave to the little child when it was placed out on the water. At that same time an inscribed tablet of great worth was also placed in with him on which his noble, sinful birth could be read. The abbot of the monastery gave it to him. He preserved it, and does penance daily in his own quarters for the sinful act of concealing its repulsive contents from the Duchess. A scandal-loving maid detects his secret, betrays it to the mistress, and thereby induces the catastrophe. Even Gregor must now recognize that his journey through the world has brought him into even greater sin.

Here it is necessary to go into another aspect of his broadly conceived character. He is very firm and strict in his concept of honor, decency, and genuine piety. He constantly places the highest demands upon himself. Even this virtue of his passes the test twice. The abbot in the monastery loves the gifted foundling very much, would like to keep him to himself and preserve him from the dangers of the world which threaten him. Before the abbot reveals to him his origin and his proper legacy which has increased, he entices him with handsome offers; he wants to obtain a rich lady for him and make him his successor as lord of the monastery and the island. But Gregor confesses his ardent striving for knighthood and the feeling that he is of high birth and insists on going out into the world. Not until then does he discover the truth, whereupon he decides to intervene wherever there is distress as a roving knight of the Lord, and so atone for his sinful birth.

In his speech of departure from Sibylle, his mother and wife, he demonstrates the greater composure. She would like to keep him, even though the marriage relationship would have to cease—a completely impossible proposal which could not be carried out. Even in her last words of departure, she does not call him Gregor, but uses the name of her dead brother and beloved, Wiligis. He is 20 years old; she is approaching 40. But he determines what is urgently necessary to be done in her terrible situation. They must separate completely at once and lay the most severe penance on themselves. She is supposed to have a relative of the Duke selected as ruler and in the future serve the old, the sick, and the poor in a retreat along the way. For him a place will be found where he can do penance and pray until his death. But the final truth does not come to light until 22 years later—Gregorius has already been a gracious Pope for five years when Sibylle is making a pilgrimage to Rome in order to obtain absolution. Previously, she did not suspect that it is her son and husband to whom she is going, but she recognizes him immediately. When he has heard her confession and absolved her, he confesses that he too entered the marriage bed with his mother knowingly. As formerly, their souls play a game together, and they are once again happy with one another.

Summarized in brief, the poet shows that being chosen is a matter beginning with birth and is a rich talent of a superhuman order. The grace of God does not fall accidentally on this or that person and certainly not accidentally on the child of a great sin, the great sinner. It falls on him who is already blessed from birth with unusualness. It is this theme of the great chosen one which attracts the individualist Thomas Mann and stimulates him to creativity.

The copyist of the legends and the two medieval poets never dreamed that their texts would ever be interpreted in this way. They wanted to honor the Lord. Under Thomas Mann's hands a hymn to the intellectually superior human being has resulted from it. Only the core of the story's meaning lies in the idea that sanctity often grows out of a conquest of great sinfulness, not from the little weaknesses of everyday human beings. But the legend lends itself even less to humanization than the stories of the Old Testament, and the poet would surely also not want to exaggerate the secularization, out of his respect for the secrets of existence. The tangible, completely convincing miracles are characteristic of the legends of the saints. Thomas Mann's novel commences with a mighty ringing of the bells of all the churches in Rome, without a hand touching the bell ropes. The Lord guides the little child in his boat from Bruges in Flanders through the sleeve canal to the Normandy island, and the 17 year old Gregor is led through the heavy fog again before the besieged bastion of Bruges on the sea. The evil fisherman who distrusts the penitent pilgrim, ferries him out onto the great lake, chains him fast to the rocky cone, throws the key into the water, and rows away mocking him. It is a miracle that the penitent survives there for 17 years until the voice of the Lord admonishes the cardinals in Rome to seek out this man and crown him the representative of Christ. A fish lands in a fisherman's net

and in his belly the cast-away key is found. In a trice the unrecognizable, shriveled hermit on the rocky cone, tiny as a
hedgehog, grown over with moss, regains his human shape.
The bells in Rome begin to ring by themselves at his entrance.
All this is fitting for a proper legend, and Thomas Mann does
little to advance a natural explanation for the miracles. For
this reason some of them stand out as isolated clumps in his
realistically fashioned novel.

The language too gives testimony to the mixture of various
intellectual elements. The narrator and the abbot introduced
monks' Latin, Sibylle speaks Old French in her love ecstasy,
and in other ways also the latter language and Middle High
German often mix in. The fisherfolk on the island speak the
dialect of Messing with an admixture of Low German and English. And in addition, the learned, sensitive literary art of
the twentieth century flourishes as always. One may doubt
whether Thomas Mann's reaching into medieval legend was
fortunate. In any case the resultant work is of his greatest
virtuosity.

The Black Swan

I would like to report a personal experience about the next
story of Mann. Since the beginning of the twenties, a German-
born wholesale merchant had lived in Stockholm-Ostermalm
in a lovely home with a view out onto the harbor and with a
substantial collection of art works and books. In 1928 when I
was introduced at his "salon," many theatre people and musicians and diplomats frequented it, drawn by his vivacious,
witty wife, who also came from a wealthy mercantile house of
the same branch. My wife and I spent many exciting evenings
there in lively discussions, even when we were still in the
process of fleeing from Copenhagen to Stockholm in 1943 and
after the lady was widowed. But gradually it grew more quiet
around her. She was only able to maintain the appearance of
wealth with difficulty by secretly selling off the valuable objects
from her husband's collection. I belonged to the small circle
of those who still visited her when she was already sick and
bedridden, up until she died at 78. Oftentimes I brought her
things to read. Even to the end she was a fascinating storyteller and always knew the **chronique scandaleuse** of high

society. One evening I related to her the contents of a book which had recently appeared. "Why that is despicable! No, that I don't want to read!" "But people are talking a lot about it in Stockholm." "Well, then send it to me please." Several days after this a call came: "Tonight I read the story, I still find it repulsive, but it is well written!"

"Please, send the book back to me; I have several friends who would like to read it very much."

"No, no, I want to read it again!"

Then she called up again: "The story is not only well written but also true to life. Several years ago the wife of a local diplomat had approximately the same experience." We were talking about Thomas Mann's short story **The Black Swan.**

In a villa in Düsseldorf lives the widow Rosalie von Tümmler, about fifty years old, with her thirty-year-old unmarried daughter Anna and her twenty-four-year-old son Edward. The mother is an attractive, happy woman whose piety is expressed in a naive reverence for nature. The daughter has a club foot, was excluded from many joys early in life, and at one time had a love relationship which she felt to be humiliating because she saw in advance that it could bring no fulfillment. She has studied at the Academy of Art, and is a painter of modern abstract leanings, a serious, clever, reticent child. She is bound by a close friendship to her mother. Since they are so different in their dispositions and feelings, there is always a lively tension and opposition in their conversations, which fill up about half the space of the narrative. Both are educated and sensitive enough to understand themselves in all the ramifications of female life. In their conversations the joyous devotion of the mother to countless details of nature unfolds at length, especially of the spring, her time of the year, because she was born in May, whereas Anna was a child of winter. The mother is also gladly permitted to criticize Anna's paintings—Anna, who opposes nature with the free creations of the human intellect—and to make suggestions to Anna; for example, to transform the splendid aromas of the flowers into abstract forms— a suggestion that the daughter smilingly rejects as romantic synaesthesia and not appropriate to the times. All the differences of opinion are unable to shake the love and confidence of the two for each other. Only because these wordy duels represent a confidential exchange between two friendly women is it also possible that the most intimate and otherwise taboo-laden matters of body and soul can be discussed without reservation, which apparently lies in the artistic plan of Thomas Mann and softens the boldness of the theme.

Frau von Tümmler is underoing the change of life and complains bitterly that she is only a female wreck. To her own astonishment and to the estrangement of the daughter, she undergoes a rapidly intensifying love for a young, vigorous, and handsomely built American, Ken Keaton, who comes into the house as an English teacher for her son Edward and, through his happy nature and his enthusiasm for European cultural traditions, soon becomes a welcome member of the family. It comes to the point that the passion of the already graying mother for the charming young man develops into the main topic between the two women. Anna is very seriously worried about spiritual harmony, about moral dignity; indeed, she is even full of premonitions about her mother's physical health. Anna warns her, gives her advice, and treats her cautiously and lovingly like a spiritual physician. But the mother waxes enthusiastic about the goodness of nature which has bestowed this great experience on her and one day reveals to the daughter that her body has adapted itself to the spring of the soul; she has again become a complete human being. This is followed by a long conversation with the daughter about this physical change and its practical consequences for the mother's love. The objections of the daughter are not completely without effect. They delay the development a little bit. But on a motor boat excursion to the Rococco Castle Holterhof of the Prince Elector Karl Theodore—which gives the narrator opportunity to describe vividly the landscape along the river, the castle park, and the building itself and its interior—things progress despite everything to a declaration of love on the part of the mother, to passionate kissing, and to the promise to visit Ken Keaton in his room.

However, Frau von Tümmler is unable to keep her promise. Her appearance and her actions have already changed markedly in the last weeks through signs of sickliness and of weakness. During the following night, she suffers a severe hemorrhage that terrifies the household. The house doctor recommends her immediate transfer to the Gynecological Clinic. Abdominal cancer is quickly determined. The operation reveals a hopeless condition. The premonitions of the daughter prove to be a terrible truth. The passion itself was evidence of inner disturbance. The happy, nature-loving woman has to die. But even in death she holds bravely to her faith: "Anna, never say that nature deceived me, that she is sardonic and cruel... indeed, death is a great instrument of life, and if for me it borrowed the guise of resurrection, of the joy of love, that is not a lie but goodness and mercy...nature—I have always loved her and she has been loving to her child." (BS, 140) Those are her last whispered words.

This narrative with its delicate motif is not only well written and true to life, it also contains a spiritual message of the subjective affirmation of life that conquers sickness and death.

Confessions of Felix Krull, Confidence Man

Among the artistic creations of Thomas Mann, the novel **Confessions of Felix Krull, Confidence Man** occupies a strange and unique position: All his other writings were published in a finished form. This one appeared three times as a fragment: in bookform in Stuttgart with the subtitle "Book of Childhood," 1923; in Amsterdam "Expanded by a second fragmentary book," 1937; and in Frankfurt on Main "The Memoires, Part One," 1954 (apart from the bibliophile editions). In the commemorative work for the S. Fischer Press' 25th anniversary in 1911, the fifth chapter from the "Book of Childhood" was printed under the title "The Theatre Visit." Thus the work on the novel reaches back to 1911. It was begun after **Royal Highness** (1909), and before **Death in Venice** (1912) and occupied the poet much for four decades.

Even his own attitude toward his work is quite unusual. In 1923 he wrote a postlude: "The novel...was begun twelve years ago, but had to be put on the shelf for the sake of other tasks, although the author never separated himself from it inwardly. A certain reputation which this **unique undertaking** achieved as a result of public readings and printed samples before its time moved the editor and author to make a tentative public offering of the greatest part of what he had written. As far as the author is concerned, he is willing enough to let himself be urged on to continuation and completion as a result of the friendly interest which the fragment may perhaps find."

Thomas Mann had already said something similar on 5 November 1916 at the occasion of his reading from the manuscript in the Berlin "Secession." When had the poet otherwise ever sought encouragement from the public to complete a work?

In 1955, when Thomas Mann had closed his eyes forever, everyone was eagerly asking whether a second volume from the legacy would appear, but there was no more. He had occupied himself with other things—at the end, chiefly with a drama **Luther's Wedding**. In the **Welt am Sonntag**, of 14 August 1955, Willy Haas published a eulogy in which he said: "At that time when he was putting the final touches to the first part of his Confidence Man Krull, he wrote to me: '... I am in a hurry to get on with these Krull memoirs since there is enough manuscript at hand, so that for the time being I may take off one volume, a 'first part' and get it out to the public ... if they then find that these jokes are in fact too far beneath my dignity (I myself am not so much in awe), then I will stop altogether and think about something more worthwhile.'" There is reason to assume that the poet no longer wanted to complete the novel. His attitude toward it vacillated. What could have fascinated him for such a long time in this "unique undertaking"in spite of everything?

There are two pronouncements of the poet about his novel which complement each other in a fortunate and informative manner. The first one from 1916 characterizes the work as a parody of the typically German novel of education and development, the second from 1953 places the narrative in the tradition of the adventure novel of the seventeenth century, Grimmelshausen's **Simplicissimus**, and then continues: "Its hero, this Felix Krull, is a young man of somewhat doubtful origin, son of a bankrupt Rhenish champagne manufacturer who meets his end through suicide. The youth, endowed by nature with a very friendly disposition, very handsome, very attractive, is **a kind of artistic person,** a dreamer, a visionary, and a useless citizen." This leads back to the artist's short story **Tonio Kröger** in 1903. Mann had spent much time with Schiller's essay **On Naive and Sentimental Poetry**. In the narrative mentioned, Mann himself proves to be "sentimental." On the one hand, Tonio experiences painfully the contrast between intellect and art and, on the other, the naive life; and he longs for the "bliss of the usual." It is this love for reality which keeps his heart alive. At the conclusion Tonio writes to his lady friend: "Don't mock this love, Lisabeta, it is good and fruitful. There is longing and melancholic envy in it and a little bit of scorn and a whole lot of chaste bliss."

The existence of the artist is questionable, Tonio explains in Lisabeta's studio. He stands apart—a non-person. All that he treats in literary form is dispensed with and transformed into dead words. Tonio lists parallels to the poet: the actor, the prince, the bank director who writes short stories and ends up in prison. From this short story, threads run to the "artist" short stories, **Tristan**, and **Death in Venice**, to the nobility novel **Royal Highness**, to the musician's novel **Doctor Faustus**, and to the **Confessions of Felix Krull, Confidence Man**.

The most intimately personal interest of Thomas Mann in his theme is touched upon in the phrase **Künstlermensch**. The problematic nature of the confidence man sets the poet's fantasy in motion. Apparently Thomas Mann identifies himself— not completely, but in part—with his fictitious creation, invests him with much of himself, and describes his intellectual development with a passionate interest.

In the comparison of the three versions of the narrative, a number of changes can be established, only one of which I will cite here. In the first two versions, read in the place where they are talking about the physical beauty of the young Felix, who is posing as a nude model for his godfather, Professor Schimmelpreester: "Perhaps just my legs were relatively a little too short; but my godfather consoled me with the information that even the intellectual Prince of Weimar [Goethe] had legs that were too short and still was able to chalk up great personal successes all his life long." This is left out in the third version. The reason is obvious: In the ninth chapter of the second book, Mrs. Houpflé compares her young lover with the God Hermes, who is constantly depicted by the Greeks in perfect beauty, never with legs too short.

It is of great importance that the narrative changes its structure with the fourth chapter of the second book. The first twelve chapters of the novel average about six and a half pages each; the seventeen following, more than twenty each. Like some of his other works, this one also grew under Thomas Mann's hands into epic proportions.

In Felix Krull, the poet creates a narrator whom he places

between himself and the material, between himself and the public. In contradiction to the great rule "create, artist—don't talk!" he lets the narrator reflect often and at great length throughout the whole work about his own writing and thus parodies his inclination to write about his own complete works; right at the beginning he says:

As I take up my pen at leisure and in complete retirement—in good health, furthermore, though tired, so tired that I shall only be able to proceed by short stages and with frequent pauses for rest—as I take up my pen, then, to commit my confessions to this patient paper in my own neat and attractive handwriting, I am assailed by a brief misgiving about the educational background I bring to an intellectual enterprise of this kind. But since everything I have to record derives from my own immediate experience, errors, and passions, and since I am therefore in complete command of my material, the doubt can apply only to my tact and propriety of expression, and in my view these are less the product of study than of natural talent and a good home environment. (FK, 3)

Among other things, Felix Krull decisively rejects the comparison of his memoirs both with works of belles lettres as well as with detective novels and relies completely on the reality experienced by himself. The parodistic nature of this and similar dilettante observations is especially underscored in the use of tired phrases.

Parody is also predominant in the description of his origin. He alludes to his "good upbringing." "There was no lack of that in my case for I come from a refined middle-class family, even though debauched." The grotesque combination of "refined middle-class" with the restrictive "debauched" is characteristic of the world into which we are led. The father's love affair with the governess from Vevey is described in a completely twisted fashion: "Since a relationship of feminine rivalry had developed between her and my mother—and in fact even concerning my father." Everything is questionable in this milieu. To be sure, the villa is counted among the "charming landed estates," but it is filled up along with the garden by repulsive objects in bad taste. The parents are bored with one another to the point of "bitterness" and for this reason give parties which are notorious in a little town. Schoolmates are advised by their parents to avoid association with Felix. It is the same story also with the "good upbringing." The father's sparkling wine is bad. We think involuntarily of the sparkling word-magic of the confidence man. Everything is heading for an economic collapse, from which the father takes flight through his suicide. The "refined middle-class" situation is merely on the surface. On this swampy soil grows the strange human blossom Felix Krull.

But even though Thomas Mann maintains the fiction of the writer of memoirs from time to time, whether it be through lengthy insertions or individual turns of phrase, it is still his own calculating artistic hand which determines all the details of this description of life. In the selection in the first book from the time of childhood and youth, for example, all the episodes presented serve the character description of the future confidence man or are directly in preparation for his "profession." Felix comes into the world on a Sunday and throughout his life regards himself as a favorite Sunday-child of nature. As a small child he is already playing "emperor" and is strengthened in this fantasy by the world around him; for instance, by his godfather. As a boy his imagination is occupied all day long with being an eighteen-year-old prince. He practices expanding and contracting his pupils voluntarily before the mirror to the point of complete success. At the age of eight, he garners great applause from a distinguished public in Langenschwalbach as he plays accompaniment for a Hungarian dance with precisely imitated movements of the violinist, while clothed in a pretty sailor suit with silk stockings and patent leather shoes, on a little violin with a heavily greased bow. Thus he learns early the sweetness of success without knowing genuine accomplishment. "It was one of the most beautiful days of my life, perhaps the most beautiful of all." The painter Schimmelpreester continually garbs the young man in new costumes from every period and place and derives pure joy from the fact that his figure and his face willingly adapt themselves to each costume. Apparently, Felix has the capacity and the desire for transformation which Max Reinhardt praises in the actor and the dramatic poet. A theatre visit creates great excitement in the feelings and thoughts of the fourteen-year-old boy. He experiences the strikingly handsome figure of an operetta singer who entrances the public. Felix afterwards meets the person himself in the dressing room and finds him a disgusting individual.

Felix practices imitating his father's signature and achieves such finesse that he is often able to cut school; for this purpose he learns to simulate illnesses in such a way that the experienced physician believes him. Whenever the hospital food does not satisfy him, he reaches into his supplies of chocolate, which he has stolen—once and then again and again —from a delicatessen. Even in the first book, the Confessions proved to be truly a parody of an individualistic novel of education and development. Naturally, Thomas Mann does not identify himself with the practices of the young Felix nor with his subsequent deeds as a confidence man, but he does much to describe penetratingly his personality—his inner world, his psychic disposition, and his lively mind—so that even at the end of the first book the reader is enchanted by him and awaits his further fate. At the same time Mann apparently uses traits from his own nature.

In the second chapter, for example, Felix Krull reports of his "unusual inclination and talent for sleep." Involuntarily, one thinks of the hymn to sleep (and the bed) that Thomas Mann has written. The boy also has the same disinclination for school as Hanno Buddenbrook and Tonio Kröger, which their creator doubtlessly shared. He relates that for weeks he has imagined himself in school to be an eighteen-year-old prince, a fantasy that Thomas Mann has reported about himself.

As to many of Krull's observations, we ask ourselves whether they are his or Thomas Mann's; for example, the astute discoveries which the fourteen-year-old makes about the operetta singer and his performance—

Consider further and ask yourself what it was that impelled this miserable mountebank to learn the art of transfiguring himself every night. What are the secret sources of the charm that possessed him and informed him to the finger tips? To learn the answer you have but to recall (for you know it well!) the ineffable power, which there are no words monstrously sweet enough to describe, that teaches the firefly to glow. Remind yourself how this man could not hear often enough or emphatically enough the assurance that he had truly given pleasure, pleasure altogether out of the ordinary. It was the devotion and drive of his heart toward that yearning crowd that made him skillful in his art; and if he bestows on them the joy of life and they satiate him with their applause for doing so, is not that a mutual fulfillment, a meeting and marriage of his yearning and theirs? (FK, 30)

Apparently the poet has taken the pen from the hand of his fictitious narrator and written this himself with all the means of his mature art. This happens more frequently in the later chapters. At times the parody is dropped by the narrator, and he becomes the interpreter of these realistic living phenomena of the lower sphere. Thus, literary work with the Thomas Mann stamp arises, an adventurous experience.

Felix Krull regards his "profession" as a kind of art, which presupposes much natural talent and demands much preparation and training. During his visit to the Stoudebecker Circus in Paris, he regards the clowns and the "daughter of the air," the trapese artist Andromache—who through their achievements go beyond anything purely human—as "non-human beings," exactly in the sense of the short story **Tonio Kröger**. But in his own case he does not let himself be completely captivated like the public around him because he is "of the profession": "I was not able to feel that I was from the circus branch, from the fatal leap branch, naturally, but a professional in general, from the branch of effect, of satisfying and enchanting human beings." Is there then in his career any kind of achievement at all, which one might compare with the outstanding ones of the artist?

We could mention his appearance before the military commission. He buys a book on epilepsy for one and a half marks and practices acting out the symptoms of this sickness for months at a time so that he does not even have to use his abilities to the fullest extent to gain the desired goal, freedom from military service. His acting at this point is a clear indication of mastery. Thomas Mann's description, especially the distortion of the face and the body, is one of the artistic highpoints of the novel:

My face became contorted—but that tells very little. In my opinion it was contorted in an entirely new and terrifying fashion, such as no human passion could produce, but only a satanic influence and impulse. My features were literally thrust apart in all directions, upward and downward, right and left, only to be violently contracted toward the center immediately thereafter; a horrible, one-sided grin tore at my left, then at my right cheek, compressing each eye in turn with frightful force while the other became so enormously enlarged that I had the distinct and frightful feeling that the eyeball must pop out...if, however, so unnatural a play of expression might well have aroused in those present that extreme distaste which we call horror, it was nevertheless only the introduction and prelude to a real witches' Sabbath of face-making, a whole battle of grimaces, fought out during the following seconds on my youthful countenance. To recount in detail the distortions in my features, to describe completely the horrible positions in which mouth, nose, brows, and cheeks—in short, all the muscles of my face—were involved, changing constantly, moreover, so that not a single one of these facial deformities repeated itself—such a description would be far too great an undertaking. Let just this much be said, that the emotional experiences which might correspond to these physiognomical phenomena, the sensations of mindless cheerfulness, blank astonishment, mild lust, inhuman torment, and toothgrinding rage, simply could not be out of this world, but must rather belong to an infernal region where our earthly passions, magnified to monstrous proportions, would find themselves horribly reproduced. But is it not true that those emotions whose expressions we assume really do reproduce themselves in premonitory shadowy fashion in our souls? Meanwhile, the rest of my body was not still though I remained standing in one spot. My head lolled and several times it twisted almost entirely around just as if Old Nick were in the act of breaking my neck; my shoulders and arms seemed on the point of being wrenched out of their sockets, my hips were bowed, my knees turned inward, my belly was hollowed while my ribs seemed to burst the skin over them; my teeth were clamped together; not a single finger but was fantastically bent into a claw. And so as though stretched on a hellish engine of torture I remained for perhaps two-thirds of a minute. (FK, 99-101)

Naturally, this artistic achievement had to be dropped in the film.

The linguistic agility of the young confidence man is of equal artistic significance, even in foreign languages. The first twelve brief chapters of the work show a paucity of fully developed dialogs, whereas the subsequent epic expansion is based in large part on extensive conversations. Felix is a participant in all of them. In most of them, he is the leading partner who reveals his capabilities in them and gets his own way; in the most unfavorable situation, naked, under military force vis-a-vis the commission; at the French customs station at the border; in the interview with the hotel director; in the dealings with his hotel comrade Stanko, who gives him the address of the fence, also with the watchmaker himself; then in the decisive conversation with the Marquis de Venosta, which he deftly leads toward the desired goal; and finally, in the role of the aristocratic traveler, his arguments with the free speaking Zouzou Kuckuck about love and his social gift of entertainment in the house of the Luxembourg envoy and in the audience with the King of Portugal. He is a gifted word juggler and transforms every word-duel, every intensive conversation, into an artistic performance. The following piece from one of the arguments between the false marquis and Zouzou may bear witness:

"There you go again paying court to me, Louis, ... murmuring sweet nothings and looking at me imploringly—or shall I say 'importunately'? No, I shall say 'lovingly,' but that is the name for a lie....And what do you want? What is the purpose of your melting words and melting glances? Something that is unspeakably laughable and absurd, both childish and repugnant. I say 'unspeakably,' but of course it is not at all unspeakable, and I shall put it into words. You want me to consent to our embracing, to agree that two creatures whom Nature has carefully and completely separated should embrace each other so that your mouth is pressed upon mine while our nostrils are crosswise and we breathe each other's breath. That's what you want, isn't it? A repulsive indecency and nothing else, but perverted into a pleasure by sensuality—that's the word for it, as I very well know; and the word means that swamp of impropriety into which all of you want to lure us, so that we will go crazy and two civilized beings will behave like cannibals. That is the purpose of your flirtatiousness."

"Zouzou, you distress me dreadfully when you use such words—what shall I call them, crude, cruel exaggeratedly true, and for that very reason only half true, in fact not true at all—when you use such words to tear away the delicate mist in which my admiration for the charms of your person has enwrapped my heart and senses. Don't make fun of 'enwrapped.' I purposely, deliberately, and intentionally said 'enwrapped' because I must use poetic words to defend the poetry of love against your harsh, distorted version. I beseech you, what a way to talk about love and its purpose. Love has no purpose, it neither wills nor thinks beyond itself, it is entirely itself and entirely inwoven in itself—don't scoff at 'inwoven.' I have already told you that I am intentionally using poetic words—and that simply means more seemly ones—in the name of love, for love is essentially seemly, and your harsh words are way beyond it in an area that remains alien to love, however familiar it may be with it. I ask you! What a way to talk of a kiss, the tenderest exchange in the world, silent and lovely as a flower! This unforeseen occurrence, happening quite by itself, the mutual discovery of two pairs of lips, beyond which emotion does not even dream of going, because it is in itself the incredibly blessed seal of union with another!"

"Patatípatatá!" she exclaimed. "Enwrapped and inwoven in a lovely flowery kiss! All sugar to catch flies, a way of talking us into small-boy nastiness! **Pfui,** the kiss— that tender exchange! It's the beginning, the proper beginning, **mais oui,** or rather, it is the whole thing, **toute la lyre,** and the very worst of it. And why? Because it is the skin that all of you have in mind when you say love, the bare skin of the body. The skin of the lips is tender,

you are right there, so tender that the blood is right behind it, and that's the reason for this poetry about the
mutual discovery of pairs of lips: they in their tenderness want to go everywhere and what you have in mind,
all of you, is to lie naked with us, skin against skin, and
teach us the absurd satisfaction that one miserable creature finds in savoring with lips and hands the moist surface of another. All of you do this without any feeling of
shame at the pathetic ludicrousness of your behavior and
without giving thought—for it would spoil your game—to
a couplet I once read in a book of spiritual instruction:

> However fair and smooth the skin
> Stench and corruption lie within." (FK, 354-6)

The conversation continues for still a while in the same
style. This uninhibited speech of the young girl in matters of
physical love in defense of her virginity is also new in the
narrator's art.

There are only two lengthy dialogues in which Felix is
mostly the listener. The writer Diana Philibert, wife of the
toilet bowl manufacturer Houpflé, speaks to her young lover in
bed between embraces in the spirit of Tonio Kröger and Sigmund Freud. Professor Kuckuck with the "star eyes" lectures
to the false marquis in the dining car of the Paris-Lisbon
express train on the theory of evolution, not bookishly but ex-
citingly, with hundreds of humorous observations and so
fascinatingly and plastically that he dreams about them in the
following night. In both cases we are dealing with prose pieces
of essayistic content, stylized as monologues, with brief in-
serts of the partner as in the studio of the painter Lisabeta in
Tonio Kröger and as in the Platonic dialogues in which Socrates
is the speaker.

In addition, Felix also demonstrates his pleasure and capacity for transformation, which he had shown and practiced in
the costumes of his godfather Schimmelpreester, in the roles
which he had to play during the course of his rise, first as an
elevator boy, then above all as a waiter, finally as a distinguished cavalier.

Beyond this he develops into a master in the **ars amandi**.
Many people believe that every man receives all the prerequi-
sites in this area from nature. The author of this novel, however, is of another opinion. He has his hero taught by the

prostitute Rozsa. The course lasts six months. But if the readers are curious to find out all the details, they will be bitterly disappointed. Felix himself confesses: "In every fiber of my being I am thoroughly aware that I would never have been able to complete the little episodes of my life with such refinement and elegance, without having gone through Rozsa's evil school of love."

The writer's artistic work unfolds in the richness of the variations of one and the same theme. Felix Krull's amorous adventures are a vivid example of this point. He does not begin in his early youth with a school boy infatuation, but with the year-long liaison with the thirty-year-old housemaid Genovefa. Then comes his infatuation for a couple of sisters whom he only catches sight of for a few moments on a balcony of a hotel in Frankfurt; one would not interpret this erotically at all if the writer of the memoirs did not do it himself. In the same large city, the meeting and relationship with Rozsa takes place. The next love affair of the young Krull begins at the French customs station, where he appropriates a little jewel box of Moroccan leather from the baggage of a forty-year-old, elegant woman. In the hotel, she entices the handsome elevator boy into her apartment. In the total work of Thomas Mann, the description of their meeting stands completely isolated in its nakedness. But with Mann, vivid reality is always just the sub-surface over which the interpretation of life's problems elevates itself. At the same time, the writer permits his colleague to philosophize about the relationship of spirit and life and about the woman's passion for very young men as a substitute for her own son whom she never bore. She addresses the young Armand, as they call Felix in the hotel service, hymnically in verses. To this experience in Krull's life is added the passionate enthusiasm for the artist Andromache, whom he worships and about whom he continues to dream as he writes his book. What occupies most space is the love of the Marquis de Venosta for a double likeness (which he compares to the two sisters), for the wife and daughter of Professor Kuckuck. His eloquence serves as the art of seduction with respect to Zouzou, who invites him to a clandestine meeting and kisses him; but the watchful mother prevents anything further, gives the aristocratic guest a lecture to the effect that he has gone to the wrong address, and flies into his arms jubilantly and with a heaving bosom.

There is not the slightest repetition in the series of these love descriptions. The richness and variation comes into sharpest focus especially when we direct our attention to the partners of the confidence man. But even in these meetings his capabilities prove themselves.

When we turn to his intensified egotism, we recognize the essential core of Felix Krull's character. He writes:

> The belief in my good fortune and that I am a chosen child of heaven, has constantly been alive in my inner- most being and I can say that on the whole it has never proven wrong. The fact that all suffering and torture which has occurred in my life appears as something for- eign and originally not desired by providence, through which my true and proper destiny shines sunnily as it were, represents after all the characteristic peculiarity of my life.

On the basis of his feeling that he is of a very special type, he does not recognize bourgeois morals. Others may call it theft, when he appropriates chocolate in a store. They may berate him as a pimp when he lives together with Rozsa and accepts a part of her earnings. He adheres to the standpoint that his deeds, which are carried out in a dream-like and in- toxicated state, are his creative property which such words do not touch at all. He feels that he has the right to correct chance, which has not granted him the social position appro- priate to him.

Even when he simulated sickness to his mother for the first time, a feeling of supreme satisfaction and joy fills him which he describes at great length:

I had improved nature, realized the dream—and whoever has been able to create a compelling, effective reality out of nothing, out of the mere inner knowledge and vision of things, in short, out of fantasy by the bold thrust of his person, he knows the marvellous and dreamlike sat- isfaction with which I at that time rested after my crea- tion.

After the death of his father he is impoverished, son of a failure, lacking the final examinations from his school, in a very unhappy situation. In Frankfurt he is excluded from participating in anything which costs money. "But his senses are lively, his intellect is overwrought with attention, he looks, enjoys, he is receptive." He studies the aristocratic world as it is presented to him in the windows of the shops, above all the expensive jewelry made of precious stones and metals. He looks through the windows of the elegant restaurants. He makes himself useful during the departure of the carriages after the conclusion of the theater and in this way earns a little money for himself.

But he wants no common ground with the companions of his misery: "For an inner voice had proclaimed to me early that attachment, friendship, and warming companionship were not my lot, but that I alone was relentlessly forced to be on my own and to make my way strictly independently." To be sure, he does undertake a few excursions in Paris into life with Stanko, but it never gets as far as an intimate friendship. "That is the way it is: the shy and not so much proud feeling of a person that there is something special about him, as one giving into his fate, creates all about him an air-curtain and aura of coolness in which almost to his own regret loyal proposals of friendship and camaraderie get caught up there and stick, they don't know how." In constantly new variations, the narrator makes it clear for us that Felix Krull feels called upon by nature to lead an unusual life outside middle-class barriers, to be the creative master of his fate. Quite often one has the feeling that these confessions are very close to Mann's conception of himself and at the same time that, with deep irony, he is transferring them to the confidence man.

Felix Krull feels thoroughly up to every task which his profession and career put in his way. Before he approaches the Marquis de Venosta, he has already been thinking about an exchanging of roles among the guests of the hotel and its employees: "An aristocracy of money is an exchangeable aristocracy of chance." The thought occurs again in the joking conversation with the aristocratic guest and his beloved Zouzou, and becomes reality in the long associations on the roof terrace of the grand hotel of the Ambassador. We are definitely not amazed that he then feels very comfortable as a noble traveling about the world and moves about gracefully in all situations into which this marvellous adventure leads him.

Thomas Mann employs every trick in his realistic description of life, his psychological penetration, and his pleasure and ability in interpreting life's problems in order to make the figure of this young confidence man as fascinating as possible. The result is an individualistic novel of education and development with a parodistic stamp. The rest of the figures are scattered along Felix Krull's path and for the most part—after they have met him—disappear completely from the reader's field of vision.

Despite this, Thomas Mann individualizes a substantial number of secondary figures, each in a special way, always with various kinds of witty devices. As an example I will select the head-waiter in the Parisian hotel:

The Maître d'hôtel, Monsieur Machatschek by name, was a man of great consequence; clad daily in fresh linen, he moved his expansive belly around the dining-room with a vast authority. His clean-shaven moon face beamed. He commanded to perfection those lofty gestures of the lifted arm by which the master of the tables from afar directs the entering guests to their places. His way of dealing with any mistake or awkwardness on the part of the staff—in passing, and out of the corner of his mouth —was both discreet and biting. It was he who summoned me one morning, I must assume on the suggestion of the management, and received me in a small office opening off the magnificent **salle-a-manger.**

"Kroull?" he said. "Called Armand? **Voyons, voyons.** Eh bien, I have heard of you—not exactly to your discredit and not altogether inaccurately, as it would appear at first glance. That may be deceptive, **pourtant.** You realize, of course, that the services you have so far rendered this establishment are child's play and represent a very meager use of your gifts? **Vous consentez?** It is our intention to make something out of you if possible here in the restaurant—**si c'est faisable.** Do you feel a certain vocation for the profession of waiter, some degree of talent, I say—nothing exceptional and brilliant as you seem to be assuring me, that would mean carrying self-confidence too far...a certain talent for elegant service and all the subtle attentions that go with it." (F K, 200 f.)

It goes on like this for quite a while. The description fills us with proper respect for this courtly head waiter. Only in this dialogue does the poet incorporate the answers and gestures of Armand into the speech of the powerful gentleman. He too finds the young man with the vast self-confidence pleasing. He is most impressed by the private means of the young man. He raises the salary from 40 to 50 francs a month.

Thomas Mann gives us 44 characterizations of 17 women and 27 men without ever repeating himself in motif or nature of presentation. The individualistic career of the confidence man Krull stands out against the broad background of a variegated description of the milieu and society. On looking back one cannot avoid calling its selection and representation a critical satire of society.

Even a list of the names has a grotesque comic effect. It is put together out of many languages, which in itself suggests the international society in which the confidence game flourishes on a grand scale. The influence of Greek and Roman antiquity (Olympia, Felix, Andromache, Diana, Hector) and from German romantic tradition (Genovefa, Adelaide, Irmingard) is striking and has a parodistic effect. Coarsely humorous are names like Schimmelpreester (moldy priest), Übel, Meerschaum, Houpflé, Twentyman, Radicule (ridicule), and Kuckuck ("whose name to be sure does sound funny," says the mother of the marquis). We know the slovenly world of the manufacturer of bad sparkling wine as the point of departure for the confidence man. It is heavily caricatured. The house doctor is characterized penetratingly as "the unworthy disciple of Aesculapius." According to Krull's opinion, the whole medical profession (like all other professions) consists of the usual hollow heads to whom he feels superior as a connoisseur of the body and the soul. This is doubtlessly seen from one special point of view. The confidence man can only follow his "profession" with a good conscience, if society is built on deception and because of its stupidity deserves and is even desirous of being deceived. It is parodistic that the Catholic and spiritual counselor Château thinks he sees in Felix one of those "who are pleasing in the eyes of the Lord." It is bitter irony that it has to be a courtesan who "refines" his nature and his nerves through her love, "benerves" him, as he says, in contrast to the deprecatory word "enervates."

All the women in Krull's successful love adventures are only described from their sensual side. This is true of Genovefa, Rozsa, Diana Philibert, Senora Kuckuck, and Zouzou. The two married ladies deceive their husbands without hesitation. Madame Houpflé exposes her husband before her lover and reports in addition that he is deceiving her with an actress.

The narrator leads us, not into the theater, where literary stage craft is offered or into the opera where classical music is presented, but only to places of coarser pleasures, into the operetta theater, into the circus, to the bull fights where the desires and sicknesses of the sensation-hungry public are satisfied, and he reproduces the events of a mass-psychological nature, in a description very close to reality and sensually exciting.

It is surely an elegant, expensive hotel in which Felix Krull is employed. For their money, the guests receive from him everything which they could desire in comfort and cultivated service. The employees are minimally housed and fed. One of the hotel boys delivers a sharply anarchistic speech to Felix, the newcomer: "They ought to put the torch to this whole den of exploitation." Felix has to assume the name Armand. His handsome exterior, his good manners and his pleasant voice, in short his sex appeal, are quickly recognized by all the people in authority and fitted into the service of the operation as an attraction for the female and male guests. That leads to his quick rise.

Louis de Venosta deceives his parents, who want to separate him from his lover, the soubrette Zouzou. They have weighty reasons to prevent his marriage with her. The little Parisian is a "beauté de diable," everything about her is merely "froufrou," little "Feu d'artifice" and "deception." He however, sends Felix Krull on the world trip prescribed for himself and stays with her. Desire and deceit fill the whole bourgeois society which the confidence man describes. But Felix Krull does not want to change it in any way. He says to the hotel director: "I find society charming as it is, and ardently desire to gain its favor." Before the King of Portugal, he delivers a highly conservative speech against the democratic stirrings in the country.

How does Schimmelpreester interpret his name? "Nature," so he says, "is nothing but rot and mold and I am ordained as its priest." In **Tonio Kröger** in the chapter which describes the development of the young man into the mature and respected poet, there is the following: "But what he saw was this: comedy and misery—comedy and misery."

In the essay on Chekhov, Thomas Mann explains that all satire conceals within itself the desire for a better, more intellectual human society. The "sentimental" writer is basically a moralist who makes his ideal demands on human motivation and is outraged when he sees how very much it falls off and fails in comparison.

This insight into the "human, all too, humanness" we recognize also in the satiric social criticism of the confidence novel. But there is not a word in it about the desire for a new society. In this respect, the writer deviates from the tradition in which he himself places his work. In Grimmelshausen's **Simplicissimus**, the crazy Jupiter proclaims a utopian realm of peace and of social justice, and in Goethe's **Wilhelm Meister's Travels**, Wilhelm joins an organization which creates and tries to maintain new economic, social, and pedagogical forms of life. Thomas Mann did not build such perspectives into his novel. He is satisfied in ridiculing society in his parody on the German novel of development and education. We probably do not laugh while reading, but we accompany the career of Felix Krull, the artist, with a pleasant smile.

Whether Thomas Mann reveals his mastery of language in the dilettante bloopers of the writer of the memoirs or whether he applies them without irony to realistic descriptions—for example, the delicatessen, the appearance of the operetta singer, the show windows in Frankfurt, the various female figures, and such—or to his penetratingly psychological analyses of individual people or of the masses in the show places or finally to the searching observations embedded in the novel; everywhere we bump into unusual creative word compositions in rich variety. The novel is above all a stylistic work of art.

The first part of the confessions of the confidence man Felix Krull contains many hints and events which lie in the future. Felix Krull was arrested many times. He spent a long time in jail. He has come into conflict with the laws of society in two ways. His specialty is hotel theft from women traveling alone. He is apparently aiming at their expensive jewelry since he boasts of his reliable familiarity with jewels. He often lived under a false name. In Berlin, he appeared as a Belgian aristocrat; de Venosta belongs to the Luxemburg nobility. At one time, in fact, he wanted to have an audience with the Pope. He loves to move about in the highest circles, where one leads a hedonistic life without work. He speaks at times of the servant who is at his disposal and of handsome carriages which he maintains. He reports of his relationship to the ladies, is proud of his successes, has loved a great deal and lived dissolutely without becoming a dissolute person and libertine. The trip around the world is discussed oftentimes in great detail. For him the world is a large and endlessly enticing phenomenon. His life is eventful and full of change, an adventurous up and down.

In comparison to these prospects, the action in the novel appears quite slight. As far as deceptive deeds are concerned, if we disregard the practice sessions of his childhood and youth, it contains only the deception of the military commission, the jewelry theft in the customs station, and the acceptance of the false noble name, but this with the approval of its bearer. About this Thomas Mann has written 442 pages. This sharply illuminates the structure of the work. The emphasis definitely does not reside in the plot, but in the description of the milieu and people, in psychology and the interpretation of life. The adventure novel transforms itself under Thomas Mann's hands into a work soaked in irony which presents the problems of life and interprets them in a language elevated beyond everyday events.

Katja Mann drew attention to the memoirs of the confidence man Georges Manolescu in two volumes which appeared in 1905 in Berlin, and I read them in the Thomas Mann Archiv in Zürich. The first volume contains only partial insignificant similarities. It had great success. The publisher travelled to the United States and induced the author, who was living there, to write a second part: "Failure: From the spiritual life of a criminal." Manolescu emphasizes strongly that in the profession he must constantly wear a mask and play many different roles, and he strives for "mastery," indeed "artistry" in them. He practices each and everything carefully before the mirror and prepares himself for weeks at a time for individual undertakings. He decides to simulate madness to rescue himself from a major jail penalty, carries on his studies in the madhouse, and carries out this role successfully in two attempts. In Paris he receives instructions for a year from a prostitute as to how one conducts oneself in the big world. I shall disregard other external similarities which probably recur in the life of every confidence man. On the other hand, one could fill many pages with the differences between Georges Manolescu and Felix Krull. But doubtlessly Thomas Mann has received stimuli from this second novel which he has transformed and expanded in his own way. Felix Krull, a kind of artist, remains a highly personal artistic creation of the writer, even if more sources come to light from which he has taken over the raw material. The Thomas Mann Archiv in Zürich possesses a chest full of materials for this novel. There is certainly possible a whole series of different interpretations of the novel, depending on whether one sees the main subject matter to be satiric description of milieu and people, psychology, observations, the play of irony, or style. A thoughtful reader said to me: "Thomas Mann wants to teach us that each one of us conceals something of the confidence man within himself." Even this concept can be defended.

In the Academy of Arts in Florence, there is a hall with sculptures of Michelangelo, among them two incompleted ones called "Captives." It has been handed down that they asked the sculptor why he did not complete the two statues. The answer went: "I expressed what I had in mind." The statuary has this powerful effect on the observer. It is as if the figures, which have only come half way out of the marble, are trying to free themselves. What is the meaning? The fate of the captives, the captivity of all men in the world, or indeed that of the souls in the sensual world? The "Captives" of Michelangelo stimulate us to such thoughts. Perhaps Thomas Mann also thought, when he had concluded the first part of his novel in 1954: "I have expressed what I had in mind—the problems of this type of human being which are so related to the artist, to myself, and others. With that it may be enough."

9. RETURN OF THE WORLD CITIZEN TO EUROPE

After his emigration from Switzerland to the United States, Thomas Mann continued his political activity along with his artistic work; in fact, he increased and expanded it from year to year. At first the refugees from the Third Reich, whose numbers grew with every new territory which Hitler subjected to his reign of terror, demanded a great deal of private and public help in which Mann took part to the limit of his ability. On this subject Erika Mann writes: "Special mention should be made of his attempts by letter to be helpful to his comrades, to rescue them physically, to make their entry possible, to gain positions, contracts, stipends, financial support for them. This was not only for Germans, Austrians, Czechs, but also for refugees from all the countries overrun by Hitler." I shall report on the massive growth of the English correspondence in the United States in addition to Erika Mann's edition of the letters. From my own studies on the intellectual life of the German refugees from the Third Reich throughout the world, I can add that Mann maintained correspondence with all German centers and with countless individual writers.

In 1939 came the outbreak of the war. Klaus Mann was first to join the American Army, then later also Golo Mann. Quite a few German writers fought with weapons in their hands the man who had conquered their homeland from the inside, had given it its evil stamp, and had finally involved it in the completely untimely world war. Erika Mann was often in Europe as a war correspondent. Other German writers worked in war propaganda; for example, in soliciting war loans or in enlightening German Americans who had been flooded with National Socialist propaganda in the pre-war period. Thomas Mann was engaged in all this. There also came into being a great number of radio plays by German refugees for this inner political pedagogical enlightenment. Thomas Mann's chief contribution to the intellectual warfare in the Second World War was the fifty-six addresses to the German people which he sent from America via the British Broadcasting Company into the Third Reich. Like an angry preacher, he spoke to the conscience of his seduced countrymen, showed them the vicious meanness of the seducers whom they were following, opened their eyes to the degradation in which they were living and to the entire consequences of their senseless war, and tried to urge them on to free themselves from the destructive reign of terror. In the decade of Hitler's increasing power, Mann had undoubtedly experienced brief periods of depression from which pessimistic declarations arose, but again and again he quickly renewed his conviction that such a thoroughly evil government, which used lies, crimes, force, and all manner of false ideas for its basic principles of statehood could not exist permanently and certainly could not be victorious. The world could not tolerate it. His radio messages thus bear a moral stamp. I still remember how we listened to them in Denmark during the first years of the war, along with Winston Churchill's addresses, which undoubtedly had more political force. Even so, Mann's speeches had a strong, morally consoling effect, because they had often made it so clear against what and for what the fighting was being carried on at that time. Here is an example from the address of May 1941, when Hitler's armies invaded Greece. Mann is recalling the 300 Greeks who defended the narrow pass of Thermopylae against the Persians: "Your mighty masters have drummed into you that freedom is outmoded junk. Believe me, freedom still exists—it will... eternally be the same as it has been for 2,000 and some odd years, a light in the soul of the West; and the love, the fame of history will belong to those who died for it, not to those who ground it into the earth with tanks."

"Freedom is the light in the soul of the West." With such wonderful verbal creations, Thomas Mann became one of the most respected German refugees and revered speakers on the humanistic front against the Third Reich.

Since so many refugees from all the countries occupied by Hitler found asylum in the United States, international cooperation came into being among them. Klaus Mann, for example, published in 1941/42 in New York the English journal **Decision**, which united notable writers of various countries as **Die Samm-lung** formerly had done in Amsterdam. This time his father furnished contributions for the first and second volumes. Thomas Mann took part along with 16 other personalities in the **City of Man: A Declaration of World Democracy**, New York, 1940. The Moses story of 1943 **The Tables of the Law** is also the fruit of such international cooperation.

It is therefore not just an empty turn of phrase when, in 1944, Thomas Mann calls himself a "world citizen" on becoming an American citizen. He has outgrown German nationalism. He regards the United States of America under Franklin D. Roosevelt as the leading democratic power in the struggle for the free world. Since the German Republic, for which he broke a lance, was transformed into the Third Reich, which took away his citizen's privileges, America became the free port where one can act as an unfettered citizen of the world and work cooperatively for humanity on an earth grown small. His vision continues to expand. New questions bombard him; for example, Hitler's plan to liquidate six million Jews in the Third Empire and the execution of this plan during the Second World War. In a series of manifestos he denounces this genocide and warns, regrettably in vain, that the condemned people should be rescued. This cosmopolitan trait, which is typical of the standard bearers of humanity in the eighteenth century, had already appeared in Thomas Mann's public activity in the twenties and now becomes stronger in the United States. But soon he has to find out painfully that there are also evil influences and currents in American politics. In November 1947, the Security Council and the General Assembly of the United Nations decided to establish an Arabian and Jewish State in Palestine. The Arabians protested violently against this decision and assumed a threatening, war-like attitude. In March 1948, the American Government wanted to withdraw its agreement to this partition decision. At that point Thomas Mann published his sharp protest. He reacted not less sharply against Senator McCarthy, who dominated the Committee on Unamerican Activities and misused it for ruthless defamation and persecution against everyone who at that time had had the slightest contact with communism. During the period of this fanatic activity, there was no personal freedom and safety any longer in American democracy. This was one of the reasons why Thomas

Mann returned to Europe. This harassing anti-communism created an unbearable atmosphere for him. McCarthyism, to be sure, was beaten down a few years later by counterforces. But Thomas Mann's hope that the world forces united against Hitler—the Soviet Union and the United States—would hold together after 1945 and work together in the United Nations for the security of world peace was not fulfilled, and the "cold war" between the world powers and their allied blocs began and has not subsided even today, although at times it has thawed.

In 1952, therefore, Thomas Mann left his American refuge, where at times he felt he would spend his remaining twilight years. But it seemed impossible to him to return to West Germany, where he had lived in Lübeck and Munich. He settled down in his own house in Kilchberg on Lake Zürich in German Switzerland, where from 1933 to 1938 he had felt quite at home. But as he had already indicated in 1945 in his letter to Walter von Molo, he was not completely able to overcome the desire for his homeland. Sadness over his lost homeland —a suppressed nostalgia—consumed him. During his visit in Europe, he delivered his **Address in the Goethe Year** in the church of St. Paul in Frankfurt on 25 July 1949 and repeated it on 1 August 1949 in the National Theatre in Weimar. He did not permit the anti-communist fanaticism in West Germany to deter him from his concept that East and West would have to collaborate as he had already described it in 1944 in an essay **Fate and Mission** (in the **Deutsche Blätter**, Santiago de Chile). He also delivered his **Address in the Schiller Year** in West and East Germany on 8 May in Stuttgart and on 14 May 1955 in Weimar. He acted as a citizen of the world, who did not allow himself to be drawn away from his long-range goal—world peace—for the sake of ephemeral political opposition.

Erich Lüth, at that time press chief of the Hamburg Senate, described through letters and a newspaper report in Neues Hamburg XIV, 1959, how Thomas Mann's lectures in Hamburg were given at a time when criticism had been especially violent toward him. During the visit on 22 October 1952 in Zürich, he was able to convince Thomas Mann and even the skeptical Katja of the genuineness of the invitation to Hamburg. But Mann was still worrying about the question of his birthplace Lübeck, about whose mayor, Otto Passarge, Lüth was able to supply favorable information. During the last month of 1952 letters were exchanged, and in June 1953 the lectures at Hamburg met an enthusiastic reception. A visit in Travemünde followed, having been arranged by a delegation of four Lübeckers to Hamburg. Thus, the path was laid for the final reconciliation of Mann with his birthplace. On 20 May 1955, the city of Lübeck presented him with an honorary citizenship. During the celebration, he expressed his thanks in a short speech in which he moved the people of Lübeck to laughter and tears. Since that time even the conservative circles of Lübeck have given up their resistance. The merchants established two rooms in the Schabbelhaus as a small Thomas Mann Museum.

Before his death, Thomas Mann bequeathed to the Federal Technical Institute his total literary legacy, his diplomas and honors, the furniture from his study along with his working library and countless portraits of himself, in thanks for the award of his honorary doctorate. This legacy forms the basis for the Thomas Mann Archiv, which is housed in the Bothmer House next to the University and receives state support to develop it into an international research center of stature. A second archive of this type exists in the Library of Yale University. This is a fit monument to Thomas Mann's world citizenship and the position of his work in world literature.

His modest grave is located on Swiss soil in the little cemetery of Kilchberg near Zürich. His mortal remains and his effects are forever removed from the homeland which excluded and defamed him. It can only transform his German work and his human message into a true possession again through good will and fruitful enrichment of German tradition for the peaceful future of the German people.

IV.

THE DEMANDS OF THE DAY

READINGS AND LECTURES

In the year 1930, Thomas Mann published an anthology in Berlin in the S. Fischer Press with the title **The Demands of the Day.** It contains works whose subjects have come to the writer from the outside, diverted him from his artistic work, and brought him into direct connection with the time and the world about him. Actually, he often received the stimulus for a literary work from the outside. The publisher S. Fischer suggested to him that he write a novel. A young artist gave him the first impulse to occupy himself with the biblical Joseph. But there still remained a deep division between such stimuli and the demands of the day which had to be fulfilled within a definite period or the letters which waited for reply. All these achievements together surpass the literary writings in extent, so that one must not skip them in a study of his personality, as so often happens. There is however a bridge between them and the fictional writings—that is, the readings from his own works which begin around 1899 and are continued throughout his whole life, alternating with lectures. At first, the press complained about the fact that Thomas Mann read softly and without expression, but soon his shyness and modesty had been overcome and he developed into an outstanding and beloved reader, but he never practiced extemporaneous speaking. As long as his books brought in very little, these readings and lectures were economically necessary. Later they produced unusually high stipends. During tedious literary work, interruptions were oftentimes welcome. The daily effort could be tormenting and the work boring. Then travels produced all kinds of new impressions of landscapes, cities, people, music, and the theatre. Above and beyond this, Thomas Mann himself apparently took a great deal of pleasure in his public appearances, in stimulating conversations with the audiences which he held under the spell of his rhetoric during the readings. Mann's linguistic creativity is enhanced when the works are read aloud. In fact, only then do they achieve their full, vivid stature. The writer, himself very musical, emphasizes again and again the influence of music on his prose works—its close relationship with musical compositions. The language is not only conceived, it is heard like the tone structures of the composer. Anybody can test this on the records which preserve Thomas Mann's reading skill forever. Whoever has heard him knows what a pleasure it is to follow his expressive speech with its sonorous modulations, logical emphases, impressive pauses, and the sparse accompanying gestures and facial expressions, bringing every detail of the work into its full effectiveness. Right up to the last year of his life, his voice retained its clarity, firmness, melody, and expressiveness. Thomas Mann knew very well what an impression he made as a speaker. Like his Felix Krull, he wanted to win people over, to fascinate them and "enchant" them. This was also true for the lectures of various types, in which his temperament often was more strongly pronounced than in his literary works, where the effect is subdued and reserved for the sake of artistic balance.

10. ESSAYS AND OCCASIONAL WRITINGS

Closest to the literary writings are the thirty cultural essays which for the most part owe their origin to some kind of external demand. Thirteen are festive or anniversary lectures; ten form introductions to books; five were held at annual meetings and congresses; only two were composed completely on his own initiative: **Goethe and Tolstoi** and **Schopenhauer.** We may call these works essays because Mann had preceded all of them with very penetrating studies, especially the more extensive ones. Only ten of them are under 20 pages, eighteen from 20 to 64, only two over 100 pages, **Goethe and Tolstoy** 116, **Essay on Schiller** 183 pages.

Doubtlessly, Thomas Mann could have become a good humanistic scholar if he had devoted himself to this field. Since he was himself an artist, he penetrated quite deeply into the artistic work of the writers, poet-philosophers, and musicians with whom he occupied himself in these essays, and he was very much interested in psychology. But he was not systematic and was not methodically trained in research, for which reason all of them harbor a substantial vein of subjectivity. Added to this is a strong element of the artistic structuring of language. These ingredients give the works their essayistic character and differentiate them from scientific treatises.

The majority of these essays, whose intense language often betrays the poet's vital interests, are occupied with the personalities and works which he was exposed to during the most receptive period of his youth or which have strongly influenced his artistic creations subsequently. The "triple constellation" in his intellectual heaven unites the philosophers Schopenhauer and Nietzsche with the musician Wagner. Schopenhauer is represented with one, the others with two essays apiece. Other philosophers and musicians are represented not at all. The

"Holy" Russian literature is treated in four essays: Tolstoi in two, Dostoevsky and Chekhov with one apiece. Goethe is represented most strongly with ten contributions. Romanticism appears in three works; one on Chamisso, two on Kleist. In addition there are Lessing, Schiller, and Platen and from recent times, Fontane and Storm as marvels of style from the 19th century; from his contemporaries: Gerhard Hauptmann, Bernard Shaw, and the creator of psychoanalysis, Sigmund Freud; further, there are discussions on Cervantes and Michelangelo.

I have already discussed the works on Wagner, Nietzsche, Schopenhauer, and Goethe. To treat all the essays in such detail as the creative writings would burst the framework of my book. I want to dwell a little more closely on just two more personalities.

Schiller belongs to the early experiences of Thomas Mann. As early as 1905 he had already composed the living nocturnal picture **A Weary Hour.** In the essays on Goethe and the novel **The Beloved Returns,** there is understandably a lot of talk about him and his beneficial friendship with Schiller. 1955 saw the origin of the great **Essay on Schiller.** (To be sure, I prefer the heavily abbreviated speech that he lifted out of the ponderous essay with the aid of his daughter Erika.) The full essay is a well-balanced, moving work. It begins solemnly with the nocturnal burial of the dead man in the crypt, without accompaniment or tolling of bells, and immediately makes the transition into a hymn to the intellectual figure which rises up from the mortal remains. In order to come quite close to Schiller, the speaker quotes here, and then often later, the words of the celebrated poet in verse and prose—very often little-known passages, never the familiar, tired, quotations. He does not hesitate to illuminate sufficiently his naive boyishness, which may often call for a smile. He then refers to the sickly poet's unusually difficult, care-filled life, from which he ekes out his gigantic literary production, and especially to the long series of powerful dramas which capture the audience again and again, whenever played. He spends a fleeting moment on the poet's marriage, which brought relaxation and peace to this tense and idealistic spirit, but he dwells much longer on the tenuous friendship with Goethe, who met his passionate approaches with reservation and who did not completely realize, until many years after the death of his friend, what he lost. The relationship of the two is marvelously illuminated by boldly chosen and interpreted verses. Schiller was a poet and a political man. Thomas Mann lends the highest dignity to his address by letting it rightfully end in a political appeal. Picking up the thread of Schiller's announcement in his journal **Die Horen**, in which he calls for the intellectual conquest of narrow, fanatic nationalism, Mann calls his intellectual legacy a vitamin which is lacking in the present in frightening measure and challenges the German people to work vigorously for peace in the world. This eloquently delivered address, solemnly elevated, born along by a genuine enthusiasm, and preserved on a record, should be heard again and again at Schiller and Thomas Mann celebrations in every cultivated home. It is one of the treasures from Thomas Mann's rich legacy."

In his essays, Thomas Mann has followed the lead in Schiller's treatise On Naive and Sentimental Poetry, but the dramatist Schiller has hardly influenced his works. On the other hand, the psychiatrist Sigmund Freud, creator of psychoanalysis, influenced his work very heavily. On 16 May 1929, before the Democratic students in Munich, Mann delivered the lecture **The Position of Freud in Modern Thought**— and on 8 May 1936, as the anniversary speech for Freud's 80th birthday in Vienna. In a great essay, Gunnar Brandell, Uppsala, has put together for the first time all the various conditions and precursors in the nineteenth century that make the emergence of Freud's depth psychology understandable as a historical phenomenon. More generally, one can say that the concept of the human soul changes fundamentally in this age. It frees itself from theology more and more. One no longer conceives of the soul as a unity with these or those prophecies; its independence is recognized, the independence of the body, the independence inherited from the forefathers back to the protocell, the independence from the influences of the surrounding world. Related to this development of psychology, an essential characteristic of European literature of the nineteenth

---

*The speaker says at one point: "Providence" instead of "Research," on the basis of two errors in the manuscript which probably go back to a dictation: Vorsehung instead of Forschung.

century is the deepening and enrichment of the description of human beings on the psychological level. Thomas Mann's passionate interest in the science of the human soul is apparent; for this reason even around 1910 when Sigmund Freud was still hotly contested and brusquely rejected on many sides, Mann became attentive to the new direction which Freud was giving to science by cutting a path for it into the subconscious with his dream interpretation and throwing light onto its dynamics—the struggle between the forces of the clear consciousness and the dark ones of the emotional world.

In his observations Thomas Mann is concerned about three things: he establishes the relationships between psychoanalysis and the romantic tradition, he describes in detail what binds him and his writings with it, and he evaluates the new doctrine as a revolutionary, optimistic, and positive force. As early as 1929 he expounds the fact that many aphorisms of the early romanticist Novalis antedate the whole doctrine of Schopenhauer of the domination of the will over the intellect and many essayistic observations of Nietzsche presage elements of depth psychology. Mann does not overlook the danger which threatens humanity from the spread of the intellectually hostile doctrines of the primacy of primitive, irrational life and the possibility that preoccupation with the chaotic, subconscious world could furnish weapons for the struggle against the age of enlightenment through reason. But in contradistinction he emphasizes that Freud's doctrine has an intellectually revolutionizing effect in the genuine sense: "This revolutionary principle, it is simply the will of the future, which Novalis has called 'properly, the better world.' Psychoanalysis serves it by making the subconscious conscious, dissolving and destroying false agreements, and furthering the unity of life, the culture of the free self-conscious human being..." It is "that very manifestation of modern irrationalism which resists unambiguously every reactionary mis-usage."

Even in his festival speech of 1936, Mann speaks in detail of Schopenhauer and Nietzsche as precursors in the area of the subconscious life of the spirit. But here myth becomes the chief subject. Since his youth, Freud had nurtured a passionate interest in mythology. In the phrase, "depth psychology," 'depth' also has temporal significance. It illuminates the depth of the past back into the age of mythical thinking, as Freud has shown in his book **Totem and Taboo.** The primeval bases of the human soul are simultaneously primeval time, where myth establishes the protoforms of life, observes Thomas Mann. This concept of myth as prototype is the most important one that Thomas Mann derives from his concern with Freud's myth studies, a completely different one from that of the psychologist himself, for whom the interpretation of the myth was important.

The influence of Freudian depth psychology on Mann's writings is powerful and varied. We detect it wherever he uncovers deeper layers of spiritual events, as in the countless betraying dreams which he encapsulates, like the first dream of Mut-en-Emets which reveals the condition of her soul to her. In his festival speech Mann dwells primarily on his biblical novel. In the life of Joseph, he is representing an experienced myth in which the soul shapes its fate. This is the epic idea of the novel, which is constantly accompanied with irony. With a charming kind of religious swindling, Joseph is recalling the Tammuz-Osiris myth in his own person, is permitting the life of the one who was rent asunder, buried, and resurrected to happen again on himself: "The secret of the metaphysician and psychologist that the giver of everything given is the soul—this secret becomes light, playful, artistic, gay, indeed a tilting at straws and clownish in Joseph; it reveals his infantile nature."

Then with a series of great historical examples, he shows what an experienced myth is: "No doubt about it, the accomplishment of this typological manner of viewing the world mythically is epic-making in the life of the narrator. It signifies a peculiar elevation of his artistic mood, a new joy of recognition and structuring. ... What is gained by this is the view for the higher truth which is represented in that which is real, the happy knowledge of the eternal, that which always is, the valid, of the plan in which and according to which what is presumably completely individual lives, not suspecting in the naive limitation of his uniqueness how very much his life is formula and repetition, a journeying in deeply worn tracks." Along with Goethe, Freud exercised the strongest influence on Mann during the time after the First World War.

Finally the poet celebrates the life's work of the scholar as an important building stone toward a new anthropology and toward the foundations of the future, the edifice of a more astute and freer humanity. Psychoanalysis as the science of the subconscious is a healing method on a grand scale. "Where it was, shall I become," says Freud himself. He compares psychoanalytic work with the draining of the Zuider Zee. That gives the festival speaker the occasion to compare him with Faust, who reclaims from the ocean free soil for a free people.

There is quite an extensive relationship between Thomas Mann's essays and his narratives. Since naturalism, a great portion of the more demanding modern literature rests on all kinds of scientific studies that give it weight and also a certain ponderousness. Thomas Mann carries out extensive preparatory studies for his longer short stories and novels. In this way a substantial strain of essayistic contents creeps into his narrative art, which is fitted into the epic structure with every imaginable artistic means. Among them we could designate in **Buddenbrooks** the observation on Schopenhauer, the description of Hanno's improvisation on the piano, and at the conclusion the description of typhoid fever, rich in technical expressions, to which Hanno falls victim. In the short story **Tonio Kröger**, the rarely interrupted monologue in the studio with the painter Lisabeta stands as a nucleus in the middle—a stylized essay. In the novels **Royal Highness**, **The Magic Mountain**, **Joseph and His Brothers**, and **Doctor Faustus**, there are many pieces of an essayistic character, for the most part restructured into lectures, conversations, letters, and observations of the narrator.

Thomas Mann's shorter book reviews cannot be separated sharply from the essays according to their content. Writers and publishers sent him many books which, for the most part, he read immediately or soon after receiving them. He was apparently often eager to get to know new works of his contemporaries, in his service to literature. While he worked very slowly on his own narratives, he was in a position to form a critical judgment immediately, to illuminate the work from various points of view, and to write all this down quickly in a publishable form. Even with books of very slight value, he found something to praise in a friendly way before he passed in conclusion his negative judgment.

Only rarely did a book meet with complete rejection, as was the case with Oswald Spengler's **The Decline of the West**, in

'iew of March 9, 1924. Thomas Mann calls the title
'ely catastrophic," in spite of its gigantic international
'. He describes the intellectual situation in Germany
defeat, which brought forth an almost limitless Rus-
discussion and new kinds of books in which science
came mixed up. Counted among them are the critic
'eyserling's **Travel Diary of a Philosopher,** the
'ietzsche book by Ernst Bertram, and the "monu-
on Goethe by Friedrich Gundolf. Mann recog-
rary polish and the intuitive rhapsodic manner"
descriptions of Spengler. Then, however,
judgment:

...gler denies being a pessimist. But even less does
he want to call himself an optimist. He is a fatalist. But
his fatalism, summed up in the sentence: 'We must want
that which is necessary or nothing,' is far removed from
bearing the tragic heroic character, the Dionysian character in which Nietzsche negated the contrast between
pessimism and optimism. Rather, it bears the character of an evil apodicticity and a hostility toward the future
which disguises itself in scientific inexorability. It is
not **amor fati.** With 'amor' he has very little to do—and
that is its most repelling aspect. The question is not
pessimism or optimism: One can take a very dim view
of the fate of man who perhaps is eternally condemned to
suffering or is called; one can wrap himself up in the
deepest skepticism whenever the talk is about 'happiness,' about the 'happiness' which is ostensibly waiting
some time in the future—without gaining the slightest
taste for the pedagogical lack of sympathy of Spengler's
fatalism. Pessimism is not lovelessness. It does not
necessarily mean an ice-cold 'scientific' control over
development and a hostile disregard of such imponder-
ables as the spirit and will of man represented by virtue of
the fact that they do perhaps after all mix an element of
irrationality inaccessible to calculating science with development. Such arrogance, however, and such disregard
of the human element are Spengler's portion. If he were
only as cynical as a devil! But he is only—boring. And

he does not do well to call Goethe, Schopenhauer, and Nietzsche precursors of his hyena-like prophecy. Those were men. He, however, is only a defeatist of humanity.

On top of this harsh rejection which is like an execution, there falls naturally a brief clear presentation of Spengler's doctrine with explanations which support and confirm the judgment. It is characteristic of Mann that after 1922 he struggles against a seductive intellectual current of the time because it has a laming and restrictive effect on the ethical spirit and will of mankind leading toward affirmation of life and optimism toward the future. The positive criticisms outweigh the others by far. Thomas Mann is always willing to express his admiration for literary performances and does it by clearly underscoring their individuality. The following are some excerpts as examples:

From the introduction to a Russian anthology of the Süddeutsche Monatshefte in February 1922:

All in all, only Pushkin gives us the historic and pre-modern feeling—the Goethe of the East. He constructs a sphere for himself, a sensually radiant one, naive, gay, and poetic. But with Gogol there starts immediately what Merischkowski calls the 'critique' or the 'transition from unconscious creation to creative consciousness' and what for him in fact signifies the end of poetry in the Pushkin sense, but at the same time it is the beginning of something new, very futuristic. In a word, from Gogol on, Russian literature is modern. With him everything that up to that time had remained such closely knit tradition in its history is all at once there: Instead of poetry, there is criticism; instead of naiveté, the religious problematic; and instead of gaity, comedy. Particularly the latter. Since Gogol, Russian literature is comic—comedy originating from realism, from suffering and sympathy, from deepest humanity, from satiric desperation, even from simple vitality; but the Gogolian comic element is lacking nowhere nor in any case. Even Dostoevsky's epileptic-apocalyptic world of shadows is shot through with uncontrolled comedy—moreover he did write what are clearly comic novels, like **Little Uncle's**

Dreams, and **Stepantschikowo's Farm**, filled with the spirit of Shakespeare and Molière. Even the ponderous and learned Tolstoi can be humorous to the point of abandon, at times even where he is at his most moral, as in the folk tales. And this Russian humor in its truth and warmth, its fantastic nature and its deep, heart-warming drollness is, if we permit our heart to speak, the most charming and rewarding kind in the world—neither the English nor the Jean Paul German humor is to be compared with it, to say nothing of France, which is dry; and wherever one finds something similar outside Russia, there Russian influence is apparent, as in the case of Hamsun. But then what is it that gives Russian humor these humanly attractive powers? Without a doubt, the fact that it is of religious origin. This can be demonstrated in the case of Gogol, who established a school with it, right at its literary source. 'All my efforts,' he says in a letter, 'are intended that everyone who has heard my works can laugh to his heart's content at the devil.' 'To make a fool out of the devil'—that is the mystical sense of Russian humor and 'heart's content' in fact the exact designation for its effects.

We see here how familiar Mann is with Russian literature, and understand why he calls it in **Tonio Kröger** the "Holy Russian literature."

On 16 April 1922, a letter to Hans Reisiger, who had translated Walt Whitman's poems into German, appeared in the **Frankfurter Zeitung**:

I am thoroughly delighted at possessing your Whitman work and cannot thank you enough, just as I also think that the German public will not be able to thank you enough for this great, important, indeed sacred gift. Since I have had them I keep picking up both volumes again and again, and reading here and there. I read right away the biographical introduction and call it a minor masterpiece of love. Truly, Herr Reisiger, the fact that through enthusiastic work and long devotion you have brought close to us Germans this powerful intellect, this bursting and at the same time deep new humanity, is a service of the first order, for we are old and at the same time immature, and for us the contact with this humanity of the future can work as a blessing if we know how to receive it. With the slowness peculiar to me, I have wrestled inwardly for years with the idea of humanity, convinced that for Germany there is no more vital task than to bring this concept into fulfillment again that has become an empty hull, a mere school term. For me personally this work is a true gift of the Lord, for I see indeed that what Whitman calls 'democracy' is nothing more than what we call in an old-fashioned way 'humanity.' Likewise I also see that Goethe alone is simply not enough but that a little bit of Whitman is necessary to capture the feeling of the new humanity, especially since these two fathers have a great deal in common, above all the sensual element, the 'calamus,' sympathy with the organic... In short, their deed—this word is not too vague and strong—can be of inestimable effect and I, though no longer young and eager, still want to be among those who have knowingly congratulated you!

It is therefore not accidental that Walt Whitman slipped into the speech The German Republic in October 1922!

Under the title "Rejuvenating Books," Mann published in the Frankfurter Zeitung of 17 April 1927 a collective review from which I select a few words:

Franz Kafka's books, for example, absolutely unique structures of sublime precision, the little stories as well as the discursive fantasies The Trial and The Castle —upsetting, weirdly humorous, masterful, and sickly, the most strangely penetrating entertainment that one can imagine. It was the poet Max Brod in Prague who tore it away from his publicity-shy friend and who as executor and editor, devotedly takes care of the legacy of the writer who died prematurely, still not sufficiently thanked by the public for this intermediary work. It is rare that a productive spirit like Brod—who has written the important historical novel Tycho Brahe's Way to God and Reubeni, in addition to the moving book so rich in pleasant formulations, Paganism, Christianity, Judaism— should show himself capable of such an unselfish act of love toward a foreign intellectual property.

This is an extremely early recognition of Kafka, who since has become world famous and belongs among the most discussed modern writers. There is still another extensive evaluation of Franz Kafka and the novel **The Castle** in the American edition, 1941.

When the book-dealer C.H.E. Fritze, Stockholm, asked Mann to write the introduction to a catalogue, **Foreign Books 1929,** he wrote about twelve German writers, among others:

I begin with Alfred Döblin, whose novel **Berlin Alexanderplatz** is just now exciting great attention. By virtue of his bold and sharp artistic intelligence, his great ambition, his closeness to life, and his power of imagery, which remained original even as it was growing—this writer is about to step into the lead of the German movement. After several grand epic experiments, the Chinese novel **The Three Leaps of Wang-Lun,** a Wallenstein novel, the futuristic novel **Mountains, Oceans and Giants,** and the Indian verse epic **Manas,** this writer has now found himself completely by making his life's experiences as a doctor for the poor in East Berlin into his material. Space forbids me from dwelling more closely on the interesting work, exciting because of its artistic means, but I confess that I stand in admiration before this grandly successful attempt to lift the proletarian reality of our time into the epic sphere.

This is an especially convincing testimony for the rapid recognition of an unusual new literary achievement which Mann would probably have rejected or left unnoticed prior to 1914.

For Franz Masereel, Thomas Mann wrote introductions to two of his wood carving series, which he himself called "novels in pictures," for the German edition of the **Stundenbuch** 1926, and for the French edition of **Jeunesse,** 1948.

I regret it but I have never experienced with full force the world of the 'image,' the spiritualization of the visible through pigment or stone, but always only occasionally and secondarily. On my respectful visits of obligation and education in this sphere, I gained little enthusiasm, love, pleasure of veneration, stimulus for my own capacities. I am comparing this with the fullness of all that came to me from literature—from the art work of the highest articulation and from that mystically articulated "language of sounds," the wonderfully abstract world of figures and motion in music.

In both works he is not interested so much in the artistic principles—although he praises the "old, noble, pious" craft of the wood-cut—but for the content.

Masereel was national and real; the war Europeanized and intellectualized him. That is a typical and familiar situation: idealization under the pressure of the war experience, the compulsion toward the intellect, toward the revolutionizing thought process which it imposes. [Here Mann is apparently thinking of his own Reflections of a Non-political Man]. But rarely or never has this experience caused such an intensification and elevation of art, such a growth into that which is humanly important and of worldly validity as in the case of Masereel. He was an indifferent sensual talent who sketched in Belgian dives. The war made him an intellectual figure, an organ of public conscience.

In 1926, Mann first describes the wood-carver's masterpiece in compressed brevity, called The City:

Our whole civilization is captured in its brutal fantasm, in these hundred tablets, as viewed with a critical and pitying glance, grotesque and horrifying in inexorable communality. It is rigid with tragic, evil, damnable absurdity; all the faces of the crassest present roll by in turning the pages of this German-Dutch "block-book"....
In any case we are dealing with a meeting and a marriage, the penetration of the democratic movie spirit with the aristocratic spirit of art, the intellectualization and spiritualization of a pleasure up to that time wildly sensational.

Then he dwells at great length on the Stundenbuch and concludes with a long admonition to the readers. The beginning and conclusion go as follows:

Take his work, old but still new, aristocratic and free,

the work of his industrious hands full of tradition and the present, the master film of an artist's life! Mix with the hero into the strange and complex human world, be astonished, laugh and let yourself go! ... In turning over the pages permeate yourself with the whole puzzling nature, with this dream of human existence here on earth which is transitory since it ends and dissipates, and still, in its transitoriness, infinity is present everywhere making it real! Look and enjoy and let your staring be deepened through brotherly trust!

In 1948, Mann writes about Masereel's picture novel **Youth**:

This artist's attitude was never scorn and skepticism. With all his capacity for suffering, with all the torture resulting from the falseness of our social conditions, a certain robustness of belief and hope always distinguished him from most of those who began with him. Goodness of the highest type, today the most indispensable property of the spirit, in which love, belief, and hope are united. This goodness teaches him to be a friendly, helpful, happy, serious, advising, warning comrade for these naive bearers of a future that may still be brighter. ... His picture poem of youth is beautiful, touching, and stimulating. Is it simply poem, goodness, dream? Are rage, blood, and complete destruction to become the fate of this earth instead of work and joy? Masereel's restlessly formative love harkens to the song of the Faustian angel choir and chimes in with it:"We bid you hope."

The reviews are frequently placed in the front of books as introductions or prefaces, or else reproduced in press brochures and on dust-jackets. Quite often they take the form of letters to the authors or publishers of the books. This activity of Thomas Mann is astonishingly broad. Bürgin cites 186 such works. Only a selection is included in his edition of the works, the rest of them are scattered far throughout the world in newspapers, journals, and books. Eight letters from Germany to The Dial in New York in the years 1922-1928 form a special group. They are reports on cultural phenomena and events. During the period of catastrophic money devaluation, they were a welcome dollar source for Mann and were then continued at extended intervals.

214

Related to the essays and reviews are the eulogies and tes-
timonials,the congratulatory wishes for birthdays and jubilees,
and the elegies or memorial speeches for departed personalities. Bürgin lists 123. Mann is always endeavoring to hold
fast the nature and creativity of man. Here are some excerpts:

To Max Liebermann on his 80th birthday 1927:

In Liebermann I marvel at Berlin, which one can admire
better from Munich than if one were to live there. I find
it magnificent that he speaks the brisk,fresh Berlin jargon, pure and unadulterated, and when I am with him in
his house on Pariser Platz I feel I am at the focal point
and gathering place of gay and powerful character forces,
at a representative and symbolic place, in the residence
of the **genius loci**: a feeling to which the amalgam of
freedom, boldness, greatness, sovereignty contributes
not a little and envelopes the well-bred and charming
personality of the master of the household.
  Berlin is energy, intelligence, strictness, unsenti-
mentality, unromanticism, the lack of any exaggerated
reverence for the past—modernity as futuricity, cosmo-
politanism as the absence of Germanic teariness—and
with this I am naming the chief characteristics of a
geniality which I love with similarly pure and innocent
respect like the art of Fontane, whose Berlinism was
sublimated, refined, Europeanized through the influence
of Gascony, like that of Liebermann's by the Jewish element. The critic in me might certainly try to celebrate
him, but this present demand to write about the great
painter gives me feelings of inadequacy.

From **In Memoriam S. Fischer**, **Basler Nachrichten**, 28
October 1934:

People have called him the "Cotta of naturalism," and it
is good naturalism to bring together, as I am inclined to
do, the publishing genius of this little Hungarian Jew—
originally rather inadequately educated—with his tenderness and receptivity. I speak of genius because it is very
easy and incorrect to brush off the secret of his success
with the formula 'more luck than brains.' Without unusual **gifts** no one builds up a life's work like his, even

though it may not be so easy to determine these gifts. The peculiar Jewish love for the 'book,' for the document, for the intellect is united in him with an infallible and almost tangible artistic sense of quality—the tactile sense for purity and value of a thing according to its fiber and grain, the critical instinct with which even at an advanced age he emerged superior to those around him and all his opposition. Whenever he shook his head and said with a drooping lower lip: "That has no magic," it probably sounded a little like literary jargon, but he hit the nail on the head with it. For the product in question, written neatly and engagingly as it was in any case, was lacking transparency and higher art. Poetically there was something not quite right about it, and the author did not go to press.

Thomas Mann himself found out that Samuel Fischer recognized the "magic" in his earlier works:

Through almost four decades, my work was united with this enterprise which he established forty-eight years ago and which was to develop to such great importance, and play such an important role in German intellectual life. Part of my own life is lowered into the grave with this tired old man, and an epoch passes to which I felt intellectually and morally bound. There are still a few representatives of this epoch here and there carrying on their life's work to its end in a climate which is no longer their own.

During our last meeting he was no longer completely clear at every moment about where he was.... Suddenly however he began to pass an opinion on a young mutual acquaintance: "No European," he said, shaking his head—'No European, Mr. Fischer, how do you mean that?" "He does not understand anything about great humane ideas."
—I cannot say how shaken I was. At that point, almost out of the night, a generation was speaking which was greater and better than the one which is now taking this issue out of my hand.

On the sixtieth birthday of Bruno Walter, Mann wrote (on 27 February 1936) a congratulatory article:

I thank fate that it gave me this contemporary who was
created and gifted so completely differently from myself,
as a mediator between my sphere and the one in which
he labors as only few do and have done: music. The love
for this mysterious, exacting, and abundant art was born
in me and has become deepened through decisive cultural experiences, the meeting with great spirits who were
passionately fond of it and created out of this spirit. And
early it was my own ambition and my desire to braid together the nature and effect of music with that of the
word, to weave, to 'think,' and to combine its nature, to
relate it to music and to have the narrative arise as a
web of themes and counterpoint, as a resounding architecture of ideas. Our friend who is now sixty has recently spoken to me about these things on my own sixtieth
birthday in an open letter with greatest tenderness and
correctness. With the kind of loyal cleverness and keen-
ness of recognition, highly characteristic of his nature,
he knew how to show how music has been my guide not
only from a technical, artistic point of view, but also intellectually and even spiritually. In the role of the seducer god, music has led me as a poet from my proper
social sphere to myth and even gay mystery. At this
point I mention this document which has brought me a
great deal of pleasure, this little masterpiece of festive-
friendly character analysis, simply to indicate what
Walter, the musician and outstanding director, has contributed to my 'musical relationship,' a relationship to
literature and a critical disposition... an ardently intelligent love for the world of the spirit and of poetry, a cosmopolitan education and reading background that is revealed in conversation almost more enthusiastically even
than his passion for his own craft and without which this
tremendous artist would not be what he is: more, you
see, than a type, even a culture—a fully established, enlightened, cultured spirit whose musical genius, wonderful as it is, draws its higher superiority and authority;
his human, I would almost like to say, social right to
command, out of the sphere of articulated humanity, out
of the literary sphere.

In conclusion Mann also shows us the director:

At the podium, in front of the orchestra ... the type and gestures of his conducting and instruction, his urging, softening, and commanding with head and hands—this creative, emulative challenging pantomime of one completely in charge of the music which affected me from my youth and to which I follow for hours at a time with my eyes while my ear belongs to the notes—as a phenomenon of a very unique type: archaic and elegant at the same time, related to the dance, to the mime—entranced and exact, conjuration and culturally conscious meticulous expression.

In 1936 Thomas Mann sent along an accompanying word for Erika Mann's cabaret **The Peppermill** on a trip to America:

One would not do wrong in calling the 'Peppermill' the swan song of the German Republic...the little group bears a saucy name; but it is precisely this mixture of saucyness and purity which distinguishes it above other attempts of an externally related type. There is nothing in the songs and scenes in this cabaret of banal spicyness or of stupid obscenity.... Its scope extends from the charmingly lyrical to the burlesque and profoundly grotesque; but all the wit, exuberance, fantasy, comedy so lightly and entertainingly sprinkled throughout permits a fund of melancholy, of sorrow over the evil, over lies and force. There is a delicate concern for the better and loftier in man to shine through to the finer senses. This has gained the approbation of every gracious public for the little theatre.

In a memorial speech for Max Reinhardt, Thomas Mann said the following in Los Angeles on 15 December 1942:

The theatre—original home of sensual intellectuality and intellectual sensuality—can rightfully be called the paradigm for every mission of art. The fact that Reinhardt's theatre was theatre so completely from the heart, so joyous and devout, a high festival full of charm and magic—that is what made it into such a fascinating, such a joyful experience for all of us artists.... Indeed how very much this man and artist belonged to the 'picture,' to our world... I knew him early; the reserved, quiet masculinity of his nature, his reflective and clear manner of speaking, his shrewdly perceptive nature—in short, his personality impressed me... and to see him at work, as in rehearsals at Berlin...belonged to the most interesting experiences of my life. At that time I understood the passionately grateful devotion which the members of his theatrical company, the actors, gave to him.... As a director Reinhardt forced nothing on these artists of the most direct physical-spiritual nature that could be foreign to them. He did not tyrannize them, but with tender empathy he got out of each one of them what was most peculiar to him, his very best, and he made it live, radiate, and have its effect.... All the heights and depths of the human phenomenon which is called 'theatre,' open up when one talks about the master that we have lost.

On 29 March 1950, on the occasion of the death of his brother Heinrich, Thomas Mann wrote among other things:

A bold experimenter in the area of the novel, confessor and moralist by blood, his figure grew in time to great intellectual dignity.... He was not concerned about peace, satisfaction, spiritual safety and security, but on the contrary his lot was unrest, creative doubt, an endless approach to the truth—a lifelong wooing of it with all the means of his intellect and art...this great essayist achieved perfection in the fascinating books of memoirs **An Age is Viewed,** an autobiography as criticism of the age he had lived through—an age of indescribable severity and gay brilliance, naive wisdom and moral dignity. His work is written in a prose whose intellectually elastic simplicity appears to me as the language of the future.

Since celebrated personalities were often close to Thomas Mann, his "adulations and laurel wreaths" are rich in personal memories and confessions. This is especially true of the speech which Mann gave for the seventieth birthday of his life's companion, Katja Mann, on 24 July 1953 to an intimate circle in Zürich:

I had seen her long before I saw her then, when I was still a mere youth as a student in distant old Lübeck.... His excellency von Kaulbach in Munich had very good luck with a picture called 'Children's Carnival'...that

depicted five children with black curly hair and ivory
skin in pierrot costumes, pointed caps on their heads
next to one another in a row, four boys and a wide-eyed
sweet little girl at the end...that masterful painting in
its way caused a sensation....As a high school junior in
Lübeck, I saw a large reproduction of it in an illustrated journal and found it so charming and worth looking at
that I clipped it out and fastened it with drawing pins over
my desk.... I was just as little curious as other people
about how the artist arrived at his subject. But they
were the children of the Munich mathematics professor
Pringsheim... and so even as a schoolboy I had my future wife constantly before my eyes in unsuspecting
pleasure—the now seventy-year-old woman who has been
sharing this life with me for forty-eight years, soon for
half a century....

Did the lovely flower at that time know what she was
doing when she gave in to the entreaties of the young man
who had nothing but his love and the surprised and surprising reception of a fortunate first novel completed by
him in shy loneliness? Schiller's **Song of the Bell** sings
of the man who has to go out into the hostile life...who-
ever has to go out into this 'hostile world,' knock around
in it, deal with people...must fight in order to maintain
his external life and at the same time screen off the
dreamer's activities and ambitions delicately from the
disturbing, practical, business affairs which would exhaust him and make him useless for his life's struggle.
The one to whom this role falls is his wife—his wife for
a whole lifetime....

There she sits and types the stenograms of my dictated
letters, records, publishers' payments. She works out
the tax declarations and in between writes long motherly
letters of advice to our distant children. She diverts
some visitors and instructs others to leave again punc-
tually. Burdened down by a thousand jobs, her alert
spirit is still awake for eager participation in public life
and world events.

Her energetically mercurial temperament is full of impatience—impatience with laziness, the disturbing slowness of the world and people, the frittering away of time

which all this lethargy exacts from her quickness. And what patience she had to learn and exercise herocially as my companion who bore my burden with me! These horrible novels in which something impossible always had to be made possible, whose origin dragged out year after year in daily deliberation and insertions which also consumed years....

[There were festivals and honors.] They made me happy for her sake, because they made her happy, made her childishly proud and, as a result, unburdened my conscience. I laid them all at her feet, in a thankfulness which could not otherwise be expressed for her unshakable persistence in the face of my slowness, for the heroic patience, for which her love and loyalty steadied her natural impatience....

If any kind of after-life is accorded me, the essence of my being or my work, then she will live with me at my side. As long as people think of me, they will think of her. If posterity has a good word for me, it will apply at the same time to her, as a reward for her vivaciousness, her active loyalty, endless patience and courage.

Beyond these Bürgin reports sixty-two purely autobiographical notices. Oftentimes they also contain observations about his own works. However, the majority are truly reports on his life at various intervals. In introductory lectures or on the basis of inquiries, Thomas Mann is also very fond of writing elucidations for his own works. Bürgin cites 113 printed articles of this type. Lübeck as an Intellectual Form of Life belongs here as well as introductions to editions in foreign languages, and a lecture at Princeton. The most extensive such article is **The Origin of Doctor Faustus, Story of a Novel.** These elucidations have by no means been cited completely in Bürgin's twelve volumes of the works. Finally, there are an additional ninety-two questionnaires, for the most part on cultural matters, which Thomas Mann gladly answered.

The scope of his concern with questions of the day in the cultural sphere is astonishingly large. The few excerpts which I cite will make it clear with what an alert interest the poet follows the intellectual currents and phenomena of his time, how passionately he takes a position on these matters, what a welter of associations, points of view, and thoughts he brings to them, what a capacity he has for characterizing each individual one, regardless of the high watchtower from which he delivers his opinions and how subject to enthusiasm he is. Most of these public pronouncements contain passages of emotional language in a high style. If we survey the themes of all these literary performances using the bibliography as a guide, we grasp the all-inclusive scope of his field of vision and his sphere of interest. We become acquainted with the rich, receptive intellectual personality of Thomas Mann in them, even more directly and more broadly than in the writings that are intensified, stylized, and varnished with irony.

11. POLITICAL MANIFESTOS

When Thomas Mann climbed down into the political arena in 1914, he was entering a territory which was unspeakably foreign to him by virtue of his nature, his individualistic romantic point of view, and his artistic work. In three sections of this book, I have already presented his political development and effectiveness, in **Reflections of a Non-Political Man, Political Morality**, and **Return of the Citizen of the World to Europe.** It was a long route with unexpected, sudden turns from the Lübeck patrician son who took over the political points of view of his surrounding world—uncritically, because he had no interest in this sphere—via the "slave galley" work of the years 1915 to 1917 up to the confessor of 1922, the good European of the Twenties, the fighting humanist against the National Socialist barbarism and the Hitlerian reign of terror, and finally the world citizen of the last period in his life. The concept of humanity gained a vital new content for Mann beyond the personal "nobility of the spirit": The new man is supposed to be friendly toward other men and the future, not blocked off from social and political life. With human kindness he should join himself to fate of all in his thoughts and deeds. For this reason, without ever joining up with one party or mixing into the details of the political questions of the day, Mann more and more frequently takes a position in the struggle for humanity and against phenomena which injure freedom and the dignity of man. He himself feels and says that an inner relationship exists between his artistic creation and such political activity since as an artist he is also a moralist and critic of society.

First we shall establish at this point the great scope of his political expressions that for the most part have the character of manifestos, or energetic appeals and challenges that address themselves to the human conscience. Bürgin notes thirteen titles of separate German editions:

The German Republic, Berlin 1923.

An Appeal to Reason, Berlin 1930.

Intellectual Message, Berlin 1932.

A Correspondence, Zürich 1937.

On the Coming Victory of Democracy, Zürich 1938.

Europe, Beware!, collection (191 pages), New York and Zürich 1938.

This Peace, Stockholm 1938.

The Problem of Freedom, Stockholm 1939.

This War, Stockholm 1940.

Listen, Germany: 25 radio broadcasts to Germany (152 pages), Stockholm 1942.

Listen, Germany: 55 radio broadcasts to Germany (132 pages), Stockholm 1945.

Suffering from Germany: Diary pages from the years 1933 and 1934, Los Angeles 1946

Germany and the Germans, Stockholm 1947.

Among the widely scattered contributions, Bürgin cites one hundred and forty-nine of a political nature from the period 1922 to 1955. We are definitely dealing then not with a handful of occasional pronouncements, but with a constantly alert attention toward the political events of the time.

Politics doubtlessly made the most powerful, most stimulating, most urgent demands on the individualistic artist Thomas Mann. But even if at times he felt a little unhappy in a role which world history had forced on him—above all, whenever he became conscious of the relatively slight influence which he could exercise against the elemental forces encountered in the political battle—it is unmistakable that his personality took on very different characteristics in the political arena. Whatever he undertook, he did with all his faculties, wholeheartedly and with all his powers, not half-willing, half-forced. Thus we see in the Reflections that he sticks to the subject for years and demonstrates an unexpected aggressiveness that expresses itself in a violent tone.

The moral courage that distinguishes his actions is even more significant. Even in his artistic work he had demonstrated personal courage and intellectual toughness in his opposition to all the fashionable movements of the time. He was courageous to write Buddenbrooks about his own family and his birthplace Lübeck in such an ironic tone, truthfully, without any attempt at idealization and glorification. He refused to abridge the novel even at the risk of having the publishing house reject it. Even in his selection of themes, which break traditional taboos, he shows great courage, as in the short stories **Death in Venice** and **The Black Swan.** To begin the novel **Joseph and his Brothers** and to conclude it not without interposing a parallel Egyptian setting is a bold deed at the time of the anti-Semitic witch hunt of National Socialism, which was also directed against the Old Testament.

But his moral courage manifests itself in the political battle even more visibly and tangibly. He does not hesitate to step forward in 1922 with his surprising espousal of the Republic, although it was predictable that he would be charged with betrayal of his own convictions in the **Reflections.** His conduct in 1930, when the SA troops threatened the life of every opponent of the National Socialist party, bears witness to his personal bravery. Even in the United States, when a political event disturbed him, he came forth publicly. He used the freedom of speech which was given him for his radio broadcast to Germany in September 1942 to denounce before all the world the plan for the extermination of the Jewish people within Hitler's huge sphere of power, while all the responsible political fountainheads buried this monstrous genocide in silence. In the notes to his drama **The Deputy,** Rolf Hochhuth refers quite rightfully to Mann's deed. In March 1948, when the American Government decided to withdraw its agreement for the establishment of a Jewish state in Palestine under the threat of war from the Arabian neighboring states, Thomas Mann published a very sharp protest in **Aufbau** in New York with the title: "Ghosts of 1938," in which he compared this step with the betrayal by the Western powers of Czechoslovakia and Munich. Moral courage was necessary to deliver the lectures on Goethe in 1949 and on Schiller in 1955 in Weimar for the Germans in the East, despite the storm of indignation in West Germany's fanatically anti-Communistic circles. In 1955, when I had an interview with President Theodor Heuss, he related among other things that when the committee for the Schiller celebration was formed in Stuttgart, the officials came to Heuss and asked him whether Thomas Mann was a suitable guest speaker. He replied that a better choice was not to be found. After some time they came again and asked the President to say a few words too during this national celebration. Mann willingly shortened his speech to make room for this address by Heuss. Everything seemed arranged; but the gentlemen came for the third time and complained about the fact that Mann now wanted to deliver his lecture in Weimar also and that this was after all unheard of! Heuss explained to them that he was only prevented by his official position from addressing the oppressed brothers in East Germany too on this occasion, and he approved of Thomas Mann's decision. He received a letter of thanks from Mann, who at that time was very much under attack! But Thomas Mann also did not delay in writing a letter of two hundred and twenty-eight lines (not pages as I wrote at one time) to Walter Ulbricht in June 1951 to oppose severe jail sentences for several people mentioned by name among three thousand East Germans.

From 1922 on, Thomas Mann entered the lists in internal politics for democracy, for freedom, justice, and a dignified human existence for the masses. Thus he fought for understanding between the citizenry and social democracy. In international politics too he sought understanding among the peoples and for peace and thus for collaboration between East and West. He was against all fascistic currents which wanted to maintain outmoded social conditions with force. He felt that the world spirit in the atomic age demanded this from people in a world which had become small. In my opinion we must not measure the significance of his political activity by the political success of the day. Mankind urgently needs such personalities of intellectual significance who in the name of humanity continually place simple moral demands in the way of professional politicians who may be forced to a narrower party line. There may be hundreds of thousands who read and love his writings, but there are millions all over the world who are grateful to him for leaving his artist's workshop, exposing himself to the attack of political opponents, and becoming a champion of the idea of humanity in disturbed times. His moral courage in the struggle on the great decisive political questions of the world belongs among the noble traits of his intellectual personality.

12. LETTERS

There remains only to speak of Thomas Mann's correspondence, the daily demands of the world requiring answer. This duty he faithfully fulfilled right up to his last breath with every ounce of his strength. The number of his letters is estimated at from 15,000 to 20,000, so that they represent along with his writings his most extensive achievement. We have already seen many of them in the groups treated. Many also have related content, like the essays and occasional writings on the one hand, the political manifestos on the other. Most of them differ, however, from all Mann's pronouncements discussed to date because originally they were not destined for publication. With important writers we regard letters in general as an ingredient of their literary creation and as essential additions to their autobiographical writings. This is also true for Thomas Mann, who was quite reticent with direct confessions about his personal life, in contrast to his son Klaus. The father never wrote an extensive biography because he felt that enough self-confessions were contained in his writings.

When the letter collection of the Fischer Press is completed in three volumes, we will only have somewhat more than 2,000 letters printed—only a small part of the total, but still they already offer priceless insights into the intellectual world of the poet.

The editing of the letters, at first in the hands of Dr. Scherrer, was later taken over by Erika Mann. Up to now two volumes have appeared, **Letters 1889-1936**, and **1937-1947**, Frankfort, 1961 and 1963. The third volume with the letters of 1948-1955 is supposed to appear in the fall of 1965. * The

---

*It has appeared: **Thomas Mann: Briefe 1948-1955 und Nachlese**, Ed. Erika Mann (S. Fischer Vorlag: Frankfort on Main, 1965), p. 655. (Tr. note)

presentation is not completely satisfactory. This results only in part from editorial notes, which have been criticized especially because there are many questions left unanswered. But they do offer a plethora of very valuable explanations by the editor from intimate knowledge of Mann's whole circle of acquaintances. The large gaps which are left as a result of editorial selection, and the absence of letters from Mann's correspondents, seem to me more important. Even if one reads all the letters to one particular person, one does not get a full picture of the relationship of two people to each other. The feeling of the inadequacy of this publication is increased when one reads of personal meetings and fruitful conversations about which little or nothing at all is explained. In the second volume, for example, there is a selection of 110 letters (out of about 300) to Agnes E. Meyer, the very active wife of the owner of the **Washington Post**, the largest series of the whole collection. Up to now only nine letters have appeared in the collection from Ida Herz, London, who possesses far more than 400 letters from Thomas and Katja Mann. This illustrates how much importance is being ascribed to this correspondence with an American woman of German origin in an influential social position in the capital of the country. But one can hardly dare to characterize the friendship between her and Thomas Mann—which was not always untroubled—without also knowing him better. She writes essays about his works in the American press, plans a book on him for which Mann sends her biographical information but which finally does not materialize, showers him with presents magnanimously, and obtains for him the position as Consultant for German literature at the Library of Congress, which relieves him from economic worries during several war years. A yearly lecture was one of his obligations at the Library.

In spite of this, the selection of letters is highly welcome. We follow the artist and champion along his life's path through the years and decades, and are permitted to take part in his sorrows and joys, in his artistic work, in his rich and varied reading, in the relationships with so many various personalities—some of high rank and significance—and we are continually in his stimulating company. We discover how often this sensitive person is tormented by physical distresses beyond his due, how severely he suffers under the uninterrupted urgent demands of the day, and then even much more severely under the world events which rob him forever of his German home-land and which heap much misfortune and disgrace on his fatherland. Much nonsense has been written about Thomas Mann's coldness, which, after all, reflects only his obsession with work. His distant attitude is assumed in reaction to his excitement and over-enthusiasm, in his effort to achieve a balance, which always was for him the measure of art. In Sweden, for example, Herbert Tingsten, the chief editor of the largest Scandinavian newspaper Dagens Nyheter, published four articles not long after the death of Thomas Mann, from 9 to 21 September 1956, which deal primarily with this theme and make his coldness the main concern in describing his person-ality and his work. This seems to me just as exaggerated and one-sided as Eric Heller's concept that irony is the chief char-acteristic of his writing. The language in all the documents treated here on the fulfillment of the demands of the day, which so often sounds warm-hearted and enthusiastic, bears witness to the opposite; even more convincing, however, is the lan-guage of the letters.

In his letters, he often surrenders himself unreservedly to his passionate sympathies and antipathies and then writes a vigorous, unrestricted language which he would not use in print; whereas in his narratives he disports himself in a cool but definitely fascinating play between irony and pathos. In his public appearances, there is an atmosphere of polite, friendly reserve about him. We come very much closer to the man Thomas Mann in his letters. The study of these letters, in part highly personal, will thus deepen our understanding of his artistic work; his writings were never born out of spirit-ual equanimity and cool superiority but out of melancholy ex-perience and suffering and out of passionate interest in human existence and its problems in all their forms, requiring all his artistic critical gift for their alleviation. Thus his letters are truly, for every reader, a substantial supplement to his literary work. Above all, however, they are valuable for the scholar, who can extract from them not only this general per-ception but also hundreds and hundreds of details about his biography, the origin of his works, and the significance which the poet himself attributes to his works.

Among other things, the letters from the period of his

courtship of Katja Pringsheim and those full of worry for the growing children—full of pride and joy when he can pay tribute to their creative activities—bear ample witness to Thomas Mann's powerful, deep, and lasting feelings. As an example I will include excerpts from a letter to Klaus Mann of 2 December 1942 about his autobiography The Turning Point in the English edition of 1942:

> My judgment is naturally prejudiced and is delivered with a certain amount of hesitancy and even concern, for I am, after all, so paternally close to all that, and with anticipatory bitterness, I think it is possible that insensitive viciousness could make fun of the family intimacy of these confessions. If we know the world at all, this will probably happen to some extent.... But what autobiography worth reading could dispense with this naiveté? If it is combined with cleverness and charm, it is precisely the element which makes up a good, captivating autobiography .... It is an unusually charming, emotionally sensitive, clever, and honestly personal book—personal and direct even in the adopted language which I should imagine is handled with surprising ease, definitiveness, and naturalness. Involuntarily we look for the name of the translator and can hardly believe that it is an original literary product—as a life's story was it not a somewhat premature undertaking? That is what people will probably say, but if you had waited until you were 50, then the early remembrances might no longer have been as fresh and funny as they are here. We as parents can certainly be satisfied with the figures we cut...the beautiful passage about the motherliness, the mother's love and the children's gratefulness will reconcile even viciously minded people. This terribly European book—discouraging perhaps for American readers—gives a strongly distorted image of pre-Hitler Europe, especially through many of your distorted little friends who were your fate. But if one then reads the chapter 'Olympus'—as a critical performance, naturally, the pièce de résistance of the book and a beautiful and earnest testimony to the capacity for devotion and admiration—then once again one has the impression that it simply does not ascend to a higher sphere without frailty, even if one issues a warning about seeing

the higher sphere precisely in the frailty. It is truly a genuinely august gathering, but each one has a "tic." One could suspect that you intentionally sought out gods like those who have "tics." But then if it occurred to you and you wanted to name those who have none, then these would have them too.

At this moment I am reading a letter from Eri, in which I discover with genuine satisfaction that sympathetic critics are waiting behind the bushes. Splendid!

The reading of separate editions of letters to a particular recipient is even more fruitful, for the simple reason that these collections form a consecutive series and many of them include the letters of the receiver and his own explanations. In the postscript to the second volume of letters, Erika Mann writes:

> T.M. lived in the United States 1938–52. In 1944, he became an American citizen. But he had already been regarded as an American for a long time by his new countrymen. Different from the majority of his companions in fate...he took an active part in the life of the nation. As a result of his public activity, he made many friends and many an enemy. But above all he attracted letters—thousands of letters written in English during the course of those fourteen years. He was asked to give interviews all too frequently as he traveled all over the country lecturing in English, and he soon spoke English effortlessly. Thus everyone assumed that he wrote it just as effortlessly.

She then reports how they organized the answering of all the letters. The German drafts of the letters were not retained.

> It was not possible even to suggest a picture of the extent and the uproarious variety of the American correspondence. The German volume of letters neither permitted English contributions in substantial measure, nor did reversed translations seem in place. In the face of this situation, it must be mentioned that there was hardly a stratum of the population with whose representatives T. M. did not correspond.... Most of the extensive and important English letters fell in their totality to Alfred A.

Knopf, T. M.'s American publisher, with whom he felt bound in grateful friendship to the very end. It is to be hoped that they will be published in English. [They have been--Tr. note.]

Heinrich and Thomas Mann. The personal, literary, and philosophical relations of the brothers, Alfred Kantorowicz, Berlin 1956, contains, besides an essay of over 50 pages, 42 letters of Thomas Mann to his brother, 1900-1927, whereas those of Heinrich are lacking. A significant result of this presentation is that the reconciliation between the two is introduced by a letter from Thomas Mann of 31 January 1922 and not on 6 June 1925 at the celebration of his fiftieth birthday in Munich as the writer Elli Petersen, who was there, reports— based on his impressions from the brothers' speeches.

The correspondence between Thomas and Heinrich Mann from 1900 to 1949 is to be published by the German Academy of Art, Berlin, with a postscript by Ulrich Dietzel in an edition of the Aufbau Press, Berlin, in 1965.

Thomas Mann: Letters to Paul Amann, 1915-1952. Edited by Herbert Wegener in the publications of the Lübeck city library, new series, volume III, Lübeck 1959, contains 48 letters of Mann, but only one of Amann from the year 1915 in draft form, and has been very carefully published and commented on. The larger portion of the entries, 30 in number from the years 1915-18, are especially interesting because they are closely related to the work on the Reflections of a Non-political Man, in which the Austrian philologist and high school teacher, devotee of France and especially of Romain Rolland, is oftentimes quoted without mentioning his name. Amann raised objections to Thomas Mann's political attitude in the First World War in such a clever and engaging manner that the poet answered in detail. Then he criticized sharply the work which appeared in 1918 and caused the correspondence to be broken off. As already mentioned, Thomas Mann deleted several attacks against Rolland from the fifth edition of the Reflections in 1922, apparently under the continuing influence of Amann. In 1935, Amann resumed the correspondence with Mann, who responded in a friendly manner, so that a new friendly exchange began again between them.

Thomas Mann to Ernst Bertram, Letters from the Years

1910-55. Edited and with an epilogue by Inge Jens, Pfulling-
en 1960. This book contains 256 letters to the literary historian selected from his legacy in the Schiller National Museum in Marbach. Those of the addressee, with all that Mann
left behind in 1933 in Munich, are regarded as lost except for
two from June 5, 1916 and July 26, 1947, which are in the possession of Katja Mann. The letters are brilliantly commented
on by the wife of the well-known classical philologist Walter
Jens in Tübingen. A picture of his friendship with Thomas
Mann is sketched in an epilogue, primarily on the basis of the
correspondence between Bertram and the Stefan George admirer, Ernst Glöckner. The Rhinelander Ernst Bertram
(1884-1957) had already written about Stefan George and
Thomas Mann when he met the two of them in 1910. But while
he belonged to the George circle as just one of many, as an
admirer and devotee of Mann's narrative art, he became a
friend of the family and godfather to the daughter Elizabeth. A
lively intellectual exchange resulted between the two of them,
sometimes personal, sometimes in letters. During the First
World War, they were completely in agreement in their conservative German Nationalist, anti-French attitude. In 1918,
it was thanks to Mann's intercession that Bertram's book,
Friedrich Nietzsche, Attempt at a Mythology, appeared in the
Georg Bondi Press, although George and Gundolf had demanded substantial changes. I shall quote one part of Thomas
Mann's letter of 21 September 1918 about the book because it
forms the high point of the friendship, and Nietzsche, after all,
is one of the three masters whom Mann revered from his youth:

> How close it is to me. How my whole being is constantly
> involved in it. How like a sibling it stands in its reflec-
> tion, culture, historic dignity, its purity, its faultless-
> ness, alongside my spontaneous, uninformed, confused,
> and compromising artist's book (Reflections)...the posi-
> tion of this book in such a rarefied atmosphere, in which
> my name really occurs and resounds, is a shock to me
> every time...you have remembered me in many places
> ...I am certain of that...there were deeper feelings than
> vanity and satisfaction which move me during the reading:
> with the greatest emotion and thankfulness, with the
> feeling of a genuinely consoling exultation aware of our

friendship, a retrospective emotion while studying this intellectual landscape, the survey of one's own life, insight into its necessity, and understanding of myself, as intensive as my own groping writing never could have granted me. Which part of this round of variations on the theme of balance' do I love most of all? I don't know. For this is indeed the amazing secret of the book, from its conception, that the whole antithetical intensity of life, the whole ineffable attractiveness, all the intellectual magic of the subject is pressed into each of these essays and variations. The arrangement of the chapters with the Eleusis section as its crowning conclusion is clever, witty and beautiful.... This mixture of philology and music in the basic nature of the book, so appropriate for the subject, has indeed a novel effect, surprisingly personal in this application. An essentially philological technique has never been handled with such vibrant feeling! ... Astonishing the physical mastery of the material, the survey of a life's work which on the surface after all is so fragmented, the presence of mind in association.... Its Germanness, by the way, has been profoundly and truly developed. Unusually fine is the parallel to Goethe, who likewise is German when he is at his highest and at his most relaxed. Meanwhile in both cases the French element...but there is no sense in underscoring individual details which put me in raptures. Every citation is an injustice to what was not cited. How beautifully the chapter on justification stands among the others! How I felt at home in a roundabout way even in these thought processes!

On the basis of this work, Bertram became an instructor with Berthold Litzmann in 1919, subsequently professor in Bonn and Cologne.

The political change in course which Mann made in 1922 was unacceptable to Bertram. But their personal relationship remained intact on the basis of their common literary interests up until 1927, although the George circle rejected Thomas Mann completely, as it did so many other important figures in the past and present. Bertram never belonged to the uncritical following of Stefan George but saw incorporated in him the idea of an aristocratic Germanness and in 1929 proposed George for the Nobel Prize, which was instead awarded to Thomas Mann. From about 1930, Bertram developed into an anti-Semite out of racial hatred, an exponent of the North, chauvinist, and finally adherent of the "people's rejuvenation" through National Socialism. This led to the breach in 1935. When Bertram resumed their epistolary relationship in 1949, Thomas Mann answered in a friendly way, to be sure, but the correspondence remained sparse and embraces only three additional letters. The other 253, however, along with the commentary, contain the life and fate of a man who stood between Thomas Mann and Stefan George in a disturbed period of German literary history. It is the largest cohesive series of letters which has been published up to now.

Karl Kerényi, the Hungarian classical philologist, published **Novel Writing and Mythology**, Zürich 1945, for the 70th birthday of Thomas Mann, when he had already been driven out of his mother country and had settled in Switzerland. It is an issue of the **Albae Vigiliae** which contains the letters of both of them with the commentaries of Kerényi. In 1960 there appeared **Thomas Mann—Karl Kerényi**, Zürich 1960, a book which he calls in the preface "humanism—a difficult happiness" and which contains the earlier letters and the rest of them from 1934-55 up to the death of the poet.

In the preface Kerényi reports that he discovered Thomas Mann's Hermes-nature in **The Magic Mountain**, the figure of the Greek god of mischief who moves about as a messenger between the realms of men and the dead. The works of this mythologist made the writer, Thomas Mann, more conscious of this disposition, since he had been familiar from his early youth with Greek mythology. He devoured them and took over many things from them into his own work, especially into the novel of the Biblical Joseph, who bears so many traits of Hermes. But when Kerényi characterizes Mann's whole personality as "hermetic," he is overlooking the artist's Proteus-like capacity for transformation. He is disregarding works like **Buddenbrooks** and is painfully disappointed in **Doctor Faustus**, which from the very beginning, after all, had as an integral part of its conception the pact of the musician with the devil. Both are agreed in the effort to make Greek myth useful for the humanization of mankind in our times. This gives their correspondence substance, dignity, and a high purpose.

Eighty-one letters of Thomas Mann are contained in this correspondence, which is intellectually the most important of those accessible up to now.

Thomas Mann—Robert Faesi—Correspondence, Zürich 1962, published by the latter, contains 36 letters of the writer with the replies of the literary historian and his explanations from the years 1921-55. Faesi very early became familiar with Mann's work. By 1913 he had already delivered lectures about the brothers Heinrich and Thomas Mann. In 1920 he published an essay C. F. Meyer und Thomas Mann, in which Heinrich Mann was referred to in comparison, and in 1955 he concluded his book Thomas Mann, a Master of the Narrative Art, for which Mann thanked him heartily. Their closer acquaintance began with Mann's visit in Faesi's house in Zollikon. The letters bear witness to Mann's sympathy not only for the scholar but also for his lyric poetry.

Hans Wysling, the successor to Dr. Paul Scherrer as curator of the Thomas Mann Archive, published From the Correspondence of Thomas Mann-Emil Preetorius with commentary, in 1963 in Number IV of the Blätter der Thomas Mann Gesellschaft, Zürich. In 1907 with his review of the illustrated edition of Chamisso's Peter Schlemihl in Hans von Weber's Hyperion Press, Thomas Mann contributed toward making Preetorius overnight into a sought-after illustrator. Subsequently he illustrated a whole series of Mann's books. The picture on the dust jacket of the first edition of A Man and His Dog is included in the correspondence along with Preetorius' article "Thomas Mann and Gluck's Iphigenie," in which he confesses that his "great friend" made him a stage designer in 1921. He also describes the visit of Thomas Mann and Bruno Walter, who talked him into this new activity. There follow six letters by Thomas Mann from the years 1935-55 and three of the addressee. An appendix furnishes a view of the total correspondence between the two, of which some letters have been lost and some have been printed in other places.

In addition Bürgin lists about 300 more letters which have appeared scattered individually or in smaller or larger groups in many publications which I cannot discuss in detail. The series I have discussed herein show that every correspondence has its own center of gravity, determined by the personality of the recipient and the relationship of the poet to him, on which the intellectual exchange revolves. As a result of this, each of them affords an insight into another sphere of interest for Thomas Mann and illuminates his intellectual world from a new aspect. We may still expect all kinds of surprises from subsequent publications of this nature—for example, the fifth issue of the Thomas Mann Society, Zürich, contains 15 letters of Thomas Mann to Otto Basler, a small selection out of about 150 letters.

13. CONCLUSION: SERIOUS CONDUCT OF LIFE

If in conclusion one asks what motivates the originally individualistically romantic artist to fulfil the powerful "demands of the day," the answer does not seen simple to me. To be sure, he loves his art passionately and is convinced that it is indispensable to the life of mankind and therefore imperishable, if its practice is carried on seriously, using all one's best efforts. But despite this, Mann is always aware of art's questionability, of its origin from dark drives of the human soul. Again and again he speaks of the demonic element which must be contained by the light forces of the spirit. At times this undoubtedly creates a lingering dissatisfaction with the "game." Perhaps his opinion is that one does not quite fulfil his task as a human being if one does not make himself useful additionally in direct service to mankind and the human community, especially in disturbed times. In his lecture **Lübeck as an Intellectual Form of Life**, Thomas Mann confesses that in the conduct of his life his father stood as a secret model before his eyes. The son was similar to his father in appearance and was called in Munich "the honorable Senator." Thomas Mann's total achievement shows that he really has to thank the legacy and model of his father for his "serious conduct of life." Thomas Mann was always a conscientious, responsible citizen, except that he was also a world citizen because of his activity in many countries. His art and his timely service to the world about him are expressions of his rich personality. When we celebrate him, we always praise him simultaneously as a creative artist and as a champion of Humanism.

14. THE CREATIVE ARTIST

If one wants to characterize with justice the artistic work of a writer of Thomas Mann's stature, one must not select a scale foreign to the arts with which to measure and evaluate it. This error can be made in various ways.

The Marxist, for example, investigates above all what Thomas Mann has contributed to the political revolutionary development of his time and the world about him. This contribution is not a little and is important enough for a full picture of his personality. Political elements also forced their way into his writings, like fascist Italy in **Mario and the Magician,** the political oppositions at the time before the First World War in the verbal duels of Settembrini and Naphta in **The Magic Mountain**—the isolationist attitude of the Amun Temple in **Joseph and his Brothers** can be regarded as parallel to National Socialism, the great curse at the end of the short story **The Tables of the Law** is invented for Hitler. But in the totality of Mann's artistic work, these political elements are peripheral, not central.

Orthodox Jews and Christians can reject the novel **Joseph and his Brothers** because Thomas Mann does not share their biblical beliefs. This is understandable; but if they do so, they exclude themselves from the enjoyment and from the judgment of his artistic achievement.

It is also not admissible to explain and evaluate Mann's work purely with philosophy as the starting point. In spite of astute intelligence and rich intellectuality, in spite of the superstructure of life's problems and their interpretations through a realistic grasp of external and internal reality, Thomas Mann is after all not a systematic thinker and strict logician. He often uses concepts in quite another meaning from what is generally customary. Indeed, in his usage, their

238

scope and content often vacillates and wavers considerably. From the reservoir of ideas handed down to us, he takes what moves and excites him and seems to him at that time fruitful for his own development and the work under consideration. Whatever he adopts for his own at any time sticks like glue in his memory and can be effective in his creative work again and again. Extremely contradictory elements come together in the archive of his memory. It is indeed possible to follow an intellectual line of development in his work up to the biblical novel, but in Doctor Faustus he returns with a theme selected early to many thoughts of his initial period which are fruitful for this work. This is no reason to condemn the book. If one dissolves the conceptual elements from a piece of writing, one is dealing with an abstraction, not with the unity of a work of art. I would like to illustrate this in a particular case. Käthe Hamburger has written a series of brilliant, searching essays on Thomas Mann's writings which she sent to him and which he praised highly in his letters to her. In the Göteborg newspaper Handels-och Sjöfertstidning for 27 November 1947, she published quite a negative criticism on Doctor Faustus, in which she regretted the introduction of the narrator Zeitblom, who is the artistic means to transform the whole novel into a powerful lament on the disintegration of the genial musician. This criticism from a philosophical point of view seems remote from art and pained the author terribly with respect to the clever interpreter of his earlier works that were influenced by Goethe's humanity.

Not only philosophically oriented literary historians are in danger of neglecting artistic work through their methods—so are all literary historians, if they try to classify a work historically before they have completely grasped its individual nature. Even the greatest writer belongs in a powerful literary tradition. Just as with Goethe, we will also put together a substantial library about Thomas Mann in order to establish all the "sources" from which he has drawn; for, throughout his life, he read an unusual amount of material thoroughly and receptively. But more important than the raw material which he takes from books is the way he transforms it in his workshop into poetry of his own crafting. Many literary historians are mired in their studies of sources, ideas, themes, forms, and styles, and if they think at all that they can derive a literary work of importance from the prehistory established in this way, then they are in error. No matter what the writer of rank learns and takes over, he uses it all in his artistic work in a unique manner, governed by his own laws, which can have the effect of making history and creating a great influence.

The literary historical methods mentioned are thoroughly justified in themselves, and the person who places the written work of art at the focal point of observation will also gratefully exploit the factual results. These results need supplementation through an aesthetic method, a structural and stylistic study, which aims at the unity and uniqueness of the literary work of stature. This is the basis of my contributions to Thomas Mann research.

It is important first of all to stake off the boundaries of his art. In spite of a number of first writings, he is not a lyricist who expresses the inner emotion of the ego directly and without reservation. He is also not a born dramatist, in spite of **Florence**, and many dramatic scenes in his narratives. The tensions and contrasts inside him are not so strong that the battle of ideas, interests, and passions in the world outside him could become the chief theme in his writings. The dichotomy in the individual person, the inner difficulties which grow out of it, and the possibilities of overcoming it—the problems of life as he experiences them and suffers them within himself—fascinate him far more. This also determines his position in the art of narration. There are many novels and short stories of the same period, whose authors are passionately interested in economic, social, and political life and hence embed the individual fates which they depict in the mass fate, which then has a determining effect for all. Many of these authors are "involved," they want to make reading people conscious of their social situation; they want to contribute to changes in the world because the situation seems to them disturbing. Before 1914, Thomas Mann considers the social element unpoetic and even later only permits it to penetrate into his writing as background material for individual fates. As a poet and individualist all his life, he wants to serve humanity by shedding light on representative individual fates.

At one time earlier I cherished the concept that Thomas Mann in his writings establishes a mighty superstructure of life's problems over a narrow foundation, but after renewed studies I can no longer hold this view. The intellectual super-structure is certainly large and decisive for the importance of the works. However, the reality experienced is also rich and varied. The poet by no means lives in loneliness and seclusion, and his thoughts definitely do not always circle around his own ego, although he speaks, like Goethe, of the confessional character of his creations. My former impressions rested on the fact that he has so little sense for the salutary force of human society (in spite of its inadequacy) and for the far reaching dependence upon it of even the gifted individual. Regardless of how many sciences Mann may have studied, sociology is not one of them.

Doubtlessly the reading experiences in Thomas Mann's intellectuality take up an unusually large amount of space, even in his writings. This is related to his origin from a well-to-do, educated, patrician family and his intellectual talent. One need only think of writers like Maxim Gorki and Martin Andersen Nexö who came from the people, to have a tangible grasp of the difference. For each of his large novels, Mann carried out extensive studies that are evident in essayistically colored sections. But his interests go far beyond the book world. In first position next to it stands music; then follows the theater. Naturally, his educational experiences also have limits, at least to the extent that they are fruitful in the work itself. The two chief sources of European culture lie in Greece and Palestine. The Judeo-Christian circle of ideas is much more strongly effective in the writings of Mann than the Greek. In **Death in Venice**, a living picture from Plato's "Phaedra" is conjured up in connection with Aschenbach's love for the young boy; in **The Magic Mountain**, Castorp experiences a dream-vision of Grecian nature in the snow storm; and the Greek god Hermes plays an essential role in several writings. On his trip into the Near East, the poet also saw the Acropolis in Athens. But in his works we hear nothing about Hellas as the rejuvenating "life of the world" (Albrecht Schaeffer), and the description of the Renaissance (Grecian culture) is in his case without radiance. In the essays on the German standard bearers of humanity like Goethe and Schiller, the powerful significance of Greece for their world view and writings is not stressed.

Beyond the cultural experiences in his case there is a many-sided reality. Thomas Mann is not a vagabond and adventurer. While his brother Heinrich to some extent, and his children Erika and Klaus, have much of this, he loves the serious conduct of life in his home and family as a firm anchor. He is definitely disinclined to all intoxication and does not need it as a stimulus to his creativity. But he has a large stimulating youthful life into the house. He loves to travel a great deal, even for the sake of new impressions. On his lecture tours he comes into stimulating contact with people from all strata and occupations. His gigantic correspondence gives us a welcome insight into the variety of his relationships. From this basis a broad stream of experienced reality, both external and internal, penetrates his work. We can read it in the variety and number of characters in his writings. The children's world with its fantasy and its own laws is represented least of all. **The Child Prodigy**, the precocious, introverted, lonely boys Hanno Buddenbrook and Tonio Kröger, Benjamin in the company of the 17-year-old Joseph, and Frido in **Doctor Faustus** are unusual, unchildlike, unique cases. But masculine and feminine youth, mature men and women and also age (Jakob, the 67-year-old Goethe) are depicted with searching insight. To be sure, all the heroes of the novels of development and education, the main figures of the major and minor narratives, the carriers of the ideas and problems are, by far, men; the short story **The Black Swan** with the vivacious Frau von Tümmler forms an exception. But a glance back at the writings does recall a long series of perceptively described female figures. From **Buddenbrooks**, Tony above all remains unforgettable; from **Royal Highness**, the young Emma Spoelmann; from **The Magic Mountain,** Claudia Chauchat ("the hot cat"); from **Joseph and his Brothers**, the beautiful Rachel, the unhappy Mut-en-Emet, and the clever Teje, the mother of Ikhnaton; also Sita with the beautiful backside from **The Transposed Heads**, who is torn between two men; from **Doctor Faustus**, Ina Roddes, who makes a mess of her life all by herself, and Mother Schweigstill, who has so much understanding for her lonesome houseguest. Even from the picaresque novel **Felix Krull**, the courtesan Rozsa, the one enthusiastic about early manhood, Madame Houpflé, and the outspoken Zouzou Kuckuck stick in our memory. Behind them a whole throng of secondary figures pops up who do not want to be overlooked because Thomas Mann has represented them so impressively; but I shall name only the musical Gerda Buddenbrook, the resourceful sister of Prince Klaus-Heinrich, Dietlinde, the little Danish girl who in the role of a medium fetches the spirit of Joachim Ziemssen while in the birth throes of two hours duration, Tamar who, as a devoted listener, cheers up Jacob's aging heart, and the charming daughter Anna von Tümmler.

Of these women only a very few take part in the action in their motherly capacities. The rest, however, are certainly not represented as free-standing, cool marble statues, but rather in their relations to the opposite sex. The eternal theme of world literature, love, also occupies its proper space in Thomas Mann's writings. Beneath the cool, intellectual stratum, there is a bubbling and seething of passionate lust of the senses to which is joined much heart-rending suffering and torment of the soul, as fate ordains. In describing women, the narrator proves to be knowledgeable in matters of the soul. A withdrawn, egocentric man would never have been able to create so many vivacious female figures and equip them with a personal individuality and their own destiny. There is not one duplicate in these descriptions of women. This is creative, artistic work.

Basically, the situation is not different with the male figures. They too show a great variety, with numerous clearly defined profiles and forms of life. This comes into sharper focus with the secondary figures than with the chief characters, because the writer has mixed traits of his own being with theirs, which may conceal their independent peculiarity on superficial observation. Thomas Mann thus demonstrates in his work a rich knowledge of people and life.

Tonio Kröger writes to his Russian friend, the painter Lisabeta, of his love for life that transforms the dilettante into a poet and of his longing for the "blisses of everyday life." But has Thomas Mann represented the naive, unintellectual, banal life in an engaging manner in his writings? It always appears in a satiric light, as "misery and comedy." Those things which fascinate and interest him seriously are almost always unusual, out of the way, strange, indeed oftentimes touchy, sensitive motifs. Think of these: a man who punishes and kills a dog in order then to demonstrate his sympathy with him, a fat man devoted to his wife like a dog who appears obediently at her party as a female dancer in a ridiculous costume and who collapses dead when he suddenly grasps that she has been deceiving him for a long time with another person, a musical boy who is incapable of life (Hanno), a cripple who falls in love with the beautiful society lady and takes his life when she rejects him, a man who dies of cholera in Venice because he cannot tear himself loose from a handsome young boy whom he loves, a large number of incestuous relationships, a young man who goes to a lung sanatorium for three weeks to visit a cousin and stays for seven years, a man who worships a woman but also marries three others and produces eleven children with them, a politically important woman in a false marriage who falls in love with her slave and is rejected by him, an epileptic youth on the throne, a musician who intentionally contracts syphilis from a lady of the evening, an older woman who believes in a rejuvenation of love but dies of abdominal cancer. This is not the naive, usual, unintellectual life. But these and similar themes stimulate Thomas Mann, and he transforms them into intellectual experiences, into writings which illuminate strange human fates. Reality is for him a raw material which is made transparent under his hands, thus permitting the problems of life, the intellectual world, to become visible, material, ennobled through his art.

Thomas Mann is a master of realism. Nature lays its strongest hold on him near the sea and in the high mountains. He represents man's immediate world with thousands upon thousands of sharply observed details. But above all, the description of man himself fascinates him. The invention of passionate tales of conflict is not his forte. Where they do occur in his work, they are taken over either from reality or from literature. He always diverts our attention quickly from the external happenings to the inner world, to the spiritual experiences, and to their accompanying thoughts.

He works slowly, every day only a few morning hours, which add very few pages to his work. Demands of the world about him force interruptions; difficulties delay the progress; fatigue and decline of interest make a conclusion difficult. In this way the completion of a work can take many years. Thomas Mann does not write quickly and fluently. His writings are cumbersome and profound. Anyone who does not enjoy their details and can gain nothing from the problems posed will never enjoy reading them.

His description of reality makes his work lively, but it is never an end in itself—simply the basis for the interpretation of life. **Buddenbrooks,** for example, is represented on the basis of the chronicle of the Mann family so realistically that in the Schabbelhaus in Lübeck a little museum has been equipped with the appropriate family pictures and such things; but the poet has depicted the biological decline of a family with the accompanying intellectual phenomena out of which rose the musican Hanno, incapable of life. This poetic clan intellectualizes and transforms reality.

Sickness is a very frequent motif in Mann's works. Sometime in the future, there will surely be a solid book written on this subject by a specialist who will investigate whether the sicknesses have been presented correctly; that is to say, whether they reflect reality. But Thomas Mann is neither a doctor nor a naturalist. Several examples may illustrate this. The short story **Tristan** takes place in a tuberculosis sanatorium. A hemorrhage makes a sudden end to Frau Klöterjahn's life. The essential content, however, is that the writer Spinell experiences a spiritual union with her in the music referred to in the title. In **Death in Venice,** cholera kills the aging poet Aschenbach, but basically the handsome Polish lad is the leader of souls who entices and guides him into death. **The Magic Mountain** also takes place in a high mountain sanatorium for tuberculosis patients, but Hans Castorp matures there to a new humanity. The Pharaoh Ikhnaton in **Joseph and his Brothers** is an epileptic, but he draws salutary divine wisdom from his ecstatic circumstances. In **Doctor Faustus,** the devil's pact with the composer Adrian Leverkühn takes the form of a syphilitic infection, which he seeks for the sake of breaking through to a new music. **The Black Swan** dies of abdominal cancer, but she is grateful to nature, which presented her in the end with a happy illusion of a love fulfilment. It is always the same thing: the disturbances in life are always only the basis for life's problems and their interpretation, for the shaping of intellectual experiences and unusual human fates.

The "heroes" of Mann's short and long narratives are chiefly lonesome people who, for the most various reasons, stand

outside the naive life of human society, whether they feel themselves to be in contrast to it because they are marked and excluded or whether they are alienated by their special dispositions. Very often it is their profession which transforms them
into "non-humans"—poets, artists, actors, confidence men,
and the like—or their social position as princes or as wealthy
independent people, so that they do not need to perform everyday work. In this manner the poet can often present the intellectual problems which he wants to present, completely freed
of the web of economic, social, and political life. For the
most part it is the personal, moral, intellectual world that interests him. The majority of his narratives end tragically or,
if the "hero" matures, his success is not represented in practical life. But one must not overlook the fortunate rise in
Royal Highness, Joseph and his Brothers and **The Holy Sinner,**
nor that Castorp proves to be a fellow man in the sanatorium
circle and that at the tragic end of Leverkühn his creative
work remains extant and bears witness to the result of his
sacrifice of human happiness. Almost all the chief figures
presented are fascinating as a result of their spiritual receptivity and intellectual gifts.

Mann's chief works are developmental and educational novels in which we follow the "heroes" along their life's paths.
This is his favorite form in **Royal Highness, The Magic Mountain,** the **Joseph** novel, **Doctor Faustus,** and **Tonio Kröger.**
Describing slow intellectual developments corresponds to the
working habits of this narrator.

In my opinion it is impossible to establish a uniform, clear-
cut attitude toward the world and life in the totality of Thomas
Mann's poetic work. He himself developed and changed just
like his main figures. Until 1914, he is by and large a pessimistic observer of the misery and comedy of life. He longs
for a solution to his inner dichotomy and tries to achieve it.
After the First World War, he withdraws initially into a narrow personal circle for self-contemplation and then turns as a
"sentimental" to the "naive" type of Goethe, from whom he
learns all kinds of things—above all friendliness toward man
in the future and the intellectual bridge of pedagogy leading to
the social life. Above and beyond this, his active participation
in political events changes his world view markedly. Since
that time, educational elements stand out more and more frequently in the observations of his writings. In the **Joseph**

novels, the new humanity has gained a shape and a wise expression. In the personal conduct of his life, Thomas Mann remains loyal to the Goethean ideal. But when he again takes up the theme of his early period about the questionability of the artist in **Doctor Faustus** after more than four decades, much of his pessimistic view of the world returns, and there arises his deeply tragic work furthest removed from Goethe.

The problem of Thomas Mann's religiosity is not insoluble. He stands under the strong influence of Protestantism, in which he grew up and was educated. In the **Reflections of a Non-political Man**, he uses a number of traditional religious phrases without any reservation. But he is free of dogma, believing neither in a personal god nor in the devil. It is clear from a letter of 7 October 1936 to Professor Karl Kerényi, who sent him a study about "Religion," that he dares to regard himself as a religious person if "religion is to be conceived of as the opposite of carelessness and disregard, as watchfulness, obedience, consideration, conscientiousness as a cautious attitude, indeed as reverence and finally as concerned, watchful sensitivity toward the movements of the world "spirit." This is a secularization of the religious concept, a displacement into the ethical realm. Accordingly, however, Thomas Mann employs religious words anew, God and the whole series of composita like God's concern, God's cleverness, God's stupidity, grace, blessing, and such without, in so doing, surrendering his freedom from dogma. Such a highly personal religiosity is indeed in our times widespread among intellectuals.

In accordance with these observations, I naturally consider it completely wrong when Thomas Mann is called the "ironic German" (Erich Heller) and his poetic creation is described as parodistic or, indeed, nihilistic, although I do not deny that the writer himself has given emphasis to this attitude in many ambiguous pronouncements. The irony which can transform a whole work into a parody is an artistic means taken over from romanticism in order to soften the work's creative pathos, to counteract the center of gravity of a serious theme and to give the work a charming equilibrium and an attractive beauty in intellectual freedom. It is after all quite impossible to conceive of his writings with their unusually grave and often macabre themes, which Thomas Mann selects, completely as parodies! No, the poet has respect for life in all its moving phenomena, and his cutting satire is directed only against stupidity and moral corruption, conceit and evil, not against genuine suffering and unfortunate fate. But the more the work induces tears of emotion, the more it requires a counterbalance. Therefore Mann overlays the surface of his works with the glittering veil of his ironic play. To experience this contrapuntal structure, this opposition of pathos and irony, belongs to the precious charms of reading Thomas Mann's works. But the pathos controlled in these works often breaks out in essays, manifestos, and letters without reservation. He himself coins the term "erotic irony" (or "parody") and means it to include love and respect.

The polarity between pathos and irony can be convincingly represented from a literary viewpoint. In his language, which unfolds and blossoms where he is heavily involved, one can read precisely what excites him and sets his fantasy in motion. Naturally it turns out that the quantitative mixture of pathos and irony is various in the dissimilar works. The ironic cast is stronger in **Tristan** than in **Death in Venice**, in **Royal Highness** and **The Magic Mountain** than in **Doctor Faustus**, and strongest in **The Confessions of Felix Krull, Confidence Man.** In the deeply serious works, the blossoming of style is restricted in his irony to peripheral arabesques; whereas in the pathetic works it takes up much space and is grand.

Novels and short stories are above all literary works of art. Their language structure decides their poetic rank: the how is more important than the what! To evaluate Thomas Mann's literary achievements with the necessary examples would require a special book of the same scope as this one. But in describing his literary performance I have at least included copious quotations throughout—on the one hand, in order to make clearer the essential character of the individual and, on the other, to furnish outstanding pieces of artful literary creation—a small selection from his inexhaustible store and variety. At this point a few indications must suffice. Thomas Mann says: "Style is the secret coalescence of the personal with the objective." One must take this explanation literally: The subject codetermines the appropriate literary configuration. In each work the poet makes an effort to adapt the style to the theme selected. His literary configuration, therefore, alternates sharply from work to work. But even within each individual work there are various styles. Each personality which is described in detail and participates in conversations receives his individual language. Beyond this, each of the various areas, such as the description of the world about, the external depiction of people, their inner world, the observations which they make, and those of the narrator, demand their own literary style. In looking back at Mann's total art we recall with special pleasure the musical experiences, the landscape of high mountains, the sea and other waters, the endless scope of the conversations and discussions, the deep-reaching spiritual knowledge, and the intellectual observations of the poet.

The style of the answers to the demands of the day shows once again a completely different character from the writings and a number of the various language forms in the essays, manifestos, letters, and such, so that the style of the fiction stands out clearly from them. Often there is criticism of Thomas Mann's long sentences. Yet if one reads them aloud, one finds for the most part that they are well structured and that they gain a great deal when heard. In general, although it takes its origin at the desk and is sharply differentiated from colloquial speech, Thomas Mann's language is not only formed with the eyes but is "heard." Again and again Thomas Mann stresses its relationship with music. He goes as far as to say that writing and the reading of literary efforts are actually only detours. One should really tell his stories, just as the term "narrator's art" preserves this concept. This is characteristic of his language. One can definitely not maintain the same of all writings of a high order.

Thomas Mann is very fond of outlining subjects and concepts boldly in three-part formulae, but he can also pile up verbs, adjectives and substantives, if necessary. He likes to vary the same subject in many ways. He commands all the rhetorical means of the language to intensify the emotions and uses countless antithetical forms. He enriches the language through the application of foreign words, his own new coinage, and a great many vivid and ingenious images and comparisons. Sometimes he selects a foreign language instead of German; for example, when Hans Castorp declares his love during the Fasching Night to Claudia Chauchat. Thomas Mann's language reveals an astonishing wealth of variation and invention; at each renewed reading of the work, we hit upon new little treasures of an inimitable personal stamp.

It is a sure sign of the great, highly gifted writer that we can never predict what his next work will bring us. There are poets whose selections of theme and style repeat themselves when they once find their own way. Thomas Mann surprises us at every new station of his creativity. There are certain recurrent problems—for example, the questionability of the artist. But problems are, after all, only an ingredient of the living work of art. In form and content, Thomas Mann never repeats himself. He may carry over details from one literary form of the language into another; he may move from essays into creative works; but he never creates a series of writings of an identical or related character. He is wealthy enough always to furnish something new.

If one constantly singles out certain pairs of opposites like artist and citizen, art and life, intellect and life, soul and body, etc. and mixes them into the main subject, or if one improperly over-estimates the elements of his own nature which Thomas Mann bestows upon his figures without trying to achieve identity—which would justify the phrase "secret self-portraits" (Jonas Lesser)—the impression can be gained that as a narrator Mann moves about in a narrow circle or even constantly circles about his own ego. To be sure, his works bear a subjective stamp; otherwise, it would be without personal charm and would fascinate no one. He is an outspoken individualist. But this prevents him in no way from comprehending a gigantic objective world and incorporating it into his work. This becomes convincingly apparent if we view the multiplicity of human destinies created by him and of the individualized secondary figures, the wide range in conversations, milieu descriptions, descriptions of people and observations, the various forms of the creative writings, their continually new tones related to music, their richly developed language structure—in short, the whole exalted work, the work of a creative artist. The great writer's fantasy creates in accordance with the principium individuationis, individualizing right into all the details, just like nature, which never repeats itself; no tree in the forest, no branch in the tree, no leaf on the branch, no vein in the leaf is completely like the others. Thus in Thomas Mann's case every narrative, every scene, every figure and its language bears its own individual stamp.

But no matter what varied insights one may gain from the penetrating analysis of the individual works or from a systematically comparative survey of the total artistic work, one must never forget in the process that all these narratives are finished works of art, complete in themselves. They are composed like oratorios, symphonies, or sonatas. For the most part, they have a clear structure with a well calculated beginning and conclusion; they are well balanced in their parts, which are joined by countless relationships with one another. No matter from what sources of life and literature they may be nurtured and enriched, they are full of observed reality, endured suffering, thoughts confirmed by experience, from Thomas Mann's inwardly experienced world. Whatever may have penetrated into it by way of ideas and problems, there are above all vivid human characters who make the idea attractive, fascinating, and fruitful for the receptive reader. Mann's writings are places of refuge, inviting man's introspection into life's problems high over the chaos of wildly disturbed times.

From my description of his great artistic achievement, which aimed seriously at objectivity, it becomes completely understandable that Thomas Mann attained a firm place in world literature even during his lifetime.

BIBLIOGRAPHY

Hans Bürgin, Walter E. Reichert, and Erich Neumann, Das Werk Thomas Manns: Eine Bibliographie. Frankfurt/Main: S. Fischer Press, 1959.

Hans Bürgin and Hans Otto Meyer. Thomas Mann: Eine Chronik Seines Lebens. Frankfurt/Main: S. Fischer Press, 1965. Compared to this chronicle, any other chronology would appear insufficient and full of gaps. (A revised, augmented, and updated translation of this chronicle has been recently published by The University of Alabama Press.)

Klaus W. Jonas. Fifty Years of Thomas Mann Studies, A Bibliography of Criticism. Minneapolis: University of Minneapolis Press, 1955. A second volume of this bibliography of Thomas Mann literature appeared in 1967 in Philadelphia from the University of Pennsylvania Press and added over 3,000 works to the over 3,000 of the first volume.

Since any selection from the huge literature on Thomas Mann would necessarily be arbitrary and incomplete, I refer to these two outstanding bibliographies by Jonas and Bürgin/Meyer.

INDEX OF MANN'S WORKS

The numbers in bold type designate the principal passages where the work is treated or where it is quoted.